D1481734

Backgrounds
of Shakespeare's
Thought

by

John Erskine Hankins

ARCHON BOOKS
1978

©John Erskine Hankins 1978
First published 1978 as an Archon Book,
an imprint of The Shoe String Press, Inc.
Hamden, Connecticut 06514

ISBN 0-208-01743-7

Library of Congress Cataloguing in Publication Data

Hankins, John Erskine, 1905-
Backgrounds of Shakespeare's thought.

Includes bibliographical references and index.
1. Shakespeare, William, 1564-1616—Knowledge and learning.   2. Shakespeare, William, 1564-1616—Sources.   1. Title.
PR2952.H27   822.3'3   78-2273

To Clyde Hyder and Carroll Edwards,
former colleagues and longtime friends

Contents

Preface

THIS VOLUME is an attempt to bridge the gap between what Shakespeare read and what he wrote and to trace the connections between the two. I have tried to fill in the backgrounds of his reading and of some other materials he may have known indirectly by hearsay. In section II.7 I have used a few passages from Milton's *Paradise Lost* to show the different ways in which the two poets developed the same theme from the same or similar sources.

I have chosen for the title the word *backgrounds* instead of the word *sources*, for I recognize that one cannot always pinpoint the particular book from which Shakespeare derived an image or idea. There may be intermediate versions I have not found or Shakespeare may have heard the material orally. Sometimes the current fund of general knowledge may explain an image without recourse to literary sources. For instance, at the end of section VII.2 "appetite, an universal wolf" may simply reflect the well-known voracity of wolves; but the word "universal" suggests a cosmic destroyer like the wolves in the Icelandic Prose Edda, which I cite without being able to trace clearly the path by which it could have reached Shakespeare. It was a part of the cultural background of his time.

In quotations from the Latin, whenever the verbal parallels with Shakespeare's lines demand a visual comparison, I have included both the Latin and the translation in the text. In other cases I have used the translation only, relegating the Latin original to an appendix. Italics emphasize significant words and phrases. The notes provide references relevant to the subject in hand but make no attempt at comprehensiveness. Sections II.7, VI.6, and VII.1 are reprinted, with changes, from *PMLA*; sections VIII.5, 8, 9 have appeared in Thaler and Sanders's *Shakespearean Studies* (Tennessee), in *Modern Language Notes,* and in *The Explicator,* respectively. To avoid repetition of my own ideas, I refer occasionally to my earlier books: *The Character of Hamlet* (1941, 1970), *Shakespeare's Derived Imagery* (1953, 1967), and *Source and Meaning in Spenser's Allegory* (1971).

I am most grateful for courtesies extended to me by the libraries of Yale University, Harvard University, Columbia University, the University of Kansas, the University of Connecticut, Colby College, Bowdoin College, and the University of Maine (Orono). For reading my manuscript and making useful suggestions, I thank Maynard Mack of Yale, Burton Hatlen of the University of Maine (Orono), and my wife, Nellie Pottle Hankins.

J. E. H.

Oxford, Maine

I

Introduction

TO THE STUDENT of literature it is an exhilarating task to trace the working of a poet's mind. Poets themselves often attempt it. In Wordsworth's autobiographical poem *The Prelude,* he used the subtitle "Growth of a Poet's Mind" and sought in the events and impressions of his life from childhood the explanation of his poetry. Goethe attempted much the same thing in his prose *Dichtung und Wahrheit.* Shelley, in his *Apology for Poetry,* and Poe, in his *Marginalia,* thought that poetic vision and utterance must proceed ultimately from a divine source. Sir Philip Sidney, in his *Apologie,* found in poetry the culmination of all learning, which raises men to their fullest potentialities:

> This purif[y]ing of wit, this enritching of memory, enabling of judgment, and enlarging of conceyt, which commonly we call *learning,* vnder what name soeuer it com forth, or to what immediat end soeuer it be directed, the final end is, to lead and draw vs to as high a perfection, as our degenerate soules made worse by theyr clayey lodgings, can be capable of.[1]

He then adds that the astronomer, mathematician, historian, and philosopher find in poetry a means of elevating and humanizing their several disciplines. Platonically speaking, the soul's "clayey lodgings"—in Shakespeare its "muddy vesture of decay"[2]—impedes its complete apprehension of divine perfection, but through *learning* it can make progress on the road toward that perfection. Learning provides the content, poetry the method, of a poet's work.

11

This noble concept of *learning* should give aid and comfort to practitioners of so-called "historical" scholarship who seek in the background of a poet's knowledge for clues to a fuller understanding of his verse. In Shakespeare's works these clues are found in single phrases and short speeches. My own research has frequently involved the detection of verbal parallels as clues to Shakespeare's reading. In 1964 Kenneth Muir wrote a short article, "The Future of Source-Hunting," for the *Shakespeare Newsletter*. He concluded that with the completion of Geoffrey Bullough's work on Shakespeare's sources, there is little more to be discovered of plot sources but that our knowledge of Shakespeare's reading is only fragmentary. He suggested an organized effort by a group of scholars to investigate the area of Shakespeare's reading.[3]

A principal difficulty in promoting Muir's proposal is the lack of agreement among scholars as to the validity of verbal parallels. Many of them regard source hunting and its discoveries as less intellectual than solving crossword puzzles. Their attitude may seem justified by the excessive claims of some source hunters, but they should not uniformly condemn all source hunting. In the first chapter of my *Shakespeare's Derived Imagery*, I tried to formulate methods of judging hypothetical sources objectively: availability, repetition of unusual words or of several words together, similar contexts, and so forth. There is some advantage in knowing that an image is not original but derivative, even if one mistakes the particular source from which it is derived. At its best, source hunting may provide the key to an author's mind through a knowledge of the materials with which he worked.

This study is concerned primarily with Shakespeare's use of science and philosophy. The theme of the book is "the world and man." There are numerous general studies in the area, such as Hardin Craig's *The Enchanted Glass* (1936), W. C. Curry's *Shakespeare's Philosophical Patterns* (1937), Theodore Spencer's *Shakespeare and the Nature of Man* (1942), E. M. W. Tillyard's *Elizabethan World Picture* (1943), Herschel Baker's *Dignity of Man* (1947), P. H. Kocher's *Science and Religion in Elizabethan England* (1953), and Robert H. West's *Shakespeare and the Outer Mystery* (1968). The best short statement is William R. Elton's "Shakespeare and the Thought of His Age," in Muir and Schoenbaum's *New Companion to Shakespeare Studies* (1971). Seldom has so much well-informed comment been packed into so little space.

In my opinion, many of Shakespeare's lines were no more intelligible to an Elizabethan audience than they are to an audience today. Shakespeare has a habit of "talking to himself" in obscure phrases and literary allusions. These do not interrupt the flow of the action, though they come perilously near it on several occasions in *Troilus and Cressida*. They seem to be a necessary part of his poetic style, as distinguished from his dramatic style. In some ways he is an allusive poet like Ezra Pound or T. S. Eliot, though not to the same degree. By contrast, Ben Jonson's plays have few obscure allusions; he seems deliberately to have avoided them except in his poems and masques. Shakespeare's allusions, when we understand them, do much to enrich the meaning of his lines; but they are difficult to catch "on the wing," as it were. I hope that this book will provide a fuller understanding of many Shakespearean lines.

Shakespeare's knowledge or ignorance of Latin is another question that will arise in these pages. We are still under the spell of the "small Latine and lesse Greeke" that Ben Jonson attributed to Shakespeare in his commendatory verses to the First Folio (1623). J. Dover Wilson, in "Shakespeare's 'Small Latin'—How Much?" reviews most of the critics who have debated the subject.[4] Dr. Johnson thought that Shakespeare could read Latin but not with ease. Wilson thinks that Shakespeare could read it fairly well but is uncertain as to how much he did read. T. W. Baldwin's *Shakspere's 'Small Latine and Lesse Greeke'* (1944) demonstrates that as a student at Stratford Grammar School he would have had a considerable exposure to Latin.[5] It is clear that Shakespeare had the linguistic equipment to read Latin if he cared to do so.

I have long suspected that Jonson's comment on Shakespeare's "small Latine" referred to the latter's inability to write or speak Latin gracefully rather than to lack of a reading knowledge. The correct composition of Latin was a major objective among Elizabethan scholars.[6] In his Epigram 101, "Inviting a Friend to supper," Jonson writes that after the meal his serving man would entertain the company by reading aloud a page from Virgil, Livy, Tacitus, or some other author in Latin; he assumes that his visitor would understand spoken Latin. Jonson received commendatory verses in Latin from John Donne and John Selden, among others. After his death, *Jonsonus Virbius*, a collection of poetic tributes to him, included five poems in Latin and one in Greek.[7] We need only recall

13

Milton's original works in Latin to realize how much composition was stressed until the time when Latin was no longer used as a language of communication. Today the study of Latin is devoted primarily to reading it, not to writing or speaking it, and may thereby give a false emphasis to Jonson's remark.

Shakespeare doubtless drew a good many ideas and images from conversations with his friends, but some must have come from his independent reading. Perhaps it would be well to summarize here what I think Shakespeare read in Latin, in whole or in part. He probably used a translation with the Latin whenever he could find one, but he was not limited to translations only.

Of Latin poets, I think that Shakespeare shows familiarity with Lucretius's *De Rerum Natura*; Virgil's *Bucolica, Georgica,* and *Aeneid* (with Phaer's translation); Ovid's *Metamorphoses* (with Golding's translation) and *Ars Amandi;* Mantuan's *Eclogae* (with Turbervile's translation); Palingenius's *Zodiacus Vitae* (with Googe's translation); and the *Sententiae* of Publius Syrus. Of prose writers, he seems to show familiarity with the moral works of Cicero and of Seneca; with Augustine's *De Quantitate Animae;* with the works of Macrobius and Censorinus; and with Claudius Minos's comments on the *Emblemata* of Alciatus. I also suspect that he read Natalis Comes's *Mythologiae* and Erasmus's *Adagia.* I quote from several of the Latin church fathers besides Augustine, but I cannot be sure that Shakespeare read them; the quotations illustrate points he may have learned from some other source.

As we should expect, Shakespeare shows interest in the Greek philosophers Plato, Aristotle, and Plutarch. He seems to me to be familiar with Plutarch's *Moralia* in Philemon Holland's English translation (1603), with Plato's works in Ficino's Latin version (many editions), and with Aristotle's *Nicomachean Ethics.*

In Ficino's one-volume translation of Plato's works (1551 and others) are included Ficino's "argument" to each dialogue and his commentaries on the *Symposium* (Lat. *Convivium*) and the *Timaeus.* These I think Shakespeare knew. I have also noted several other passages from Ficino's *Opera Omnia* (1561, 1576).

Shakespeare twice refers to Aristotle by name, in both instances to the *Nicomachean Ethics.*[8] The only translation in English, John Wilkinson's abridged *Ethiques of Aristotle* (1547), cannot account for Shakespeare's borrowings from the work. After examining a num-

14

ber of Latin commentaries, I found one with significant resemblances to Shakespeare's work in Argyropylos's translation, with a commentary by Donatus Acciaiolus (1565).[9] He may also be indebted to Thomas Aquinas's commentary on the *Nicomachean Ethics*, as well as to the *Summa Theologica* and several minor works of Aquinas and to his commentary on Aristotle's *De Anima*.

Besides these, Shakespeare probably read in Phaedrus's Latin version of Aesop's *Fables*, in the Roman historians, and in the Roman dramatists (*The Comedy of Errors* is adapted from Plautus). These authors, however, do not come within the scope of the present study.

The works I have listed are those an intelligent Elizabethan would read in order to improve his knowledge of science and philosophy. The total amount of Latin text is quite large; but if we consider that Shakespeare probably read excerpts instead of complete books, the amount is not excessive. An eager and inquiring intellect would not find the difficulties insuperable. Mantuan, Palingenius, Virgil, Ovid, Cicero, and possibly Seneca and Lucretius could have been read in the grammar school at Stratford-upon-Avon.[10] At least Shakespeare could have been introduced to them there and have finished them for himself. The tradition that he once served as a schoolmaster would seem to indicate a fair knowledge of Latin.

Sixteenth-century compilations of knowledge in English have been explored by Hardin Craig[11] and his numerous successors, but they still yield significant information for the study of Shakespeare's intellectual background. Most of them are translations from Latin or French. Over the years much debate has centered upon Shakespeare's possible use of Montaigne's *Essais* (1588) in the English translation by John Florio (registered in 1600, printed in 1603). My opinion is that he did use Florio's translation, even before 1600, which means that he must have seen portions of it in manuscript (below, p. 183). He may have read it earlier in French, but the verbal parallels are not so marked as they are to the words of Florio. Alice Harmon in 1942 and Margaret T. Hodgen in 1952 warned against too ready acceptance of Montaigne as a Shakespearean source, since his images and ideas also appear elsewhere.[12] There is no better evidence of the difficulty of finding any consensus on verbal parallels and of the widely varying susceptibilities that different readers bring to the study. Some advocates of Montaigne's influence on Shakespeare have been J. M. Robertson, George Coffin Taylor, Suzanne Türck, W. B. D. Henderson, Max Deutschbein, Eleanor Prosser, Frank Kermode, and J. R. Brown.[13]

In my *Shakespeare's Derived Imagery* I have already demonstrated Shakespeare's heavy debt to the English translations of Palingenius's *Zodiake of Life* and La Primaudaye's *French Academie;* some further use of them is found in this volume. He also used treatises by Timothy Bright, Thomas Wright, Reginald Scot, Ludwig Lavater, Levinus Lemnius, and Bartholomaeus Anglicus (in Batman's translation).

We shall now study the transmutations in Shakespeare's mind of the materials he had read and their resultant contributions to his poetry.

II

The Universal World

SHAKESPEARE'S INTEREST in man, the microcosm or "little world," is paralleled by an interest in the macrocosm or "great world," of which man is the model.[1] Macrobius (fourth century) had written, "The physicists said that the world is a great man, and man a little world,"[2] similitudes echoed by many authors, notably by La Primaudaye (below, p. 200). Shakespeare uses each phrase. Lear rages "in his *little world* of man" (III.i.10). In *The Merchant of Venice* Portia complains, "My little body is aweary of this *great world*" (I.ii.2). The idea of such a resemblance or "cosmic sympathy" is prevalent in Shakespeare's plays and contributes to their "larger than life" portrayals.[3] The physical world seems to echo or foretell disasters in the world of men. Perhaps this theme is most evident in *Julius Caesar* and in *King Lear*.

An immediate problem is the meaning of the word *world*. Sometimes in Shakespeare it is a synonym for *earth*. At other times it refers to all eight spheres within the *primum mobile*, that is, to the entire visible universe of Ptolemaic astronomy. This second meaning is given by Macrobius, who writes that *mundus* properly refers to the sky[4] and by Barnabe Googe, who notes in *The Zodiake of Life* that "the vniuersal world" refers to *Cosmos* or *Mundus* or *Totum vniuersum*, since these are all the same.[5]

The confusion that can arise from the double usage of *world* is illustrated by the use of the phrase "pendent world" by Shakespeare and by Milton. In *Measure for Measure* Claudio names as one punishment after death to be blown about "the pendent world"

17

(III.i.126). The punishment is that named by Cicero in the last sentence of *Somnium Scipionis* (below, p. 58). The world here is the earth, and *pendent* was probably suggested by Ovid's *Metamorphoses* (I.12), where the earth hung *(pendebat)* in the surrounding air, poised by its own weight. In *Paradise Lost* (II.1051–1052) Satan sees at a great distance heaven "and fast by hanging in a golden chain This *pendent world.*" It seems likely that Milton recalled the Shakespearean phrase, but his "world" refers to the entire cosmos enclosed in an opaque shell; the "golden chain" comes from the *Iliad* (VIII.18–27), where Zeus boasts that if the gods should attach a golden chain to the world, he could draw it up by his own strength even if all the other gods pulled against him. The chain had been often used figuratively, but Milton chose to use it literally. In "pendent world" he and Shakespeare use the same words, but they refer to different things.

A similar ambiguity attends Shakespeare's use of the word *center* as applied to the earth. Sometimes he means the center of the earth; at other times he means the whole earth as the center of the world. I have reviewed elsewhere his uses of the *center,* together with his figurative use of the law of gravitation as a form of love, of the earth as the universal mother, and of the earth as an emblem of firmness and stability.[6] The essential qualities of the earth are briefly summed up in *Batman upon Bartholome:*

> As for the Earth, it is the Bace, and the Foundation of all the Elementes: for it is the obiect, the subiect, and the receiuer, of all the beames and influences of heauen. It contayneth in it the seedes, and seminall vertues of all things, therefore is she called Animall, Vegetall, and Minerall, which beeing made fruitfull by all the other Elementes and Heauens, is apte to beget all things. Of it selfe, it is receyuer of all fruitefulnesse, and as it were also, the first springing Parent of all things, the Center, foundation, and mother of all things.[7]

1. The World's Diameter

The earth itself is fixed and immovable; at the same time it furnishes the support for the revolving spheres. The entire cosmos revolves around the earth every twenty-four hours, while within the *primum mobile*, the outermost sphere, the several planets revolve at a more sedate pace. But all revolve upon the same invisible axis, which extends through the poles of the earth to the poles of the outermost sphere. Philemon Holland, translating from Plutarch's *Platonic Questions*, no. 7, calls it "the axletree or pole that passeth thorow the world."[8] Robert Allott, in *Wits Theater of the Little World* (1599), explains it at greater length:

> The Spheare of heauen goeth vpon two Poles, the North and the South, which are neuer seene of vs.
> The Center of the Spheare is the middle poynt of the same, and the Axe of it is a right line, passing from one side of the same (by his Center) to the contrary side, about which the roundnes of heauen moueth, as a wheele about an Axletree, but the line it selfe standeth still.
> The ends of this line *Axis* are called *Cardines coeli*, because they mooue about the hollownes of the Poles.[9]

This axis received its principal support at the center, from the earth, somewhat like cantilever construction in modern buildings; but its tremendous length made desirable some additional support at each end. Lucretius explains in these words:

> If from the beginning the great sphere of heaven revolves, we must say that an *air* presses on the pole at each end and confines it in the outside and closes it in at both ends.[10]

The Venerable Bede, in his *Mundi Constitutio*, expands this explanation in connection with his description of the firmament:

> But each of the elements of which the world consists takes its place according to its nature: fire the highest place because of its lightness, earth the lowest place because of its weight; around it the water flows, and the air around them both. But above the firmament, in the realm of divine things, are the super-celestial waters, and above these the spiritual heavens in which the angelic virtues are contained. Indeed, the one earth is so located in the midst that it is equally distant from the firmament at all

19

points, except for the surface irregularities of mountains and valleys; and through its middle point there crosses an intellectual line [perceived only by the intellect] from the Arctic Pole to the Antarctic, which is so bound (*ligatur*) by the surrounding pressure of the *air* that it may never be deflected.[11]

In *Troilus and Cressida,* when the Greeks are in council, Ulysses urges them to pay attention to Nestor's words, which are but air and yet are powerful:

> and such again
> As venerable Nestor, hatch'd in silver [gray-haired],
> Should with a *bond of air* (strong as the *axle-tree*
> On which the heavens ride) knit all Greek ears
> To his experienc'd tongue. (I.iii.64–68)

The "bond of air" that supports the "axle-tree" of heaven and is equally strong resembles Bede's *ligatur* but could also have been suggested by Lucretius's infinitives *premere, tenere, claudere.* Shakespeare wishes to demonstrate the strength of an "airy word" (*Romeo and Juliet,* I.i.96) such as Nestor's when its wisdom determines a course of human action.

Shakespeare has other figurative uses of the earth's centricity in the world. In *Hamlet* after Polonius's death King Claudius speculates on means of minimizing the public reaction against the royal family:

> Come, Gertrude, we'll call up our wisest friends;
> And let them know, both what we mean to do,
> And what's untimely done. So, haply, slander,
> Whose *whisper* o'er *the world's diameter,*
> As level as a cannon to his blank [target],
> Transports his poison'd shot, may miss our names,
> And hit the woundless air. (IV.i.38–44)

This passage represents a combination of sources. We are helped in our understanding of it by Macrobius's discussion of the world's diameter. He explains that the Egyptians, in order to predict eclipses of the moon, wished to determine the relative magnitudes of the earth, the sun, the moon, and their orbits. To do this, they sought to determine the circumference of the sun's circle by first determining the circle's diameter:

> In every orb or sphere the middle is called the center, and the center is nothing but a point by which the middle of the orb or sphere is distinguished by most careful observation. Again, a line drawn from any point of the circle which is called the ambit [circumference] to any other extreme point of the same circle will necessarily separate a certain part of the orb. But not in every case is it the middle of the orb which this division separates. For, if that line divides the middle orb into equal parts, so reaching from one extreme point to another extreme point that it necessarily crosses through the center and thus divides the orb equally, it is called the *diameter*.... But the earth, in the midst of the celestial circle through which the sun runs, was placed as a center; therefore a measure of the celestial diameter may show the middle of the earth's shadow; and if also from another part of the earth an equal measure is extended to the same circle, the whole diameter of the circle through which the sun runs is discovered.[12]

Macrobius had already pointed out that the earth is the center of all spheres as well as of the sun's sphere and is thus the center of the whole world: "But the earth is the center of the world-sphere."[13] Later he declares that, since the earth is the center of the universe, all things fall toward it from all sides.[14] He has made it clear that there is no one diameter; any straight line drawn through the center from opposite points in an outer sphere will be a diameter of that sphere.

This discussion associated itself in Shakespeare's mind with Ovid's account of the palace of *Fama* (fame, rumor) at the midpoint of the world-sphere to which all sounds in the world fall. This description was used by Chaucer in his House of Rumour, which follows after his description of the House of Fame. Ovid writes;

> There is a spot in the middle of the world (*orbe locus medio est*), between the land and the sea, and the regions of heaven, the confines of the threefold universe, whence is beheld whatever anywhere exists, although it may be in far distant regions, and

every sound pierces the hollow ears. Of this place Fame is possessed, and chooses for herself a habitation on the top of a tower, and has added innumerable avenues, and a thousand openings to her house, and has closed the entrances with no gates. Night and day are they open. It is all of sounding brass; it is all resounding, and it reechoes the voice, and repeats what it hears. Within there is no rest, and silence in no part. Nor yet is there a clamour, but the murmur of a low voice, such as is wont to arise from the waves of the sea, if one listens at a distance, or like the sound which the end of the thundering makes when Jupiter has clashed the black clouds together. A crowd occupies the hall; the fickle vulgar come and go; and a thousand rumours, false mixed with true, wander up and down, and circulate confused words. Of these, some fill the empty ears with conversation; some are carrying elsewhere what is told them; the measure of the fiction is ever on the increase, and each fresh narrator adds something to what he has heard. There is Credulity, there rash Mistake, and empty Joy, and alarmed Fear, and sudden Sedition, and *Whispers (Susurri)* of doubtful origin. She sees what things are done in heaven, and on the sea, and on the earth; and she pries into the whole universe. (trans. Riley)[15]

Shakespeare recalls this description in *Titus Andronicus:*

The Emperor's court is like the House of Fame,
The palace full of tongues, of eyes, and ears. (II.i.126–127)

The location of Ovid's house of *Fama* at the midpoint of the world-sphere places it on the earth. The various slanders and whispers falling straight down "as level as a cannon to his blank" must necessarily traverse the world's diameter, or its many diameters. The king, comparing himself to the earth, wonders if he could step aside enough to let the "poison'd shot" pass by harmlessly and hit the "woundless air" beyond.

This proposed evasion seems to be suggested by Macrobius's argument for the earth's centricity. Rain falls to the earth from every quarter of the sky. If the earth were not central or could be moved from the center, much of this rain would fall past the earth and into the air beyond and out again into the sky. Since this does not happen, the earth must be central.[16] Claudius's plan to evade the "whisper" by slipping our of its way is analogous to Macrobius's speculation as to moving the earth from a central position so that the "world's diameter" would no longer pass through it. It was a forlorn hope at best. Until Copernicus, no one thought it could be done.

The words "so, haply, slander" do not appear in the original texts of *Hamlet* but were supplied by Capell's emendation. I suggest "so, haply, rumour" as more probable. In the prologue to *2 Henry IV* Rumour personified appears "in a robe painted full of tongues." This detail comes from Virgil's *Fama* (*Aeneid*, IV.183) and Chaucer's *Fame* (*House of Fame*, line 1390); and these combined in Shakespeare's mind with Ovid's *Fama*, whose house is at the midpoint of the world. Since this personification was in the king's mind and since Shakespeare elsewhere calls her Rumour, this name is probably the one that Claudius would have used.[17]

Yet another use of the earth as the world's center and of the diametric line running through it appears in *A Midsummer Night's Dream*, when Hermia refuses to believe that Lysander has deserted her:

> The sun was not so true unto the day
> As he to me; would he have stolen away
> From sleeping Hermia? I'll believe as soon
> This whole earth may be bor'd, and that the moon
> May through the center creep and so displease
> Her brother's noontide with the Antipodes. (III.ii.50–55)

The fancy that the earth may be bored, with an open passage through the center, appears twice in Plato's works. In *Phaedo* (112) he describes the cavern of Tartarus which pierces through the whole earth and through which great rivers flow. Ficino refers to it as follows:

> And also hard by the center itself of the world, rivers of fire, water, and air flow from all sides through the terrene gulfs.[18]

In the Vision of Er in Republic X (616), Er sees a straight line of light extending right through the whole heaven and through the earth. This would seem to be the "axle-tree" of the universe, though

23

Plato does not call it so. Vincent de Beauvais speculates on what
would happen if the earth were bored *(perforatus)* and a stone were
dropped into the opening; the stone would stop at the exact center of
the earth.[19]

Hermia describes as something unbelievable an astronomical
game of tag between the sun and the moon. Macrobius explains that
when the sun and the moon are both in a direct line with the earth,
one or the other of them is necessarily in eclipse. If the moon is on the
side of the earth away from the sun, her light is eclipsed by the
conical shadow of the earth projected through space; but if the moon
is between the earth and the sun, the sun is eclipsed because his light
cannot reach the earth through the solid moon.[20] Macrobius also says
that "without *her brother's rays* the moon may not shine."[21] He
discusses and explains at some length the Antipodes or side of the
earth directly opposite one's present location and changing as one
changes that location.[22] He defines the meridian as the highest point
of the sky that the sun occupies at "noon-tide"; when the moon is in
eclipse, it occupies the meridian directly opposite.[23] Palingenius
writes,

> And as the Sunnes eclipse doth showe; wherein appeareth well
> Howe great the Moon in body is while vnder him she glides,
> And darkning all with shadowes blacke, *hir brothers beames she*
> *hides.*[24]

Hermia's conceit involves yet another impossibility: that the
moon should abandon its circular orbit and progress in a straight
line. Macrobius points out that the motion of the heavenly bodies is
necessarily circular.[25] If all the impossibilities could be overcome, the
astronomical action would be as follows: Hermia is speaking at
night, while the sun shines on the Antipodes, on the other side of the
earth. If at noontide there the moon should be in eclipse here and if
the moon could creep through the center of the earth in a straight
line, she would automatically reverse the situation by putting the sun
into eclipse "and so displease Her brother's noontide with the
Antipodes." She would thus play a joke upon her lordly brother; he
could not be "true unto the day" because day is turned into night for
the period of the eclipse.[26]

2. *The Sun and the Moon*

The sun and the moon are included among the "wandering stars" or planets (*stellae erraticae* or *stellae errantes*) in contrast with the fixed stars above and the fixed earth below. As the most eminent of the planets, the sun is the middle one of seven, with the moon, Mercury, and Venus below him and with Mars, Jupiter, and Saturn above him. Palingenius hails the sun as "the Prince of all the Starres."[27] Macrobius, writing of the sun, says,

> Therefore he is a leader *(dux)* because he precedes all other lights in majesty; a prince *(princeps)* because he is so far eminent *(eminet)* in brightness that he may appear *solus* (alone), from which he is called *Sol,* the moderator of the remaining lights, because he governs their turnings and returnings within a certain defined limit of space. For a certain defined limit of space is that to which, when a particular wandering star receding from the sun shall have come, as though it is prohibited from continuing it seems to go backward; and again, when by receding it shall have touched a certain part, it is recalled to its accustomed direct course. So the strength and power of the sun govern the motion of the remaining lights by a constituted dimension.[28]

In Ulysses' speech on degree in *Troilus and Cressida*, he seems to make use of this passage:

> The heavens themselves, the planets and this center
> Observe degree, priority, and place,
> Insisture, course, proportion, season, form,
> Office and custom in all line of order;
> And therefore is the glorious planet *Sol*
> In noble *eminence* enthroned and sphered
> Amidst the other; whose medicinable eye
> Corrects the ill aspects of planets evil,
> And posts, like the commandment of a king,
> Sans check to good and bad. But when the planets
> In evil mixture to disorder wander,
> What plagues and what portents! (I.iii.85–96)

The sun and the moon, among the planets, maintain a constant distance from the central earth; the other planets "wander" farther from the earth at some times than at others. But the sun sees to it that they do not wander too far and thus introduce confusion into the affairs of men. Likewise the constituted leader of men—Agamemnon in this case—must be recognized and obeyed if the Greek army is to function effectively.

Macrobius refers to the sun as the *igneus oculus* (fiery eye) of the heavens.[29] Shakespears calls the sun "heaven's fiery eye" in *Love's Labour's Lost* (V.ii.375) and a "burning eye" in *Romeo and Juliet* (II.iii.5). Palingenius calls the sun "the syght and eye of all the worlde."[30] He is called "the all-seeing sun" in *Romeo and Juliet* (I.ii.97).

Macrobius explains Virgil's reference to zones in the sky. The earth has one tropical or "burning" zone bounded by the tropics of Cancer and Capricorn, which mark the northern and southern limits of the sun's path around the earth. The corresponding zone in the sky is also a burning *(perusta, ardens)* zone. Likewise, the sky has temperate and frigid zones corresponding to similar zones on earth.

This analysis is based on Virgil's lines from the First Georgic.[31] Macrobius comments,

> Nunc, quoniam constitit, easdem in caelo et in terra zonas esse vel cingulos—haec enim unius rei duo sunt nomina. (Now, since he demonstrates that in the sky and in the earth there are the same zones or girdles—for these are two names for one thing.)[32]

This analysis explains Hamlet's words to Laertes at Ophelia's grave:

> And if thou prate of mountains, let them throw
> Millions of acres on us, till our ground,
> Singeing his pate against the *burning zone*,
> Make Ossa like a wart. (V.i.303–306)

Ossa is the proverbial mountain upon which the Titans heaped Mt. Pelion in order to reach the dwellings of the gods on Mt. Olympus. Hamlet proposes a mountain to reach the "burning zone" or sun's circle in the sky, which would make the Titans' effort seem insignificant.

Macrobius's alternate term for *zone* is *cingulum* (girdle). This may have suggested Puck's remark in *A Midsummer Night's Dream:*

> I'll put a *girdle* round about the earth
> In forty minutes. (II.i.175-176)

He refers to his speed, which he estimates at 37,500 miles per hour.

Puck's reference to "the wandering moon" designates the moon as one of the planets (IV.i.102). His reference to the swiftness of the moon's sphere (II.i.7) denotes the fact that the moon circles the earth in twenty-eight days, while all the other planets take much longer. The change of shape of the moon during its course makes it an emblem of inconstancy (*Romeo and Juliet*, II.ii.107; *Antony and Cleopatra*, V.ii.240). In *Timon of Athens* the moon is termed a thief for shining by the reflected light of the sun (IV.iii.68,440). In *Troilus and Cressida* Thersites sarcastically remarks that when Diomedes keeps his word, the sun will borrow light of the moon; neither circumstance will ever happen (V.i.101).

Macrobius repeats the well-known fact that the moon controls the ebb and flow of ocean tides; and he gives a calendar thereof, with the highest tides coming on the new moon and on the fourteenth day thereafter.[33] Shakespeare uses this figuratively. In *The Winter's Tale* Camillo remarks that "you may as well Forbid the sea for to obey the moon" as try to change Leontes's mind (I.ii.427). In *1 Henry IV* Falstaff characterizes himself and his fellow night prowlers as "minions of the moon . . . being governed, as the sea is, by . . . the moon." Prince Hal replies that their fortunes ebb and flow like the sea, being governed, as the sea is, by the moon (I.ii.29-37).

The moon's control of the tides caused her to be associated with moisture. Shakespeare refers to her as "the moist star" (*Hamlet*, I.i.118) and "the watery moon" (*Midsummer Night's Dream*, II.i.162, III.i.203; *Richard III*, II.ii.69). Macrobius says that the union of heat from the sun and moisture from the moon is the cause of all generation of life.[34] In the soul's passage from the heavens to the earth, it acquires from the moon "naturam *plantandi* et augendi corpora" (the nature of planting bodies and causing them to grow).[35] Among Troilus's vows to Cressida, he promises to be as true "as *plantage* to the *moon*" (III.ii.184), that is, crops mature on the full moon. The moon's influence upon the human body is stated by Macrobius:

> Nor is there any doubt that the moon is the author and conditioner of mortal bodies, so much so that some bodies experience growth with the increase of her light and are diminished when her light is decreased.[36]

In *Measure for Measure* the Duke-Friar names such changes among the ills of life:

> Thou art not certain,
> For thy complexion shifts to strange effects
> After the *moon*. (III.i.23–25)

The lunar moisture can cause illness and even insanity, Macrobius says,

> For if one has given himself to sleep for a long time under the moon, he is excited by illness and becomes nearest to the insane from the oppressive weight of the humour which in all his body is diffused and dispersed by the lunar property, which opens and relaxes all the passages of the body as it infuses the body.[37]

Othello pretends to explain to Emilia the catastrophe being visited upon them:

> It is the very error of the moon;
> She comes more nearer earth than she was wont,
> And makes men mad. (V.ii.109–111)

Batman states that the moon is a cause of madness because of the effect of her rays upon the brain.[38]
Macrobius expands at some length upon the debilitating effect of the moon's rays as evidenced by the fact that they cause meat to decay. He insists that, in hunting, if wild boars are killed by day the meat will stay fresh, but if they are killed at night by moonlight the meat will putrefy:

Nullius enim rei fit aliquando putredo nisi calor humorque convenerint. Pecudum autem putredo nihil aliud est, nisi cum defluxio quaedam latens *soliditatem carnis in humorem resolvit.* (For decay of anything is not accomplished at any time unless heat and moisture come together. But decay of the meat of animals is nothing else than when a certain hidden down-flowing *resolves the solidity of flesh into moisture.*)[39]

A few lines later Macrobius adds,

Sed nescio quae proprietas, quam Graeci *idioma* vocant, et quaedam natura inest lumini, quod de ea defluit, quae humectat corpora, et velut *occulto rore madefaciat;* cui admixtus calor ipse lunaris putrefacit carnem, cui diutale fuerit infusus. (But I know not what property, which the Greeks call *idioma,* and particular nature is in the light which from her [the moon] down-flows, which moistens bodies and *soaks them as by a hidden dew;* added to which the admixed lunar heat itself putrefies the flesh into which it shall have been infused for such a long time.)[40]

We find a possible verbal reminiscence of these passages in Hamlet's first soliloquy:

> O that this too, too *solid flesh* would melt,
> Thaw and *resolve itself into a dew.* (I.ii.129–130)

I do not propose to debate the Folio reading *solid* as opposed to the Quarto reading *sallied* (usually emended to *sullied*) except to say that *solid* seems more logical to me as the opposite of *thaw* and *melt.* It is quite possible that Shakespeare himself used both forms, for the Folio version of *Hamlet*[41] involves a considerable revision of the Quarto versions.

In the two passages from Macrobius the "downflowing" represents the "influence" of a heavenly body, an influence that "falls" from the sky to affect the world of perishable things. The "moisture" of the first passage becomes a "hidden dew" in the second. The Latin *madefaciat* does not quite mean *thaw* or *melt* but is the first stage of thawing when the flesh becomes "soaked" before decomposition. Macrobius sums up his argument in these words:

Ita undique versum probatur, ad humectandas dissolvendasque carnes inesse lunari lumini proprietatem; quam magis usus, quam ratio deprehendit. (So it is proved at every turn that in the lunar light is a property towards moistening and dissolving flesh, which experience demonstrates more than reason does.)[42]

Here the "dissolving" process of flesh into dew is made complete. There seems to be no rational explanation why lunar light should dissolve flesh, but experience shows that it does so. The verbal resemblances to the several passages suggest that Shakespeare had a keen memory for Latin phrases as well as for English ones.

The moon's moisture is also used in witchcraft. In *Macbeth* Hecate says,

> Upon the corner of the *moon*
> There hangs a *vap'rous drop* profound;
> I'll catch it ere it come to ground;
> And that, distill'd by magic sleights,
> Shall raise such artificial sprites
> As by the strength of their illusion
> Shall draw him on to his confusion. (III.v.23-29)

In classical mythology Hecate herself is one form of the triformed moon goddess: Cynthia in the heavens, Diana or Artemis on the earth, Hecate in the underworld.[43]

In *The Tempest* Prospero says that the witch Sycorax, when living, could control the moon and the tides (V.i. 269-270). Francis Douce long ago pointed out a marginal note in William Adlington's translation of Apuleius's *Golden Ass* (1596):

> Witches of old time were supposed to be of such power that they could pul downe the moone by their inchauntment.[44]

The source of this belief is probably Virgil's *Bucolica* (VIII.69): "Carmina vel coelo possunt deducere Lunam" (Magic songs can even draw down the moon from the sky).

3. The Great Globe

The sun and the moon are not alone in their power to affect the lower world of change and mortality, which includes everything below the moon's sphere. According to Palingenius, God uses the whole universe enclosed by the sphere of the fixed stars to implement the decrees of destiny. God is

> In one estate remaining still, and chaunging in no time,
> The chiefest cause that rowling ay the *Globe* where starres do shine,
> Doest guide by fixed law thappointed force of destenie.[45]

Like *world*, the word *globe* may refer to the earth alone or to the whole universe. Macrobius mentions its use in both ways. The heavenly sphere or "globe" of the fixed stars does not of itself determine the fates of men, "cum *globus ipse,* quod caelum est, animae sit *fabrica*" (since the *globe itself,* which is the sky, is a *fabric* of the world-soul).[46] This conjunction of *globe* and *fabric* appears in Prospero's visionary speech in *The Tempest*:

> And, like the baseless *fabric* of this vision,
> The cloud-capp'd towers, the gorgeous palaces,
> The solemn *temples,* the great *globe itself,*
> Yea, all which it inherit, shall dissolve
> And, like this insubstantial pageant faded,
> Leave not a rack behind. We are such stuff
> As dreams are made on, and our little life
> Is rounded with a sleep. (IV.i.151–158)

Macrobius elsewhere quotes Cicero's reference to "illum *globum,* quem in *templo* hoc medium vides, quae *terra* dicitur" (that *globe,* which you see in this *temple* at the middle point, and which is called *earth*).[47] He explains that the "temple" is the universal world that God conceived and built, while the "globe" or earth is the central point of this great temple. It seems likely that Macrobius's verbal conjunctions of "fabric" with the "globe itself" and of "temple" with "globe" are echoed in Prospero's speech, for these three words do not appear in the other probable sources of this passage.[48]

Prospero's description of life as being "rounded with a sleep" has caused much debate. Some readers find in it a denial of immortality, death being "only a sleep eternal in an eternal night."[49] Others view it as a promise of immortality, a relief from the perils and dangers of this life. Perhaps Macrobius can shed some light on this debate. He pictures each human soul as being fashioned by God, then "falling" through the sphere of the fixed stars and the lower planetary spheres until it reaches the body it is to inhabit while on earth. In its passage it receives various qualities from the different constellations and planets. When it reaches the boundary line where the Zodiac and the Milky Way touch each other, "anima descendens a *tereti*, quae sola forma divina est, in conum defluendo producitur" (the soul, falling from its *roundness*, which is the only divine form, by downflowing is stretched into a cone). After the body's death and the soul's purgation from any vices it may have acquired, it ascends to the light of perpetual life and is returned into its original form.[50] Earthly life is an imprisonment of the soul as compared with its better life above the stars.[51]

Here is a logical meaning for Prospero's word *rounded*. The soul's change of shape in falling was probably suggested by raindrops, which lengthen into conical shapes before striking the ground. Our death on earth is a "sleep" that "rounds" our life by restoring the soul to its natural rounded shape that it enjoys before and after its tour of duty here below. Some readers may prefer the simpler explanation that the wheel of life has come "full circle" (*King Lear*, V.iii.174).

According to Macrobius, Cicero uses *globe* or *globosity* to express the density or solidity of a sphere and uses *rotundity* to express its round shape:

> But when he calls the stars *globosas et rotundas*, he expresses not just the species of individual stars but of those which gather together in forming signs [of the Zodiac]. For all stars among themselves, though they have some difference in magnitude, yet have no difference in species. But through these two terms is described a solid sphere, which cannot be achieved by globosity lacking rotundity nor by rotundity lacking globosity, since in the one case it is abandoned by form, in the other case by solidity of body. But we here name as spheres those bodies of

the stars themselves which have all been formed according to this species.[52]

Macrobius here uses "solidity" to refer to any degree of density or "thickness," including that possessed by the fire of the stars and the aether of their spheres; for without some density a sphere is nothing but a mathematical diagram. Relatively, the earth's solidity is greater than any other, since it was formed by the dregs of the sky;[53] but the spheres above have lesser degrees of density and therefore have some weight. In 1596 Johann Kepler published his early efforts to measure the "thickness" of space in order to determine the weight of the universe that rested upon the earth as its foundation.[54] His work may have renewed scientific interest in the theory here set forth by Macrobius.

Hamlet uses this imagery to stress the heinousness of his mother's conduct in wedding Claudius:

> Heaven's face doth glow;
> Yea, this solidity and compound mass,
> With tristful visage, as against the doom,
> Is thought-sick at the act. (III.iv.48–51)

Both the sky and the solid earth experience the same fear that they will feel before their destruction on doomsday. The sky blushes with shame; the earth's face is sad. The earth is a "compound mass" of different elements; stars above the moon are not compound, being made wholly of fire. Hamlet's speech is another instance of the "cosmic sympathy" between the macrocosm of the universe and the microcosm of human beings.

Yet another instance is Lear's furious cry to the thunder:

> Strike flat the *thick rotundity* of the *world!*
> Crack *nature's moulds,* all *germens* spill at once
> That makes ingrateful man! (III.ii.7–9)

The *thickness* of globosity and the roundness of *rotundity* are both necessary parts of the earth, of a star, or of a starry sphere. We cannot say with certainty whether Lear's "world" in the quotation refers to the earth or to the sphere of the universe. It does not matter very much which answer we give; for if the great sphere were flattened, the earth at its center would be flattened, too. In a similar image from *The Winter's Tale,* Prince Florizel says that if he should break faith with Perdita,

> Let Nature crush the sides o' the *earth* together
> And mar the *seeds* within. (IV.iv.488–489)

This reference to the earth suggests that Lear is likewise referring to the earth and to the storm upon its surface.[55] Had he thought about the matter, he would have known that a local thunderstorm did not extend to the outer stars.

4. Seeds and Germens

The "germens" appear once more in Shakespeare when Macbeth invokes the aid of the witches:

> Though you untie the winds and let them fight
> Against the churches; though the yesty waves
> Confound and swallow navigation up;
> Though bladed corn be lodg'd and trees blown down;
> Though castles topple on their warder's heads;
> Though palaces and pyramids do slope
> Their heads to their foundations; though the treasure
> Of *nature's germens* tumble all together
> Even till destruction sicken; answer me
> To what I ask you. (IV.i.52–61)

This continues the imagery from the speech by King Lear.

In *Macbeth* Banquo addresses the witches, who have just hailed Macbeth as thane of Cawdor and future king of Scotland:

> If you can look into the *seeds of time*
> And say which grain will grow and which will not,
> Speak then to me. (I.iii.58–60)

Since a germen is a sprout or germinated seed, the four passages using "seeds" and "germens" are obviously related to each other.

The word *seed* has several meanings. It can refer to the seeds of plants, in which the principle of life lies dormant. Its Latin form *semen* can refer to the seminal fluid of animals. As used in accounts of the creation, it has two distinct meanings. One meaning refers to atoms of matter, the smallest units of which go to make up all things in the universe. These atoms, in a confused and disorderly mass, constituted the first matter (*prima materia*) of chaos. The theory of atoms is usually accredited to Democritus, but it was popularized by Lucretius, whose *primordia* (first beginnings) are hard and indestructible and are called *semina rerum* (seeds of things).[56] But he quotes Anaxagoras as thinking that the seeds are weaker and subject to injury when the world falls to destruction:

> Nam quid in oppressu valido durabit eorum
> Ut mortem effugiat, leti sub dentibus ipsis?
> (For which of those will endure the crushing pressure, that it
> may escape death, under the very teeth of dissolution?)[57]

This does envision an injury to the "seeds of things" when the earth is crushed flat and offers a probable suggestion for Florizel's speech. Lucretius thinks that the seeds or *primordia* will survive to become part of a "sea of matter" (*materiae . . . in pelago*).[58] These atoms are also the *semina rerum* in Ovid's description of chaos.[59] They are not seeds that can sprout into life but are the basic particles of matter of which all things are made. They also seem to be the "seeds" Virgil found in the songs of Orpheus:

> Namque canebat, uti magnum per inane coacta
> *Semina* terrarumque, animaeque, marisque fuissent
> Et liquidi simul ignis: ut his exordia primis
> Omnia, et ipse tener mundi concreverit orbis.
> (For he sang how through the great void the *seeds* of earth and
> air and water and clear fire had been all driven together; how
> from these first things the fragility of the world's sphere hard-
> ened into all the elemental beginnings.)[60]

Here the "seeds" combined in such a way as to produce the four elements they were designed to produce. The seeds themselves seem to be atoms.

A seed that can sprout into a plant carries in miniature all the qualities of the parent plant and by its own decay produces a new plant like the parent. These qualities that it transmits exist within it as seminal reasons *(rationes seminales)*, according to Saint Augustine.[61] In the first creation of the world there were no prepared seeds and plants sprang into being directly from the seminal reasons, which were mixed into the first matter of chaos. An analogous process took place in animal and human generation. The first crossing of the seminal power into concrete existence was in the sprouting "germen" that would eventually grow into a new plant or animal. The seminal reasons of all future living things were mixed into the matter of the world from its beginning.

In an illuminating essay, W. C. Curry traces Shakespeare's "germens" to the *rationes seminales,* though he does not sufficiently clarify the distinction between seeds as atoms and seeds as germens. He points out that all seminal reasons were originally mixed into the matter of the world, though they might wait many centuries before emerging as new forms or species and some might never emerge at all. Consequently, he identifies Banquo's "seeds of time" with the *rationes seminales,* since some grains will grow and some will not grow.[62] This is a highly ingenious supposition and I think a correct one.

Augustine uses *germen* to mean a sprouted seed.[63] In the Vulgate version of Isaiah 61:9-11 *semen* and *germen* are used metaphorically in reference to one's descendants. Ficino writes that the soul enters the body "potestate *naturae* foecundae pullulantis in *germen"* (by the power of fecund *nature* sprouting into a *germen*), for the bodily form is the offspring of the fecund soul.[64] Again, Ficino relates the propagation of seeds into germens to the impulse of love, both divine and natural, which brings orderly existence out of chaos:

> Love compels the *seeds* to sprout into a *germen,* brings forth their qualities in its bosom, conceives a foetus and as if by opening with certain keys brings the conceived thing into the light; for which reason all parts of the world, because they are the works of one Maker, members of the same machine alike in being and in living among themselves, are reciprocally bound to each other by a certain mutual love, so that rightly love can be

called the perpetual knot and coupler of the world, the immovable support of its parts, and the firm base of the whole machine.[65]

The description of love as the support and the base (*sustentaculum* and *fundamentum*) of the world recalls Batman's description of the earth in the same terms; he also adds that the earth contains the seeds and the seminal virtues of all things (above, p. 18). Perhaps Shakespeare recalled the two passages together in Cressida's words when she finds that she must leave Troilus:

> Time, force, and death,
> Do to this body what extremes you can;
> But the strong *base* and *building* of my love
> Is as the very center of the earth,
> Drawing all things to it. (IV.ii.107–111)

Ficino and Batman may also have jointly contributed the image of earth as a storehouse of "nature's germens." These are the sprouts proceeding from the *rationes seminales,* which determine the appearance and qualities of the bodies to be produced and which may be accurately characterized as "nature's moulds."[66] The earth as a reservoir of the "seeds of all things" is also described by Timothy Bright:

This earth he [God] had endued with a fecunditye of infinite *seeds of all things*: which hee comaunded it as a mother, to bring forth, and as it is most agreable to their nature, to entertaine with nourishment that which it had borne, & brought forth: whereby when he had all the furniture of this inferiour worlde, of these creatures, some he fixed there still, and maintaineth the seedes, till the end of al thinges, and that determinate time, which he hath ordained, for *the emptying of those seedes* of creatures, which he first indued the earth withall. Other some, that is to say, the animals, hee drew wholly from the earth at the beginning, and planted seede in them onely, and food from other creatures: as beasts, and man in respect of his bodie.[67]

The last sentence indicates that man's physical body and the seeds that make it shall perish along with the beasts but that the rational soul, created separately by God, shall not perish in the world's destruction at doomsday. The "emptying of those seedes" may have suggested Lear's image of "spilling" the germens.

5. Chaos and the Elements

Bright's belief that earth will contain and that God will maintain the "seeds" to the end of all things on doomsday serves to identify the Last Judgment with the destruction of the world envisioned by Lear, Florizel, and Macbeth. Shakespeare is fond of using doomsday figuratively. "Up, up, and see The great *doom's* image," cries Macduff on discovering the murdered Duncan (*Macbeth*, II.iii.82–83). "Is this the promis'd end? Or image of that horror?" ask Kent and Edgar when Lear brings in the dead Cordelia; Albany replies, "Fall, and cease!" (V.iii.263–264).[68] After the murder of Julius Caesar, "men, wives, and children stare, cry out, and run As it were doomsday" (III.i.96–97). "What less than dooms-day [death] is the prince's doom?" Romeo asks of Friar Laurence after the death of Tybalt (III.iii.9).

The world's destruction on doomsday is often envisioned as the return of ancient chaos. Somewhere in or outside the world, chaos still exists, waiting to overwhelm the orderly cosmos. It is identified with the "deep" or "abyss" (Vulgate) of waters in Genesis 1:2. Hence its action is described in terms of a flood.[69] In *2 Henry IV* Northumberland cries out on hearing of his son's death:

> Let heaven kiss earth! Now let not Nature's hand
> Keep the *wild flood* confin'd! Let order die . . .
> And *darkness* be the burier of the dead. (I.i.153–160)

The "wild flood" is the same as Lucretius's "sea of matter" (above, p. 35). The "darkness" may stem from "darkness . . . upon the face of the deep" in Genesis 1:2. Northumberland, in his grief, seems to feel that the whole world should fall to destruction to match his sense of loss.[70]

Ficino, in his chapter "The Origin of Love from Chaos," expands upon the concept of love as a creative force. The impulse of love brought life, order, and harmony out of the confusion of chaos.[71] Othello uses this figure in stating his love for Desdemona:

> Excellent wretch! Perdition catch my soul,
> But I do love thee! and when I love thee not,
> *Chaos* is come again. (III.iii.90–92)

His love for her cannot fail as long as the principle of love exists in the universe. But after he has killed her, he exclaims,

> Methinks it should be now a huge eclipse
> Of sun and moon, and that th'affrighted globe
> Did yawn at alteration. (V.ii.99–101)

The globe or sphere of the world would be changed from its present form as the lights of heaven went out. The sun and moon could both be in eclipse only by extinction of the sun's light.

Before the destruction of the cosmos and the final victory of chaos, there are occasional lesser confusions among the elements of the world and among the seasons of the year. Plato relates these to a failure of harmonious and orderly love as a guiding principle in the operations of natural things (*Symposium*, 188). I translate from the Latin of Ficino:

> For the constitution of the seasons of the year is full with one or the other [kinds of love]. When, as I was just saying, [the qualities of] hot and cold, dry and moist, share a concordant love among themselves and sustain a suitable harmony and temper, they will bring a healthful and fertile year to all men, animals, and plants, nor will they injure anything. But, contrariwise, when petulant and contumelious love prevails in the seasons of the year, it corrupts things with much harm. Plagues are accustomed to be born from them, and many other diseases spring up in various animals and plants. Then frost, ice, hail, rust and rottenness of the corn, proceed from the immoderate and excessive love among the qualities.[72]

In his commentary on this passage, Ficino writes that "from moder-

ate love come pleasingly temperate air, tranquility of waters, fertility
of lands, and health of animals; from immoderate love, their op-
posites."[73]

The passage in the *Symposium* was spoken by Eryximachus. The
four "qualities" that fall into disarray through immoderate love are
hot and cold, dry and moist, which characterize the four elements of
earth, water, air, and fire; and Eryximachus's reference, "as I was just
saying," is to a remark on harmonizing the hostile qualities of the
four elements (*Symposium*, 187). According to Macrobius, the elements are bound together by their similar qualities and pressed apart
by their hostile qualities, thus holding themselves in equilibrium:

Earth	Water	Air	Fire	Earth
Cold	Cold	Hot	Hot	Cold
Dry	Moist	Moist	Dry	Dry

The stability of the elements depends on this equilibrium of their
qualities.[74] In primeval chaos, according to Ovid, there was no
equilibrium: cold fought against hot, moist against dry.[75] God's act
of creation was to separate the elements and to recombine them in an
orderly manner, maintaining an equilibrium of their qualities.[76]

In *A Midsummer Night's Dream* Titania has a long speech upon the
unseasonable weather, which she attributes to the quarrels and
disorderly love between herself and Oberon:

These are the forgeries of jealousy;
And never, since the middle summer's spring . . .
But with thy brawls thou hast disturb'd our sport.
Therefore the winds, piping to us in vain,
As in revenge, have suck'd up from the sea
Contagious fogs . . . and *the green corn*
Hath rotted ere his youth attain'd a beard.
The fold stands empty in the drowned field,
And crows are fatted with the murrain [diseased] flock . . .
That rheumatic *diseases* do abound.
And thorough this distemperature we see
The seasons alter . . . the spring, the summer,
The childing autumn, angry winter, change
Their wonted liveries; and the mazed world,

By their increase, now knows not which is which.
And this same progeny of evils comes
From our debate, from our dissension;
We are their parents and original. (II.i.81–117)

This speech suggests that Titania and Oberon are a personification of the "love" that should keep the elements of the world in harmony; their failure to do so betokens a flaw in their "love."

Honorius of Autun equates the four elements and the four qualities with the four seasons of the year:

Earth	Cold	Dry	Autumn
Water	Cold	Moist	Winter
Air	Hot	Moist	Spring
Fire	Hot	Dry	Summer

This serves to explain how confusion and discord among the elements could cause confusion and discord among the seasons of the year.[77]

Macrobius explains that the elements originally proceeded from "the seeds of things" but that this operation ceased in those parts of the universal world that were perfected in all their parts and had already received a plentiful supply of elements. The office of generating by means of moisture the eternal propagation of animals was assigned to Venus, so that thenceforth all animal creatures should be born from coitus of male and female.[78]

Fire and air are the lighter elements; earth and water are the heavier elements. In *Henry V* the Dauphin of France praises the nimbleness of his horse:

He is pure air and fire, and the dull elements of earth and water never appear in him. (III.vii.22–23)

This remark is figurative, for it could not be literally true.

Cicero explains that the human soul is made entirely of air and fire, lacking any traces of earth and water.[79] Cleopatra, in *Antony and Cleopatra*, echoes this statement just before her suicide:

I am fire and air; my other elements
I give to baser life. (V.ii.292–293)

She feels in anticipation the freedom of her soul released from the clogging weight of her body with its heavier elements. In sonnets 44-45 the poet fancies that his thought, being made of air and fire, flies to his friend, leaving behind with his body the heavier elements of earth and water; his spirits revive when the two lighter elements return with news of his friend's well-being.

In *Timon of Athens*, when Timon's household is broken up and his servants are all discharged, they feel that their parting is like death and one remarks that "we must all part *Into this sea of air*" (IV.ii.21-22). This echoes Lucretius's phrase, "aeris in mare."[80] In *The Tempest* Prospero uses the elements of earth and air to heighten his dramatic contrast between Caliban and Ariel. To the first he says, "Caliban! Thou *earth*, thou!" (I.ii.314). To the second he says, "Thou, which art but *air*" (V.i.21). The elements thus play a considerable part in Shakespeare's delineation of character.

6. The Elemental Spirits

Since Plato describes the confusion of the seasons in terms of disordered love among the elements and their qualities and since Shakespeare assigns the confusion of the seasons to the disordered love of Titania and Oberon, it follows that these two may be elemental spirits. Spirits were popularly believed to inhabit each of the four elements. Ficino explains that the nine heavenly circles, including the *primum mobile*, were inhabited by heavenly spirits and that these were identified by Dionysius the Areopagite as nine hierarchies of angels. The region above the moon has only one element, that of fire. But below the moon, in descending order, are four levels of elements: fire, air, water, and earth. It is reasonable to suppose that these levels are also inhabited by spirits who share the qualities of their particular elements. The rational creatures that inhabit the earth are human beings. In the upper levels below the moon are "daemons" of ethereal fire, of pure air, and of moist air— akin to water; and these experience pain, emotions, and passions. They also love good men and hate bad men.[81]

Honorius of Autun names the same three orders of "daemons"

below the moon. The ethereal and aerial spirits are good spirits, called *calodaemons*. But the watery spirits proceeding from foggy air are evil spirits, called *cacodaemons*. They ensnare men into evil and are the *Incubi* who cohabit with women. All three of these groups are elemental spirits.[82] Honorius thinks they can live in the air until doomsday and can become visible to men whenever they so desire.[83]

Aquinas, in his short essay *De Substantiis Separatis,* quotes numerous authorities on the nature of spirits or "daemons." St. Paul, in Ephesians 6:12, calls the devil "the prince of the powers of the air." Augustine admits that daemons are airy beings not subject to death but denies that they can be the souls of men. Chrysostom denies it also; when the airy body or ghost of a dead man appears and speaks, he is really an evil demon who takes that form to deceive his hearers. Plotinus and Porphyry believe that the souls of dead men do become daemons. Dionysius assigns to daemons certain passions of concupiscence and phantasy that pertain to the sensible soul, not to the rational soul. Aquinas also mentions but does not quote Apuleius's *De Deo Socratis* as a source of information on daemons.[84]

Paracelsus, the medieval Swiss physician, developed his own categories of elemental spirits, using older titles. Those that live in the bowels of the earth are *gnomes,* those that live in the waters are *nymphs,* those that live in the air are *lemures,* those that live in the sky are *penates.*[85] He thinks that the fallen angels may inhabit the elements as their hell, which consists in deprivation of paradise.[86] Elsewhere he adds to his list of spirits the *salamanders,* who dwell in fire; the *sylphs,* airy spirits who inhabit desert places; and the *pigmies,* who are the same as the gnomes.[87]

The reader should remember the distinction between *demon* and *daemon.* Today we usually use *demon* in reference to an evil spirit. In Shakespeare's two uses of the term (*Henry V,* II.ii.121; *Antony and Cleopatra,* II.iii.19), the First Folio gives the spelling *Daemon,* referring once to an evil spirit and once to a good spirit. This accords with the usage in Latin and Greek; the *daemons* could include evil spirits but also fairies like Oberon and Titania and spirits such as Ariel.

Ariel seems to be a self-contained spirit, without ties to any member of the opposite sex, whereas Oberon and Titania are lovers whose jealous quarrels disturb the elements they inhabit. Perhaps a hint for this came from Vincent de Beauvais, who attributes to Seneca a belief that each of the elements had two sexes, masculine and feminine.[88] It would logically follow that spirits inhabiting the elements might be of two sexes also.

Paracelsus states that frequently tempests are nothing but the apparitions of spirits. Lightning is the appearance, thunder the words of the spirits.[89] This statement applies to Ariel, who causes the tempest by bringing turbulent air from a storm in the Bermudas and blowing it up to a tempest in the Mediterranean. And Ariel describes to Prospero the violent thunder and lightning he produced (I.ii.195-200). He again appears to Alonzo, Sebastian, and Antonio in thunder and lightning (III.iii.53). He identifies himself and his fellow spirits as "ministers of fate" serving the decrees of destiny (III.iii.53-66). Ficino calls the airy spirits the "executors of fate":

> Animas in generationem labentes ducunt daemones, electae iam vitae sortisque *fatalis executores.*(Daemons, already the chosen *executors of fate* in the lot and life [of man], lead the fallen souls into generation.)[90]

Again, Ficino writes that under the moon daemons of pure air are the rulers of generation and will live until the end of time *(sempiterna);* daemons of impure air are perishable and after a long time will cease to exist.[91]

Oberon and his fellow spirits have the duty of leading human souls into generation. They will supervise the bridal beds of the three newly married couples to make sure that they generate good offspring:

> To the best bride-bed will we,
> Which by us shall blessed be;
> And the issue there create
> Ever shall be fortunate.
> So shall all the couples three
> Ever true in loving be;
> And the blots of nature's hand
> Shall not in their issue stand;
> Never mole, harelip, nor scar,
> Nor mark prodigious, such as are
> Despised in nativity,
> Shall upon their children be. (V.i.410-421)

It seems quite likely that this duty of the spirits had passed into popular folklore, for the fairies were eager to have good offspring themselves and would sometimes exchange an imperfect fairy babe for a newborn human babe; hence retarded or deformed children were sometimes regarded as "changelings" or babes exchanged by the fairies.[92]

The spirits in *A Midsummer Night's Dream* combine the theories concerning elemental spirits with the traditions of popular fairy lore. *The Tempest* is more concerned with the elemental spirits whom magicians may control by the practice of theurgy or white magic, though Stephano and Trinculo vulgarly call Ariel a "fairy." The practice of theurgy has been analyzed by W. C. Curry and others.[93] The opposite of theurgy, necromancy or black magic, had been practiced on the island by Caliban's mother, Sycorax, and was used to imprison Ariel in a cloven pine, from which Prospero's theurgy later released him.

The fairy lore of Shakespeare's time was early studied by Nathan Drake and was continued by other authors up to Minor Latham's *The Elizabethan Fairies* (1930), a more extended study.[94] Miss Latham concluded that the tiny fairies, such as Queen Mab in *Romeo and Juliet* (I.iv.53-94) and Titania's tiny attendants, were a Shakespearean invention; for earlier works, such as Spenser's *Faerie Queene*, describe the fairies as indistinguishable from human beings.

Curry cites a most interesting work for the appearance of fairies and spirits: *A Discourse concerning Devils and Spirits*, Book II of which first appears in the 1665 edition of Reginald Scot's *Discoverie of Witchcraft*, the first edition of which appeared in 1584 and was used by Shakespeare. There is no evidence for the date of composition or for the authorship of *A Discourse*, Book II; conceivably it could have appeared early enough for Shakepeare's use, though not in print. It conveniently synthesizes in one place much material drawn from Paracelsus, Hector Boece, and other authors. All references here quoted are from Book II in Brinsley Nicholson's edition of *The Discoverie of Witchcraft*.

In this work chapter III is entitled "Of the Astral Spirits of Men Departed" and chapter IV, "Of Astral Spirits or separate Daemons." An astral spirit is a form imparted by the stars; but the spirits, whether ghosts of men or daemons by creation, inhabit the airy region or dwell upon the earth. The two kinds of spirits associate with each other, for observers had watched banquets of the fairies, among whom appeared former friends who were quite oblivious of the presence of the observers (pp. 505–506). Sometimes spirits of the dead can be evoked by witchcraft, as the spirit of Samuel was called up by the Witch of Endor (p. 504). Sometimes spirits appear because of an unrevealed murder or a hidden treasure, the thought of which torments them; but they have great difficulty in communicating to living persons by voice or by gesture unless they are actual souls of the dead persons and not merely their astral forms. (On its first appearance to Horatio, the ghost in *Hamlet* shows manifestations of this kind.)[95]

The separate spirits—not souls of men—are classified according to the planets under which they have most influence. If unfavourably disposed, they blast vegetation with mildew, blind or paralyze animals, or bring plagues, pestilence, famine, storms, and tempests upon the earth; if favourably disposed, they bring sweet and excellent influences upon animals and vegetation. They principally inhabit the airy region and are ignorant of the language of other groups of spirits; therefore they use the services of such spirits as dwell *in omnibus Elementis* (in all the elements) to be their interpreters (p. 509). While they can sometimes be forced into service of the devil, in themselves their nature is wholly harmless, as to any "innate Evil, having nothing in them that is eternal as the Soul of Man: consequently nothing in them that is able to make them capable of enjoying Heaven, or induring the torments of Hell" (pp. 509–510).

This last conception seems to characterize Ariel, who lacks the emotions of human beings and does not have a human soul (V.i.20).[96] He is made of air but is *in omnibus Elementis,* for he can move through all elements at will when Prospero sends him

> to tread the ooze of the salt deep,
> To run upon the sharp wind of the north,
> To do me business in the veins of earth
> When it is bak'd with frost. (I.ii.252-256)

Here are named the water, air, and earth; he moves in fire when he simulates the lightning. As Prospero releases him from service, he says, "Then to the elements Be free, and fare thou well!" (V.i.317-318).

The unfavourable conduct of the elemental spirits in destroying crops and bringing plagues, pestilence, storms, and tempests resembles closely Titania's speech on the confused seasons and Plato's words on the same (above, pp. 39–41). This is sufficient to identify Oberon and Titania as daemons by creation, or separate spirits of the airy region. It is painful, says *A Discourse,* for spirits of one element to manifest themselves to the outward world in all four elements, as they must do to become tangible or visible. Consequently, they are seldom seen, preferring to remain in their own element; when they leave it, they are like a fish out of water or a man with his head under water (p. 503).

The planet that governs Oberon, Titania, and their train is the moon, which they follow around the earth in "the night's shade" (IV.i.100) and "following darkness like a dream" (V.i.393). They are differentiated from the souls of men who walk the earth as ghosts but must disappear at cockcrow (III.ii.381, V.i.388). Oberon says, "But we are spirits of another sort," who are allowed to remain until the sun is well advanced in the sky if there is need for them to do so (III.ii.388–393). Notwithstanding their difference from human beings, they offer to make Bottom one like themselves. Titania says,

> And I will purge thy mortal grossness so
> That thou shalt like an *airy spirit* go. (III.i.163–164)

She also explains that "the summer still doth tend upon my state" (line 158), a fact that helps to explain why her agitated and disordered love causes the confusion of the seasons.

Puck, or Robin Goodfellow, is not of the same order as Oberon and Titania, who are aerial spirits.[97] He is a terrestrial spirit, subordinate to spirits of the air, according to *A Discourse.* Terrestrial spirits inhabit "Woods, Mountains, Caves, Fens, Mines, Ruins, Desolate places, and Antient buildings." They are variously called "Nymphs, Satyrs, Lamii, Dryades, Sylvanes, Cobali, etc." Of this group are the Faeries, who often appear clothed in green. "Such jocund and facetious Spirits are sayd to sport themselves in the night by tumbling and fooling with Servants and Shepherds in Country houses, pinching them black and blew, and leaving Bread, Butter, and Cheese sometimes with them, which if they refuse to eat, some mischief shall undoubtedly befall them by the means of these Faeries" (p. 509). Finally, the author names *Robin-goodfellows* as fairies of this kind, giving Hector Boece's *History of Scotland* as his authority (p. 510).

The account of Puck's practical jokes given in *A Midsummer Night's Dream* (II.i.32–57) very much resembles the passage quoted above. Terrestrial spirits, as described in *A Discourse,* live on the earth's surface and move through the air, unlike Paracelsus's terrestrial spirits, or gnomes, who travel through earth as their accustomed medium. In *A Discourse,* these are defined as subterranean spirits (p. 517).

The angels who occupy the spheres above the moon can and do visit the mutable world below, but they do not establish a residence there. They powerfully affected Shakespeare's imagination. I should note in *The Merchant of Venice* the angelic song of the spheres as played and sung for the "young-ey'd cherubins" (below, p. 203). Looking up at Juliet's balcony before his presence is known, Romeo says,

> O speak again, bright angel, for thou art
> As glorious to this night, being o'er my head,
> As is *a winged messenger of heaven*
> Unto the white-upturned wond'ring eyes
> Of mortals that fall back to gaze on him
> When he bestrides the lazy-pacing clouds
> And sails upon the bosom of the air. (II.ii.26–32)

And Macbeth, meditating the murder of Duncan, says,

> Besides, this Duncan
> Hath borne his faculties so meek, hath been
> So clear in his great office, that his virtues
> Will plead like *angels,* trumpet-tongu'd, against
> The deep damnation of his taking-off;
> And pity, like a naked new-born babe
> Striding the blast, or *heaven's cherubin* hors'd
> Upon the sightless couriers of the air,
> Shall blow the horrid deed in every eye,
> That tears shall drown the wind. (I.vii.16–25)

The poet seems always to have preserved the faculty of looking at the universal world with the sense of wonder expressed in *The Tempest* in Miranda's words:

O brave new world
That has such people in it. (V.i.183–184)

7. The Pains of the Afterworld[98]

A fascinating and too often neglected area of literature is the medieval visions of the afterworld, the detailed conceptions of hell, purgatory, and paradise, which were to reach a culmination in Dante's *Divina Commedia*. Several of these visions became widely popular, both in Latin and in vernacular versions. They have been carefully studied for their possible influence on Dante's writing.[99] I propose to explore one aspect of them, the threefold pains of punishment by fire, wind, and ice, and to show how differently this material was used by Milton and by Shakespeare.

In Dante's *Inferno* and in Milton's hell, the most prominent topographical features stem from the contrasting punishments of extreme heat and extreme cold. There are certain vital differences, both in the manner and in the regions in which these punishments are used. Dante punishes the gluttons in the Third Circle with storms of cold rain and snow. In the City of Dis he changes to punishments by fire, only to change back to punishments by cold in the Ninth Circle, freezing the traitors in a lake of solid ice. Furthermore, the inhabitants of any circle stay in that circle and eternally receive the same punishment without change, whereas in Milton they are forced to change at intervals from heat to cold and back again. Dante considers such change a boon to be denied; Milton considers it a penalty to be enforced. Milton has no lake of ice but rather a frozen continent encircling the fiery continent and separated from it by the river Lethe. He uses the Virgilian rivers of Hades, as Dante does, and adds the biblical lake of fire (Rev. 20:10, 14–15). The winds appear as storms in the frozen continent.

When we read medieval visions of the afterworld,[100] we can see at once that Milton does not borrow his details from Dante but was probably influenced by the visions that were Dante's own sources. In the elaborate Vision of Tundale (ca. 1149),[101] for instance, we have the two traditions separately followed by Dante and by Milton. Here we find a lake of ice into which vow breakers are thrown after being swallowed by a horrible winged beast. The resemblance to

49

Dante's Lucifer gnawing sinners in the midst of an icy lake is at once apparent. But Tundale has traitors punished on a great desert mountain, one side of which is a region of fire, the other a region of ice, snow, and horrible winds. The souls dwelling thereon are forced to cross from one region to the other and after a time to cross back again. This is the arrangement used by Milton. The Dantesque lake of ice appears in the Vision of Alberic (1127),[102] where it is used to punish adulterers, and in the Vision of Lazarus from the medieval *Kalendar of Shepherds*,[103] where it is used to punish the envious. The Miltonic regions of fire and ice between which sinners alternate are found in the Vision of William (twelfth century),[104] in Bede's Vision of Dryhthelm (699),[105] and in the Vision of the Monk of Evesham (1196).[106] In this last account the two regions are separated by a foul-smelling lake or river through which the souls are dragged, somewhat similar in function to Milton's use of the river Lethe.[107]

Why Milton chose to use Lethe in this connection is something of a puzzle, since Virgil had placed it in the Elysian Fields and Dante in the Earthly Paradise. Possibly Milton took a hint from Lucian's satire *The Tyrant*, which pictures the arrival of Charon's ferryboat in Hades. Cyniscus advises the judge Rhadamanthus to punish the wicked tyrant Megapenthes simply by depriving him of the usual draught of the waters of Lethe, the means to forgetfulness. We recall that the severest pang suffered by Milton's demons comes as they cross the river Lethe and are denied the care-quelling draught of oblivion they so eagerly desire.

Since the regions of ice and fire occur in Hebrew, oriental and classical mythology[108] and since the range of Milton's reading was so wide, we cannot limit his sources to the early medieval visions; but we can be reasonably sure that the *Inferno* of Dante was not his principal source for the topography or the punishments of hell. While he drew physical details of hell from the visions—including some details that the visions assign to purgatory—he also seems to have studied the comments on hell of St. Gregory the Great (ca. 600).[109] Gregory was perhaps the first important Christian theologian to set forth explicitly the doctrine of purgatory.[110] He bases his belief on Christ's statement that the sin against the Holy Ghost cannot be forgiven in this world or in the world to come (Matt. 12:32). The inference is that some other sins can be forgiven in the world to come. He also uses St. Paul's figure of the purifying fire (1

Cor. 3:11–15). The works of all who build on Christ as a foundation shall be tried in the fire. Those who build of gold, silver, and precious stones shall be rewarded because their building will survive the fire. Those who build less securely, of wood, hay, or stubble, shall suffer loss; but they shall be saved through purification by fire. Gregory defines the wood, hay, and stubble as venial sins, which can be consumed by the fire. Mortal sins, he says, might have been represented by iron, brass, or lead, which are not consumed by fire. A record of good actions in this life is necessary to anyone who is permitted to expiate venial sins after death.

Only after Gregory's work appeared did Christian visions of the afterworld make a clear distinction between hell and purgatory.[111] Yet the idea of such a distinction was already implicit in classical literature, and the Christian purgatory drew heavily upon this classical material for its physical details. Since Milton makes no use of purgatory, he does not distinguish it from hell; but Shakespeare makes the distinction—though not always clearly—and it plays a significant part in his references to the afterworld.

In Shakespeare's *Measure for Measure* the pains of the afterworld are summed up in Claudio's words:

> To bathe in fiery floods, or to reside
> In thrilling region of thick-ribbed ice;
> To be imprison'd in the viewless winds
> And blown with restless violence round about
> The pendent world; or to be—worse than worst—
> Of those that lawless and incertain thought
> Imagine howling. (III.i.122–128)

A problem arises in the last three lines, where the word "or" seems to set off the three punishments of fire, ice, and wind against a fourth punishment: to be among those who are imagined howling. Who these howling ones are is indicated by Romeo's words to Friar Laurence:

> Banished?
> O friar, the damned use that word in hell;
> Howling attends it. (III.iii.46–48)

51

Likewise, at Ophelia's grave Laertes exclaims to the priest who will not allow her a requiem:

> I tell thee, churlish priest,
> A minist'ring angel shall my sister be,
> When thou liest howling. (*Hamlet*, V.i.263–265)

The implication is clear. Shakespeare uses "howling" to describe the despair of those who are damned in hell and hence are eternally lost. Since their fate is "worse than worst," the other punishments of fire, ice, and wind are probably in this instance purgatorial pains, which are easier in that they do not last forever. We should remember that Hamlet's father temporarily undergoes the punishment of fire until his sins shall be burned and purged away (I.v.9–13). As Shakespeare had used purgatory in that instance, it is not improper to assume that Claudio may be contrasting the pains of purgatorial expiation with the eternal pains of hell.

An examination of the medieval visions tends to confirm this view. Almost all of them distinguish between purgatory and hell; the companion regions of fire and ice are usually characteristic of purgatory, while hell is filled with fire, smoke, and despairing cries. This is true, for instance, in the visions of Dryhthelm, Alberic, Tundale, and the Monk of Evesham. Alberic says that he came to the mouth of the infernal gulf, from which issued horrible screamings and howlings, and was permitted to look within but that it was too dark for him to see much that went on there.[112] This arrangement has a classical precedent, for it is much like Plutarch's account of Timarchus's vision in the Cave of Trophonius (ca. A.D. 100); there Tartarus appears as a vast gulf from which issue the howls and groans of living beings, heard as though from a great distance.[113] A similar arrangement seems to be indicated in the Greek *Revelation of Paul* (third century),[114] where Paul sees various souls punished by whipping, darkness, fire, a river of fire, and a pit of blood, after which is unsealed for his view a deep, murky well of worse sinners for whom no angels intercede; these had denied the divinity of Christ. Paul does not enter the well but only looks into it to behold the torments. In the medieval visions the dreamer is usually permitted to look into hell but seldom actually to enter it, since from there none are supposed to return.[115] Dante's vision is the most notable exception to this practice.

While the ultimate source of Tartarus is probably Book VIII of the *Iliad* (line 13), for the Middle Ages the immediate source was unquestionably Book VI of the *Aeneid*. When Aeneas approaches Tartarus, he hears the cries and horrible clamour within. Finally the gate opens and he looks inside while the punishments are described by the Sibyl, but he is not permitted to enter. Instead, she draws him away toward Pluto's palace and the Elysian Fields. There his father Anchises points out to him the souls beside the River Lethe waiting to be reborn. These have undergone purgation during a thousand years. Purgation is accomplished in three ways: by wind, water, and fire. Some souls are suspended in the *inanes ventos* (empty winds); for others, at the bottom of a vast gulf, the wicked infection is washed away or is burned away in fire. Since these pains are not eternal, they obviously correspond to the pains of purgatory. Gawin Douglas, the medieval Scottish translator of the *Aeneid* (perhaps following the commentator Ascensius, whom he mentions by name), declares that these pains are an image of the Christian purgatory, while Tartarus is an image of the Christian hell. He adds that Virgil also foreshadows the limbo of infants—since he places in Hades the souls of children slain in infancy—and the limbo of the fathers.[116]

These points suggest that Virgil had considerable influence upon medieval ideas of hell and purgatory.[117] Dante's professed devotion to him would indicate as much, yet in some respects the earlier visions follow him more closely than does Dante. The conventions of approaching hell, of hearing the horrible clamour of human voices, and of looking in but not entering seem almost certainly patterned after Aeneas's conduct before Tartarus. Another borrowing seems to reflect Virgil's puzzling inclusion in Hades of men who were unjustly slain. The Monk of Evesham places in purgatory not only poisoners but their innocent victims, not only thieves but travelers who were slain by thieves, though allowing the victims a lighter punishment than the criminals.[118] He apparently considers Virgil's unjust homicides to involve death without warning, thus giving the victims no chance for absolution and the last rites of the church and, as with Hamlet's father, forcing them to undergo a period of purgation after death.

When we recall the reverence accorded to Virgil in the Middle Ages, assigning him almost the rank of a holy prophet,[119] and realize that the doctrincs of purgatory and limbo were developed from very slight scriptural evidence,[120] we can see that Virgil's influence was probably strong upon the physical details, if not upon the inception, of these doctrines. I may add that Plutarch, writing in the classical tradition a century later, has very clearly developed in his Vision of Thespesius the doctrine of purgatory, even to allowing a shorter period of purgation to those who have partly expiated their sins while on earth. He also used the alternating punishments of extreme heat and extreme cold, having demons drag the souls from one lake to another.[121]

Shakespeare's use of "howling" to designate souls in hell may proceed from the groans (*gemitus*) and great cries (*tantus plangor*) of Virgil's souls in Tartarus (*Aen.* VI.557, 561) and from the later visions that follow the same convention. The fact that hell is not usually entered or clearly seen but is a place of "darkness" viewed from without may have suggested that its penalties are imagined by "lawless and incertain thought," that is, unrestrained thought that, uncertain of the exact punishments of hell, imagines the worst of horrors and takes the outcries to be the screams of tortured sufferers. In this connection a sentence from Natalis Comes's description of Tartarus may be significant. Comes disagrees with those who think that Tartarus is at the North or South Pole in a place of extreme cold. He adds,

> Ego sane potius accesserim Zesae opinioni, qui Tartarum sub-terraneum incendium esse credidit, quia vapores ibi gignantur, quare et *clamores et strepitus incerti*, et tremores apparent, unde Tartarus appellatus est a Graecis quia multae ibi *tarachai* sive perturbationes existant. (I rather more reasonably may agree with the opinion of Zesa, who believed Tartarus to be a subterranean fire, because vapours are produced there, where *clamors and uncertain noises* and earthquakes appear, whence it was called Tartarus by the Greeks because there many *tarachai*, or perturbations, exist.)[122]

In Comes the noises are "incertain." In Shakespeare "incertain thought" imagines what the noises are. If Claudio's howling ones refer to souls in hell, then his fire, wind, and ice afford a clear parallel to Virgil's purgatorial punishments of fire, wind, and water. Immediately following Virgil's lines on purgation occur the words,

"Quisque suos patimur Manes" (VI.743), translated by Gawin Douglas as "Ilkane of vs his ganand purgatory Mon suffir" (Each one of us must endure his own purgatory). I stress the word *Manes* because it guides us to a line in Virgil's First Georgic. He has described the zones of the sky as corresponding to the five zones of earth: the torrid zone parched with fire (above, p. 26), the frigid zones congealed with bluish ice and dark rains, the temperate zones habitable by men. What form of life is in the southern temperate zone, in the opposite region underneath our feet? There, he says, are the dark River Styx and the *Manes profundi*, or ghosts of the deep (line 243). Servius, the most popular and authoritative of all Virgilian commentators, glosses this phrase as supporting the opinion of philosophers that souls that die here are allotted new bodies in the Antipodes, that there is the otherworld of man's belief. He quotes in support Lucan's line, "There the same spirit rules a new body born in another world." Since the soul is purged by fire or wind or water, says Servius, such purgation must necessarily take place while it is passing through the frozen plains and the fiery plains toward its destination in the Antipodes.[123] He evidently thought of the soul as traveling around the globe directly north or directly south, in which case it would necessarily cross the torrid zone and one of the frigid zones before reaching a place directly opposite its starting point. Its punishment by water would take place in the regions about the North or South Pole. Since Servius's commentary was written near the end of the fourth century, it preceded most of the medieval visions and demonstrates how Virgil's punishment by water was equated with the already traditional region of ice. We have just noticed Comes's later reference to those who would place Tartarus at the North or South Pole. The punishment by cold is also to be found in other sources available to Shakespeare, notably in Palingenius's *Zodiacus Vitae*, a book well known to him.[124]

The theologians themselves were uncertain of the location of purgatory. Dante's placing it on a mountain beneath the Earthly Paradise was not the opinion most generally accepted. In medieval visions purgatory is frequently underground.[125] Aquinas quotes Gregory as authority for making it a higher circle in the cavern of hell, where the same fire punishes the damned and cleanses those who are destined for paradise. Others, says Aquinas, think that the soul undergoes its purgation at the scene of its crime, inhabiting the

55

air.[126] Occasionally we find the fancy that the souls of the damned are also punished in the air. Peter Lombard suggests that they will be punished in the air until Judgment Day and afterward in the gulf of hell.[127] These varied interpretations suggest that the essential difference between purgatory and hell is not one of location or of specific punishments but consists rather in the hope or lack of hope for an eventual release.

Tundale's description of the desert mountain beset with ice and horrible winds, already mentioned, has a striking resemblance to certain lines in Shakespeare's *Winter's Tale*. After announcing Hermione's death, Paulina reproaches Leontes in these words:

> But, O thou tyrant!
> Do not repent these things, for they are heavier
> Than all thy woes can stir; therefore betake thee
> To nothing but despair. A thousand knees
> Ten thousand years together, naked, fasting,
> *Upon a barren mountain, and still winter*
> *In storm perpetual,* could not move the gods
> To look that way thou wert. (III.ii.208–214)

Since Leontes's crime is unpardonable, according to Paulina, it will be useless for him to implore mercy or have others to implore it for him. The final sentence envisions some form of purgatorial expiation, though it is not clear whether she is referring to the pains of purgatory in the next life or to expiatory sacrifices in this life for the salvation of Leontes's soul. The barren mountain, winter, and perpetual storm seem reminiscent of Tundale's vision.[128]

Shakespeare's indebtedness to the medieval visions appears again in Lear's "wheel of fire" (IV. vii.47). Virgil has some of the sinners in Tartarus stretched upon whirling wheels but mentions no fire. However, an ancient vase painting shows Ixion bound to a fiery wheel,[129] indicating that the image is classical in origin. Vincent de Beauvais recounts the vision of a novice who saw Judas Iscariot bound to a vast fiery wheel and whirled down into hell amid universal shouts of execration.[130] James Mew reproduces from the medieval *Pélerinage de l'âme* a woodcut showing two sinners spiked to a wheel that turns above a slow fire (p. 255). In the Vision of Owen (1153), who visited St. Patrick's purgatory, some souls are whirled on a great wheel of fire, while others are scalded with molten lead.[131] Lear uses both of these punishments in his words, "but I am bound Upon a wheel of fire, that mine own tears Do scald like molten lead" (IV.vii.46–48). The probable origin of these images is further suggested by Hamlet's exclamation "by Saint Patrick" (I.v.136) when speaking of a ghost that purports to come from purgatory.[132]

In the medieval visions there appear punishments by other molten metals as well as by lead. A lake of molten gold appears as a punishment in Plutarch's Vision of Thespesius (cf. n.121). These punishments are reflected in *Timon of Athens*, when Timon's servant Flaminius angrily flings back the small coins offered him by Lucullus:

> May these add to the number that may *scald* thee!
> Let *molten coin* be thy *damnation*. (III.i.54–55)

A different version of the threefold pains appears in Othello's tortured self-accusation over the body of Desdemona:

> When we shall meet at compt,
> This look of thine will hurl my soul from heaven,
> And fiends will snatch at it. . . . Whip me, ye devils,
> From the possession of this heavenly sight!
> *Blow me about in winds! roast me in sulphur!*
> *Wash me in steep-down gulfs of liquid fire!* (V.ii.273–280)

Here the winds and the "fiery floods" occur, but no ice. Instead, burning with sulphur is added. It seems likely that Shakespeare may be recalling directly Virgil's words describing the purgatorial pains already mentioned:

> Aliae panduntur inanes
> suspensae ad ventos; aliis sub gurgite vasto
> infectum eluitur scelus, aut exuritur igni.
> (*Aeneid*, VI.740–742)
> (Some hang suspended in the empty winds; for others, at the bottom of a vast gulf the wicked infection is washed out or is burned out with fire.)

In the last line "washing" is mentioned, but washing by water is not specified; hence Shakespeare could have associated the word *igni* with both verbs, reading "is washed out with fire or is burned out with fire." Such a reading would suggest the washing with liquid fire and the burning with sulphur. Thus it is possible that Virgil's words are recalled directly in Othello's lines but only indirectly in Claudio's speech, where ice has become one of the three punishments.

Another discrepancy is noted in the winds. Virgil's phrase seems to suggest that the sinners are suspended, like clothes hung out to dry in the wind. Claudio's phrase "viewless winds" could very well proceed from Virgil's "inanes ventos."[133] But Claudio envisions an image unlike Virgil's, for his sinners are not attached to any fixed point and can be blown all the way around the world.[134] There is nothing quite like this in Virgil or in any of the medieval visions, though Plato has a somewhat similar description in the *Phaedo* (109–114) and Dante's guilty lovers are blown about by winds within the confines of hell (*Inferno*, V.31). Much the closest resemblance that I have observed is Cicero's account of the punishment of the wicked at the end of his *Somnium Scipionis*:

> Corporibus elapsi, circum terram ipsam volutantur, nec hunc in locum nisi multis exagitati saeculis revertuntur. (IX.iii) (Released from their bodies, they are whirled around the earth itself, nor are they returned to this place [the heaven of fixed stars] except after being agitated for many centuries.)

W. W. Skeat, in his edition of Chaucer, noted that these lines are used in *The Parlement of Foules*[135] and also noted their resemblance to Claudio's words. He did not, however, note Macrobius's interpretation of the passage as meaning that the souls so whirled about shall eventually reach paradise.[136] In Christian doctrine this would make such punishment an equivalent of purgatory.

The medieval visions, supplemented by Virgil and Plutarch, help us to realize how extensively Shakespeare used the imagery of both hell and purgatory. A notable contribution to our understanding of this point has been made by Roy W. Battenhouse, who thinks that the ghost in *Hamlet* comes from a pagan purgatory, not from the purgatory envisioned in Roman Catholic theology.[137] If my own assumptions are correct, the two were not sharply differentiated in the English public mind, since the Christian purgatory drew so many of its physical details from pagan sources. This type of confusion becomes evident in John Webster's *The White Devil* (1612), when the villainous Flamineo identifies purgatory with the Hades pictured in Lucian's *Dialogues of the Dead*:

> Whither shall I go now? O Lucian, thy ridiculous *purgatory!* to find Alexander the Great cobbling shoes, Pompey tagging points, and Julius Caesar making hair-buttons! Hannibal selling blacking, and Augustus crying garlic! Charlemagne selling lists by the dozen, and King Pepin crying apples in a cart drawn with one horse!
> Whether I resolve to fire, earth, water, air,
> Or all the elements by scruples, I know not,
> Nor greatly care. (V.vi.108–116)

Flamineo, a materialist who scorns all religious and moral values, is expressing his contempt for the notion of life after death; he expects his body to be dissolved, Lucretian-like, into its original atoms. The essential point here is the identification of the classical Hades with purgatory, a point that supports Battenhouse's contention. It seems likely that such recognition of purgatory as an element of classical and folk tradition made possible its use in the drama, for we can hardly believe that Elizabeth's or James's government would have allowed the presentation of plays that seemed to be open propaganda for Roman Catholic doctrines.

The evidence here given controverts the popular impression that later writers on the afterworld borrowed their descriptions primarily from Dante. Instead, it reveals the influence of a body of writings that contributed much imaginative detail to religion and literature but have largely faded from the modern mind. They are interesting, nevertheless, as a highly significant chapter in the history of ideas.

* * *

The physical world as the abode of man, both before and after his death, was a subject of engrossing interest to Shakespeare. From hell, at the center of the earth, through the stars to the place of the blest in the Empyrean, the universe presented to him a fascinating backdrop for the working out of human destiny.

III

Numbers

MOST RECENT studies of numerology as used by Shakespeare and other authors have to do with structural patterns: stanzaic arrangements, numbers of lines per section, and similar questions.[1] I have made no investigations into patterns of this kind. But I find in Shakespeare a few allusions that show a knowledge of numerology and some interest in it. An understanding of the subject serves to illuminate passages that would otherwise seem obscure.

1. The Ages of Man

Perhaps the most common use of numerology is its significance for the various ages of man. The perfect number is 10, since all higher numbers are compounds involving the use of 10 or its multiples. Of numbers below 10, the most important ones in regulating human life are 7 and 9. The square of any number is of especial importance, multiplying the power of that number.

Macrobius briefly discusses the part played by 7 in the regulation of human life.[2] But this is more clearly stated in Censorinus's short work on birthdays, *De Die Natali*, frequently bound with the writings of Macrobius.[3] In 1604 Thomas Wright published in English *A Succinct Philosophicall declaration of the nature of Clymactericall yeeres, occasioned by the death of Queene Elizabeth*, based largely upon the work of Censorinus.[4]

According to both authors, human life progresses in a series of "steps" (*gradus*), and the time of change from one step to another is always critical and sometimes hazardous. These are the climacterical years. In addition there is the grand climacteric, likely to be marked by great change and great danger in the life of the individual. If he passes safely the year of the grand climacteric, he may live in relative security thereafter.

Some lives are governed by nines, some by sevens, and some are mixed. Hence the climacterical ages may be 9-18-27-36-45-54-63-72-81 or 7-14-21-28-35-42-49-56-63-70. The grand climacteric is the square of the original number, 81 (9×9) or 49 (7×7). Where both numbers influence a life the grand climacteric is 63 (9×7). Wright adds 70 (10×7) as a fourth grand climacteric not mentioned by Censorinus. This addition was doubtless prompted by the fact that Queen Elizabeth died in her seventieth year.

Censorinus states that some writers distinguish the two numbers as pertaining to the body (7) and to the mind (9), because diseases of the body are treated with physical remedies but diseases of the mind are treated with music, which has a healing and calming effect. Since there are nine Muses, *music* has affinities with the number 9.[5]

Shakespeare has made use of the climacterical years in *King Lear*. There the Earl of Kent is greatly moved by the suffering and death of Lear. When offered a share in the government by Albany, he replies,

> I have a journey, sir, shortly to go;
> My master calls me, I must not say no. (V.iii.321-322)

That is, he will join Lear in death. As with Enobarbus,[6] Shakespeare avoids the question of whether Kent proposes to commit suicide or realizes that he will die from the great emotional tension that he has undergone.

Kent is in his forty-ninth year. When Lear inquires his age, the disguised earl replies, "I have years on my back forty-eight" (I.iv.42). This signifies that he has completed forty-eight years and is now in the year of his grand climacteric if his life is governed by sevens.

When Lear awakens to the sound of sweet music, which the doctor has prescribed to cure his madness, he recognizes the infirmity of his great age: "I am fourscore and upward, not an hour more nor less" (IV.vii.61). Since 80 is a round number, "and upward" could mean several years or several months. The *Oxford English Dictionary* gives an instance of "thirty-two years and upward."[7] Since 32 is not a round number, the author apparently refers to an excess of less than a year; otherwise he would have given the number as 33, 34, or some other figure under 40. Lear's attempt to be specific, "not an hour more nor less," suggests that "and upward" means some days, weeks, or months beyond 80 but less than 81. He is therefore in his eighty-first year, the climacteric of his life, which has progressed according to nines.

This assumption may explain Regan's words to Lear:

> O, sir, you are old;
> Nature in you stands on the very verge
> Of her confine. (II.iv.148-150)

Since 81 is the latest age given in the lists of Censorinus and Wright, it may be considered the usual ultimate boundary or "confine" of life, though in point of fact some persons live a good deal longer. Regan is not predicting Lear's specific date of death; she is like an insurance agent consulting a mortality table to determine the probable date in terms of a national average.

That Lear reaches his year of crisis in his eighty-first year and Kent his year of crisis in his forty-ninth year seems more than a chance coincidence. Shakespeare is clearly using the two grand climacterics in the two courses of life by nines and by sevens. We are tempted to think that the Earl of Gloucester represents the "mixed" courses of life with the grand climacteric at 63 (9×7), but I can find no reference assigning to him a specific age.

In *As You Like It* Adam has almost reached his eightieth birthday when he leaves his familiar home to follow Orlando and to serve him:

> From seventeen years till now almost fourscore
> Here lived I, but now live here no more;
> At seventeen years many their fortunes seek,
> But at fourscore it is too late a week;
> Yet fortune cannot recompense me better
> Than to die well and not my master's debtor. (II.iii.71-76)

On his eightieth birthday he will begin his eighty-first year, his year of the grand climacteric. The great change involved is his departure from familiar surroundings into unknown dangers.

In *Merry Wives* Justice Shallow remarks that "I have lived four-score years and upward" (III.i.56), but there seems to be no great crisis involved in his situation except his concern for the money he had lent to Falstaff. He had entered Clement's Inn fifty-five years before (*2 Henry IV*, III.ii.224), about the time of Falstaff's birth (*1Henry IV*, II.iv.467). Therefore his past relationship with Falstaff had been like that of Falstaff with Prince Hal, an older man consorting with a much younger man.

The Duchess of York, mother of Edward IV and Richard III, sorrowfully predicts her own death to take place in or about her eighty-first year:

> I to my grave, where peace and rest lie with me.
> Eighty odd years of sorrow have I seen.
> (*Richard III*, IV.i.95–96)

This suggests that her life has progressed by nines up to her grand climacteric.

If life progresses by sevens, there must be enough steps to reach 70, the "threescore and ten" named in the Bible as man's allotted time on earth (Psalms 90:10). If there are only seven steps, or seven ages, then some of them must be longer than seven years. Wright uses multiples of 7, making one step of twenty-one years and another of fourteen years to fill out the required time. His seven ages run as follows:

1. to 7 years   Infancy (*Infantia*)
2. 7–14 years   Childhood (*Pueritia*)
3. 14–21 years   Adolescence (*Adolescentia*)
4. 21–28 years   Youth (*Juventus*)
5. 28–49 years   Man's Estate (*in Statu Virili*)
6. 49–63 years   Age (*Senectus*)
7. 63–70 or 77 years Decrepit Age (*Decrepita Aetas*)[8]

Not all estimates agree with Wright, for *Juventus* is sometimes extended to forty years. It is the period of early manhood and not of late childhood.[9]

THE AGES OF MAN

In Jaques's speech on the seven ages of man in *As You Like It,*
Shakespeare has used seven examples to match the seven ages: (1) the
infant in the nurse's arms, (2) the schoolboy, (3) the lover, (4) the
soldier, (5) the judge who becomes sedentary and gains weight, (6)
the old man whose body shrinks and whose voice becomes shrill as
his vital powers weaken, and (7) "second childishness and mere
oblivion" (II.vii.139–166).

In *Twelfth Night* Viola has lost her father by death on her
thirteenth birthday, just as she enters her fourteenth year (V.i.251).
This was the second climacteric in her life, marking the end of
childhood. The same is true of Sebastian, who is her twin.

In *Pericles* Marina at fourteen is threatened with death at Cleon's
hands but luckily escapes (V.iii.8). This crisis marks her second
climacteric.

In Macrobius's discussion of the ages of man, he states that
fourteen marks the beginning of puberty in members of both sexes,
when they become capable of begetting or conceiving offspring.[10]
Shakespeare takes note of this in *The Winter's Tale* when Antigonus
defends Hermione against the charge of unchastity:

> Be she honour-flaw'd,
> I have three daughters; the eldest is eleven;
> The second and the third, nine, and some five;
> If this prove true, they'll pay for't: by mine honour,
> I'll geld 'em all; *fourteen they shall not see,*
> *To bring false generations.* (II.i.143-148)

Shakespeare has taken pains to give fourteen as the age of two of
his heroines, Juliet and Miranda. In *Romeo and Juliet* the nurse
declares that in two weeks and several days Juliet will be fourteen,
and Lady Capulet assures Juliet that she is old enough for marriage
and childbearing (I.iii).[11] In *The Tempest* Prospero tells Miranda that
she was not yet three years old when they left Milan twelve years
ago (I.ii.41, 53). She has thus passed her fourteenth birthday but is
not yet fifteen. In each case Shakespeare wishes to portray young
love when the onset of puberty makes the girls more aware of the
nature of love itself. His purpose is similar to that of Eugene
O'Neill's portrayal of Muriel in *Ah, Wilderness.* For both Miranda
and Juliet, their second climacteric is marked by their falling in love,
one happily, the other tragically.

In *Othello* Iago gives his age as twenty-eight (I.iii.313). His treason and death occur in his fourth climacteric, assuming that his life is ruled by sevens.

From these instances we can see that Shakespeare's use of climacterical years is frequent, if not always precise. At times the age stated is one year short of the climacteric, since the climacterical birthday marks the end of the dangerous period; for example, forty-nine marks the *end* of the forty-ninth year. At other times he merely states the climacterical birthday as the present age. Juliet, just short of fourteen, is still in her climacterical year; Miranda, already fourteen, is actually in her fifteenth year, just beyond the climacteric. These variations do not obscure Shakespeare's intent to use the climacterical years as times of particular significance in the lives of men and women. They constitute a very large percentage of all his references to the ages of his characters throughout his works.

The most controversial age of a Shakespearean character is that of Hamlet, which seems not to depend upon the climacterics at all. The first gravedigger states that he began his employment on the day young Hamlet was born and that he has worked at it for thirty years (V.i.162, 177). A few moments later (line 191) he states that Yorick has been dead for twenty-three years; he therefore died when Hamlet was seven years old. But in the First Quarto version the twenty-three years since Yorick's death are stated as twelve years, and the thirty-year figure is omitted. Since the difference between twenty-three and twelve is eleven years, we may assume that the First Quarto text envisions Hamlet's age as thirty less eleven, or nineteen years.

If none of the figures stated is inadvertent, the two Quartos represent different stages in the composition of the play, and much of the first survived into the second. The nineteen-year-old Hamlet was "the glass of fashion and the mould of form" (III.i.161), but the thirty-year-old Hamlet was Shakespeare's maturer conception. I have elsewhere given a possible explanation, which may be accepted for want of a better.[12] In *Troilus and Cressida* Hector describes Paris and Troilus as "young men, whom Aristotle thought Unfit to hear moral philosophy" (II.ii.166–167). The reference is to *Nicomachean Ethics* (I.iii.5), in a passage designed to show that youths are too impulsive and inexperienced to decide objectively on questions of justice. Aristotle does not give a particular age at which these imperfections are overcome, but Shakespeare could have recalled a similar passage in Plato's *Republic* (Book VII), where the proper age for beginning the study of philosophy is set at thirty years (537 D, 539). This explanation supports those who see in Hamlet a philosopher-prince trying to regulate his life by principles of justice. If we say that Shakespeare decided that Hamlet should be less like Troilus and more like Hector, we can perhaps understand better the change in Hamlet's age.

To Shakespeare the age of a character might be an important part of his or her personality. To catch his characters at the crises in their lives, he enlisted the aid of contemporary philosophy and numerology, thereby enhancing the dramatic effectiveness of his plays.

2. *Numerical Creation*

In his commentary on Cicero's *Somnium Scipionis,* Macrobius states that the Greek philosopher Pythagoras studied the hidden meanings of numbers in his search for something constant on which to base physical laws. The change and flux of the physical world make uncertain any propositions based upon the nature of matter. But number seems to be constant. No matter what material objects they are applied to, the twoness of 2 and the threeness of 3 are always the same. Applying these to the points bounding geometrical figures, which represent material objects in graphic form, one may find a clue to the nature and processes of the physical world.[13]

Plato, in his *Timaeus,* analyzes at length the meanings of numbers and their corresponding geometrical figures. For Shakespeare's time these were summarized in the *Compendium in Timaeum* of Marsilio Ficino, a commentary included in Ficino's Latin translation of Plato's complete works.[14] Plato's position was also explained in Thomas Aquinas's commentary on Aristotle's work, *Concerning the Soul.*[15] A somewhat different tradition was set forth in Macrobius's *Commentarium in Somnium Scipionis* (II.ii.). The popularity of this work is attested by a reference to it in the *Roman de la Rose* (tr. Chaucer, line 7) and likewise in Chaucer's *Parlement of Foules* (line 111), where it is quoted as an authority on the nature of dreams.

Both Plato and Macrobius sought to explain the creation of the material world by the construction of a geometrical figure. Both began with a point, itself immaterial, that represented one, or unity. By extending the point they produced a line bounded by two points, or duality, or dimension, the beginning of materiality.

Here the two authors part company. Plato extended the two points to a third point to form a triangle, or plane surface, the second stage of materiality. He then extended the three points to a fourth point to form a pyramid, or solid, the third and final stage of materiality. Accordingly, the material world was represented by the number 4 and the stages of its creation by the progression 1-2-3-4.

Macrobius proceeded differently. From the line, instead of extending the two points toward a single point, he moved the whole line through space to establish a plane surface bounded by four points, or a square. He then moved the plane through space to form a solid bounded by eight points, or a cube. Thus the material world was represented by the number 8 and the stages of its creation by the progression 1-2-4-8, which is also the progression usually used in Euclidean geometry. He chose a modified by geometric progression where Plato had proceeded by arithmetic progression. To him the number 4 was the penultimate stage of solidity, while to Plato it was the ultimate stage.[16] In either case it was emblematic of the world made tangible and visible to the human senses.[17]

This interpretation was reflected by Stephen Batman in the sixteenth century when he declared that sense is like to "a quadrangle square" (below, p. 72). In Latin *quadrangulum* (four-cornered) usually refers to a four-sided right-angled figure. But one must be careful, for Aquinas at least once applies the term to the four corners of a pyramid. These conflicting traditions seem to have been resolved for most writers by accepting the number 4, common to both traditions, as emblematic of the physical world, and the square, found only in the Macrobian tradition, as the geometric type-figure to represent that world.

The progression 1-2-4-8 as reasoned by Macrobius found no place for the number 3. Yet this number admittedly had great significance. The Platonic Triad (Divine Will, Divine Mind, World-Soul) and the Christian Trinity (Father, Son, Holy Spirit) were the first agents of creation and were represented by the number 3. Also in the world itself the most significant components were neither tangible nor visible. These constituted the life force, or souls, of men, animals, and plants and the invisible power that caused the transmutations of animate and inanimate matter. Accordingly, Macrobius postulated a second geometric progression of numbers, 1-3-9-27, which represented the nonmaterial components of the world and seemed closer than matter to the nature of divinity.[18] This nonmaterial sequence cannot be perceived in terms of material figures but permeates the material world and aids in guiding and shaping it.

Since one (*unitas*) is the fountain and source of all other numbers, it cannot itself properly be called a number. Beyond one, the sequence 2-4-8, representing the material world, is made up of even numbers; the sequence 3-9-27, representing the nonmaterial world, is made up of odd numbers. La Primaudaye equates even and odd numbers with matter and form.[19] The one may be taken as God, from whom all things proceed;[20] and odd numbers, of which 3 is the prototype, are nearer the nature of God and are hence deserving of greater honour. Thus Virgil says, "Numero Deus impare gaudet" (God rejoices in an odd number).[21] Falstaff speculates that "there's divinity in odd numbers" (*Merry Wives*, V.i.3) and therefore hopes that his third attempt to seduce Mistress Ford will be successful. The monad one is both masculine and feminine. Odd numbers are masculine, characterizing the "superior" sex; even numbers are feminine.[22] When Menelaus tells Cressida that "every man is odd," he is punning upon the double meaning of the word: (1) queer or eccentric, (2) masculine by number (*Troilus and Cressida*, IV.v.42).

The belief that one is not itself a number is repeated by Shakespeare. In sonnet 136 he remarks that "among a number one is reckoned none" (line 8). And Capulet urges Paris to compare his daughter's beauty with that of other girls at the party:

Which, on more view of many, mine, being one,
May stand in number, though in reck'ning none.
(*Romeo and Juliet*, I.ii.32-33)

And Aumerle echoes the phrase in expressing his grief at Richard II's dethronement: "God knows I had as lief be none as one" (*Richard II*, V.ii.49). The statement that "one is no number" had become proverbial.

Some significance must be attached to Troilus's use of "unity" to express the unalterable quality of the one, or the deity. Ficino has a similar usage of the divine unity (below, p. 112). *Unitas* is the word regularly used by Macrobius in referring to one as the source of numbers. When Troilus sees Cressida go to Diomedes's arms, he cannot believe the evidence of his own eyes:

> If beauty have a soul, this is not she.
> If souls guide vows, if vows be sanctimonies,
> If sanctimony be the gods' delight,
> If there be rule in *unity* itself,
> This is not she. (V.ii.138-142)

Here "unity" is not used in its ordinary sense, which appears elsewhere in Shakespeare. He avoids an anachronism by referring to "the gods" of the Greeks and Trojans instead of to "God" as in the Christian religion (below, pp. 112, 191). Instead he uses the mathematical and philosophical concept of the one as the source of all numbers and hence of all things material and nonmaterial. If there is any constant and unalterable quality in the founder of the universe himself, then Cressida cannot be false, as she now appears to be. Shakespeare has used "unity" in the same sense as Macrobius's *unitas*.

The use of numbers and geometrical figures to express the nature of material and immaterial things is a device that stems from man's sense of form. Geometry is a science of form; as Edna St. Vincent Millay put it in one of her best sonnets, "Euclid alone has looked on beauty bare." Form and number provide us some stability in the midst of a fluctuating world.

3. The Square of Sense

One of the most stubborn cruxes in Shakespeare's writing is Regan's phrase, "the . . . square of sense." In the opening scene of *King Lear* she is seeking to surpass Goneril in expressing love for her father:

> I am made of that self metal as my sister,
> And prize me at her worth. In my true heart

70

I find she names my very deed of love;
Only she comes too short, that I profess
Myself an enemy to all other joys
Which the most precious *square of sense* possesses,
And find I am alone felicitate
In your dear Highness' love. (I.i.71–78)

The general intent of Regan's speech is clear enough; she is so engrossed with the mutual love between herself and her father that she can take no pleasure in anything else. But this would seem to involve more than love based on the five senses, for Goneril had included grace and honour in her list of "more than's," and Regan therefore includes them in hers.

The word *square* sometimes involves a reference to a carpenter's square, as in Ulysses' injunction to Troilus not "to square the general sex by Cressid's rule" (V.ii.132). It also has an ethical content, as in Antony's lament, "I have not kept my square" (*Antony and Cleopatra*, II.iii.6).[23] In a comment upon Aristotle's *Nicomachean Ethics*, Donatus Acciaiolus states that the virtuous and happy man is "squared" (*quadratus*).[24] Right angles and straight (*recta*) lines become symbols of up*right*ness and *rectitude*.

Aristotle, in his work on the soul, seeks to explain the soul's nature by analogy with triangles and a square. Where Plato had used four points to bound a pyramid, his emblem of solidity, Aristotle uses four points *in the same plane* as an emblem of the "soul sensible."[25] We may read his explanation as expanded in the words of Stephen Batman's translation from Bartholomaeus Anglicus, which appeared in 1582:

> If we take heed to the soule in comparison to his working, wee finde three manner of vertues, . . . *Vegetabilis*, that giueth lyfe, and no feeling, and that is in plants and rootes, *Sensibilis*, that giueth life & feeling, and not reason, that is in vnskilfull beasts, *Racionalis*, that giueth lyfe, feeling, and reason, and this is in men. The Philosopher [Aristotle] lykeneth the soule that is called *Vegetabilis*, to a Triangle. For as a Triangle hath three corners, this manner soule hath three vertues, of begetting, of nourishing, and of growing. And this soule *Vegetabilis* is lyke to a Triangle in Geometrie. And hee lykeneth the soule *Sensibilis*,

to a quandrangle square, and foure cornerd. For in a Quadrangle is a line drawne from one corner to another [a diagonal]
before it maketh two Triangles: and ye soule sensible maketh
two triangles of vertues. For where euer the soule sensible is,
there is also the soule *Vegetabilis,* but not backwarde [not vice
versa]. And he lykeneth the soule *Racionalis* to a Circle, because
of his perfection and conteining. . . . And therefore who that
hath the soule reasonable, hath also the power *Sensibilis* and
Vegetabilis, but not contrariwise.[26]

This passage is copied rather closely in Robert Allott's *Wits
Theater of the Little World* (1599) (ff. 37–38). Both Batman and
Allott refer to Aristotle's *De Anima,* but they may also have con-
sulted Aquinas's *De Unitate Intellectus,*[27] in which substantially the
same explanation is given.

Thus the souls of plants, animals, and men are geometrically
represented by the triangle, the square, and the circle respectively.
These are all plane surfaces. Since the soul is nonmaterial, without
solidity, the solids (pyramid and cube) are not usually used to
represent it. However, the sphere or "solid circle" is used to represent the soul (above, p. 32). Each higher form includes within itself
the functions of lower forms and becomes increasingly complex.
The sensible soul is assigned to animals but also is part of the rational
soul assigned to men. In each case its principal function is perception
through the senses.[28]

Aristotle, Aquinas, Batman, and Allott all associate the square as a
geometrical figure with the sensible soul; and this association seems
almost certainly to have provided the basis for Regan's phrase. But
we do not yet know the four qualities or "sensible" faculties that
should correspond to the four points of a square. They cannot be the
external senses, which are five in number: sight, hearing, touch,
taste, and smell. Aquinas calls these the external senses that belong to
the "apprehending" power of the soul *apprehensiva deforis.* To this
same power belong five internal senses that constitute *apprehensiva
deintus.* These are common sense, phantasy, imagination, judgment
(estimative or cogitative), and memory. These are the stages involved in perception, and Aquinas attributes their classification to
Avicenna. He adds that Averroes regarded phantasy and imagination as the same, reducing the internal senses to four.[29]

72

The five internal senses were popularly known among Elizabethans as the five wits. Shakespeare refers to them five times, most
significantly in sonnet 141:

> But my five wits nor my five senses can
> Dissuade one foolish heart from serving thee. (lines 9–10)

He also refers to the "apprehensive senses" in *All's Well* (I.ii.60),
classifying them as Aquinas had done. The context suggests a
reference to both the external and the internal senses.[30]

Batman and Allott both depart slightly from Aquinas's list of the
internal senses, or five wits. Batman, translating Bartholomaeus,
gives five powers of the soul: feeling (*sensualitas*), bodily wit (*sensus*),
imagination, reason, and intellect.[31] Allott gives feeling, wit, imagination, reason, and understanding.[32] But they both preserve the
number five and are not suitable bases for a four-pointed square.

Ficino, in his commentary on Plato's *Timaeus* (*Compendium in
Timaeum*), devotes nine short chapters (18–26) to the number four
and its properties, both in the cosmos and in individual lives. Basic to
his discussion is the supposition that the world is composed of four
elements: earth, water, air, and fire. In chapter 19 he discusses the
relations of numbers to geometric figures and equates the square of
any number with the square as a geometric figure; in this sense both 4
and 9 could be represented as a square. Corresponding meta-
physically to the four elements are four stages of creation: essence,
being, virtue (or quality), and action, represented geometrically by
the point, line, plane, and solid (chapter 22). In chapter 26, "On the
Spirit of the World," he explains the fourfold power that gives life
and perception to otherwise inanimate matter: (1) intellect, itself
unmoved but ruling the motions of the spheres as ordained by the
author of all things; (2) the soul of the sphere, movable and moving
the sphere; (3) intelligence, divinely planted by God and the superi-
or intellect; and (4) nature, the seminary and vital virtue everywhere
infused into matter. Corresponding to these in man are four degrees
of sense (using *sense* as a general term for all perception): (1) intellect,
(2) intelligence, (3) animal power, or sense in its more limited
meaning; and (4) natural power, a mere shadow of sense such as
plants might have.

These four constitute the whole range of perception of both the

external and the internal senses. Aquinas explains the difference
between intellect and intelligence. Both are based on the process of
considering (*intelligens*). The first stage, intelligence, is possessed in
some degree by the lower animals, who can perceive that a fire means
danger, a fragrant smell indicates the presence of food, and so forth.
This impression represents rudimentary reasoning powers. But
beyond this the mind of man may form an intellectual conception by
abstracting a quality from several impressions, such as *whiteness*
from several objects that are white.[33] The ability to form this
conception and to analyze its nature is marked by the ability to
express it in speech.[34] Consequently, intellect is possessed only by
human beings, intelligence by them and the higher orders of beasts.
The lower orders of beasts (shellfish, for example) have only the
corporeal senses with no power of "considering." Plants may have
vague sensations of pain and pleasure, which Ficino calls the natural
sense.[35]

Shakespeare shows familiarity with this classification. In *Love's
Labour's Lost* Nathaniel speaks patronizingly of Dull:

> His *intellect* is not replenished; he is only an *animal*, only
> *sensible* in the duller parts;
> And such barren *plants* are set before us, that we thankful
> should be,
> Which we of taste and feeling are, for those parts that do
> fructify in us more than he. (IV.ii.27-30)

Nathaniel means that Dull can exercise no perception through the
intellect and not much through intelligence. Like a lower animal, he
perceives only through the five external senses and may even be
likened to a plant, which has only the dullest feelings of pleasure or
pain.

In *The Comedy of Errors* Luciana urges Adriana to recognize her
husband's right to preëminence in the household, adducing examples
of beasts, fishes, and fowls:

> Men, more divine, the masters of all these,
> Lords of the wide world and wild watery seas,
> Indu'd with *intellectual sense* and souls,

74

Of more preëminence than fish and fowls,
Are masters to their females, and their lords. (II.i.20–24)

Here again the intellect, with its "sense" or power of perception, is used to distinguish man from the lower orders of creation. Aquinas uses this same classification for love in a general sense: intellectual, rational (or intelligential), animal, natural, and these cause "affections of the soul."[36] But Ficino's usage is nearer to that of Shakespeare.

At last we have a probable explanation of Regan's "square of sense." All human joys, mental and physical, are summed up in Ficino's four orders of sense: intellectual, intelligential, animal, and natural. These are the four points of the square.

* * *

The sense of form to be found in numbers, whether used as a pattern of the world or a pattern of human life, had a strong appeal to Shakespeare and may have contributed to the symmetry of his plots, of his characters, and of his *Weltanschauung* or way of looking at the universe.

IV

The Psychology of Perception

IT IS AXIOMATIC that Shakespeare was a keen observer of men and manners, but he also had a keen interest in the physical and mental processes by which his observations were accomplished, that is, in the psychology of perception. How the mind received its impressions of objects, why different minds formed different impressions of the same object, when reality faded into illusion, what were the causes of self-deception—these were questions that attracted him and to which he sought an answer in such psychological treatises as were available. They are reflected in short phrases and in occasional longer speeches throughout his works.

We sometimes forget that Shakespeare had access to a rather fully developed system of psychology. For the Elizabethans it began with Plato and Aristotle, was perfected by the Schoolmen, particularly by Thomas Aquinas, and was supplemented by various authors of the Renaissance. Perception is only one part of psychology; but it is a very important part, and Shakespeare made use of it in considerable detail. He was fascinated by the interplay of the physical and mental faculties, by the translation of physical sensations into impressions and ideas. Not merely the content, but the method of human thought was of great interest to him.

1. The External Senses

As Dante reminds us in the *Paradiso*, all impressions and rationalizations of the mind must ultimately be based upon impressions received through the five external senses, for these are the raw material upon which the mind must work.[1] Milton laments his blindness "and wisdom at one entrance quite shut out."[2] The autobiography of Helen Keller, who became blind and deaf at the age of two, expresses the barren quality of her mental life until her teacher devised a system of communication through the sense of touch.[3] Reason cannot function in a vacuum; it must have material upon which to work, and this material is provided by the five external senses.

Thomas Aquinas, in his commentary upon Aristotle's *De Anima* and in several shorter works, analyzes the relationship of the external senses to the internal senses, covering the whole range of human perception. Shakespeare shows a familiarity with his ideas and his terminology.

Besides the apprehensive powers of the sensible soul, it also has the power of motion.[4] Animals, possessing the senses, can move from place to place; but plants, lacking the senses (except possibly touch), cannot. Therefore motion is deemed a necessary power of the sensible soul.[5] Hamlet reflects this when he says to his mother, "Sense sure you have, Else you could not have motion" (III.iv.71–72). In *Measure for Measure* Claudio dreads to exchange "this sensible warm motion" of life for the cold stillness of death (III.i.120).

Except for touch, which is felt throughout the entire body, the external senses are limited to the sense organs designed for them. They receive the physical impressions of things, but they do not interpret these things. All of them transfer the impressions received to one "common sense," the first of the internal senses, which sets the process of rationalization in motion. The common sense can distinguish between impressions from a single sense, as white and black, sweet and bitter. It can also distinguish between white and sweet, thus receiving impressions from two different senses at the same time. This shows it to be a single power, indivisible though its perceptions through several channels might suggest that it is divisible. It remains close to reality, receiving the physical impressions of objects without itself attempting to rationalize upon them.[6] In *Love's Labour's Lost* Biron objects to forgoing food and the presence of ladies in order to concentrate upon abstract reasoning, "things hid and barr'd . . . from common sense" (I.i.57). Common sense can perceive food and ladies only when they are physically present. To enforce their absence causes the mind to imagine their presence and is more of a distraction than their actual presence would be (I.i.64).

The debate between Biron and the king repeats a similar debate in Montaigne's essay "Of Solitarinesse" and seems to use the language of Florio's translation (below, p. 183). Biron thinks that concentrated study can injure one's health and dull the mind rather than enlighten it:

> Small have continual *plodders* ever won,
> Save base authority from others' *books*. (I.i.86–87)

Florio's words are, "This *plodding* occupation of *books*, is as painfull as any other, and as great an enemie unto health."[7]

Though the common sense perceives through the five organs of sense, it does not perceive through all of them equally at all times. Sometimes the force of all the senses is concentrated on the object of a single sense to give undivided attention to that sense. Thus Dante in *La Vita Nuova* describes a meeting with Beatrice:

> When she was about to salute me, a spirit of Love, destroying all the other spirits of the senses, urged forth the feeble spirits of the sight. (chapter 11)[8]

Dante repeats the image in chapter 14.

In *Love's Labour's Lost* the same image is used when Boyet tells the princess that the king is "infected" with love for her:

> Why, all his behaviours did make their retire
> To the court of his eye, peeping thorough desire;
> His heart, like an agate, with your print impress'd,
> Proud with his form, in his eye pride express'd;
> His tongue, all impatient to speak and not see,
> Did stumble in haste in his eyesight to be;
> All senses to that sense did make their repair,
> To feel only looking on fairest of fair;
> Methought all his senses were lock'd in his eye. (II.i.234–242)

Not merely the other senses, but also the heart and the tongue concentrated their forces in the king's sense of sight to behold the princess's beauty.

In *The Winter's Tale* Autolycus says that his song was so popular with the shepherds that "all their other senses stuck in ears" (IV.iv.620), that is, the force of all five senses concentrated upon hearing. In *A Midsummer Night's Dream* Hermia notes this action with relation to sight and hearing:

> Dark night, that from the eye his function takes,
> The ear more quick of apprehension makes;
> Wherein it doth impair the seeing sense,
> It pays the hearing double recompense. (III.ii.177–180)

This again represents the ability of the common sense to concentrate its perceptive powers upon a single sense.

When a person is asleep or unconscious, impressions made upon the sense organs cannot be relayed to the mind, for the common sense is inactive or sometimes only partially active. When Lady Macbeth walks in her sleep, her doctor says, "You see her eyes are open," to which her attendant replies, "Ay, but their sense is shut" (V.i.28–29). In *A Midsummer Night's Dream* Titania "strikes dead" the senses of five mortals by putting them into a heavy slumber (IV.i.84–85). Also, a mind can be so preoccupied with internal fancies that sense impressions are not received by it. In sonnet 113 the poet says, "Since I left you mine eye is in my mind," that is, he so concentrates on the image of his absent friend that his eyes do not see clearly what is before them. Hamlet suffers a similar moment of introspection when he says,"My father!—me thinks I see my father . . . In my mind's eye, Horatio" (I.ii.184–185) and again when he says, "Farewell, dear mother," though his mother is not present (IV.iii.51). After the witches' prophecy is partly confirmed, Macbeth's imagination is so engrossed with "the imperial theme" that he cannot hear words spoken to him, causing Banquo to exclaim, "Look, how our partner's rapt" (I.iii.142). Later, seeing the air-drawn dagger before he kills Duncan, he says.

> My eyes are made the fools o' th'other senses,
> Or else worth all the rest. (II.i.44–45)

All his senses are so concentrated in the sense of sight that he is made to see what is not there.

King Lear declares that the agony of his mind prevents his feeling the violence of the storm:

> When the mind's free,
> The body's delicate; the tempest in my mind
> Doth from my senses take all feeling else
> Save what beats there. (III.iv.11–14)

Here mental anguish impedes the normal operation of the external senses. Physical anguish concentrates upon the sense of touch and is felt throughout the body, exciting sympathy in the other members. In *Othello* Desdemona remarks,

> For let our finger ache, and it indues
> Our other, healthful members even to a sense
> Of pain. (III.iv.146–148)

Plato uses this illustration in *Republic* V (462):

> As in the body, when but a finger of one of us is hurt, the whole frame, drawn towards the soul as a center and forming one kingdom under the ruling power therein, feels the hurt and sympathizes all together with the part affected, and we say that the man has a pain in his finger. (trans. Jowett)

Levinus Lemnius makes the same point:

> For all the members of the body be so lyncked and knitte together, and such participacion and consent is betweene them, that if one of the smallest ioyntes, or the little toe be hurt or payned, the whole body is distempered and oute of quite. And thus (as *Chrysostome* sayth) if the foote or one of the fingers endes bee pricked wyth a thorne or other sharpe thing, al ye other members are ioyntly greeued aswel as they.[9]

Stephen Batman has a statement to the same effect.[10]

Physical anguish does not vary with size; a large person does not feel pain more keenly than a small one. Seneca writes, "In the largest and in the smallest bodies, the pain of a wound is equal."[11] In *Measure for Measure* Isabella applies this statement to the pain of death:

> The sense of death is most in apprehension;
> And the poor beetle, that we tread upon,
> In corporal sufferance finds a pang as great
> As when a giant dies. (III.i.78-81)

The first line of this quotation seems indebted to Montaigne's essay, "That the Taste of Goods or Evils Doth Greatly Depend on the Opinion We Have of Them":

> Death is but felt by discourse, because it is the motion of an instant. . . . And I find by experience, that it is rather the impatience of the *imagination of death* that makes us impatient of the paine, and that we feele it two-fold grievous, forasmuch as it threats us to die.[12]

The basic "complexion" and health of the body depend upon its maintaining a proper balance of the four humours: blood *(sanguis)*, phlegm, choler, and melancholy. The last three of these are like the glandular secretions of modern physiology. The predominance of any one humour produces a particular type of personality, which is named for that humour: sanguine, phlegmatic, choleric, melancholic. Under stress of violent emotion any of the humours may be burned by the furnace of the heart, leaving an injurious black substance called "adust" or burnt melancholy. This substance may be compared to ashes from a fire. If not purged from the body, it will clog the passages of the veins and arteries, causing madness and finally death (below, p. 141). Sometimes the heat of the heart will dry out the brain, which is normally cold and moist.[13]

But there is a milder form of burning, when the fire in the heart boils or "seethes" the humours in the stomach (particularly phlegm, which is watery and difficult to burn), the vapours from which ascend to the brain and cause it to seethe also, obscuring the operation of the reason and sense. Sometimes, instead of steamy vapours, fumes of smoke will ascend to the brain, likewise obscuring the senses.[14]

Shakespeare uses this imagery. In *A Midsummer Night's Dream* Theseus observes that lovers and madmen have "seething brains" (V.i.4). In *The Tempest* Prospero restores the senses of the Italian noblemen who have been thrown into a trance by Ariel:

81

A solemn air and the best comforter
To an unsettled fancy cure thy *brains*,
Now useless, *boil'd* within thy skull. . . .
                                    so their rising senses
Begin to chase the ignorant *fumes that mantle*
Their clearer reason. . . . Their understanding
Begins to swell, and the approaching tide
Will shortly fill the reasonable shore
That now lies foul and muddy. (V.i.58–82)

In similar terms, Donatus Acciaiolus describes the process of sleeping and awaking from sleep:

For at first a man is awake; afterwards comes sleep, which is a certain privation of wakefulness and operation [ability to move and act]. For the senses are all bound up *(ligantur)*, whence sleep is customarily called the bond of the external senses. Then, sleep having been dissolved, again wakefulness occurs in a kind of intoxication from which vapours ascend and perturb the vital spirit and the brain, the instrument by which reason operates. But that vapour being dissolved, the spirit again begins to run pure and to return the appropriate instrument [of reason] to the exercise of its operations.[15]

The intoxication *(ebrio)* apparently refers to the first few confused and dull moments felt as one wakes from a sound sleep. Shakespeare's "approaching tide" that will fill the "reasonable shore" is the same as the stream of spirit that runs pure after the annoying fumes and vapours are dissolved. Earlier, when Ferdinand is made powerless by Prospero's magic, he says, "My *spirits,* as in a dream, are all *bound up*" (I.ii.486). This uses the same image, *ligantur,* that Acciaiolus applies to the senses.

One of the humours, blood, gives rise to the spirits that are instrumental in uniting soul and body. Lemnius and La Primaudaye name three kinds of spirit: natural, vital, and animal (from *anima:* soul).[16] Spirit is first distilled from the blood, then each successive stage represents a further distillation and is more volatile than the one before. Natural spirit dwells in the liver, vital spirit in the heart, animal spirit in the brain.[17] Vital spirit carries heat and life to the whole body, while animal spirit carries messages between the soul and the several parts of the body and becomes the vehicle of the soul, the mediator between the nonmaterial soul and the material body. It is an extremely fine mist or vapour and, with the vital spirit, courses through the arteries of the body. Ordinarily it is extremely active and always in motion, but it can become sluggish and dull from sorrow, fatigue, or boredom.[18]

In *Love's Labour's Lost* Biron warns against too much study, since "universal plodding poisons up The *nimble spirits in the arteries*" (IV.iii.305-306). In *The Tempest* Antonio is not sleepy because "my spirits are nimble" (II.i.202). In *As You Like It* Rosalind, overcome by fatigue, says, "How weary are my spirits" (II.iv.1). In *Hamlet* the player-king becomes sleepy when "my spirits grow dull" (III.ii.236), and Hamlet dies because "the potent poison quite o'ercrows my spirit" (V.ii.364); his mother thinks that he is mad when "forth at your eyes your spirits wildly peep" (III.iv.119). These uses reflect contemporary physiology.

Since animal spirit is so closely associated with the soul, *spirit* is sometimes used as an equivalent of the soul. Though a material substance, it was thought to accompany the nonmaterial soul into death and sometimes to use its vapourous substance to present the soul's form as a ghost.[19] Such is perhaps the "spiritual body" that shall arise from the grave, according to St. Paul (1 Cor. 15:44). In *Twelfth Night* Sebastian assures the onlookers that he is a spirit but a spirit still in its physical body, not a ghost (V.i.243-245). The basic meaning of *spirit* is still that of a volatile liquid, but it came to be used for all "airy bodies," such as Puck and Ariel, and for the souls of men.

When a person is happy and cheerful, the humours in his body are warm and moist and so is the body itself. At such times the spirits are very active and nimble. But sorrow tends to dry up the humours, leaving the body cold and dry, the cheeks pale, and the spirits sluggish.[20] When parting from Juliet, Romeo explains the paleness of their faces: "Dry sorrow drinks our blood" (III.v.59). In *Pericles* Dionyza admonishes Marina, "Do not consume your blood with sorrowing" (IV.i.23-24).

Ficino states that a hot and moist constitution favours sexual activity, since heat and moisture are essential to all generation of life.[21] Othello uses this imagery when he suspects Desdemona of excessive sexuality:

Oth. Give me your hand. This hand is *moist*, my lady.
Des. It yet hath felt no age nor known no *sorrow.*
Oth. This argues fruitfulness and liberal heart;
Hot, hot, and *moist.* This hand of yours requires
A sequester from liberty, fasting and prayer,
Much castigation, exercise devout;
For here's a young and sweating devil here
That commonly rebels. (III.iv.36–43)

Aquinas assigns a rank to each of the external senses in terms of its contribution to the process of perception. By this standard the sense of sight is the "noblest" and the sense of hearing is in second place. These are the most active in receiving impressions from outside the body.[22]

In his commentary on Aristotle's *De Anima*, Aquinas devotes three chapters or "lectures" to the nature of sound (II.xvi–xviii). All sound, he concludes, is a percussion (*percussio*) or a result of percussion. It is transmitted by the air; for example, voice is caused by a percussion of air against the "vocal artery." In turn voice makes a percussion against the air outside, which in turn strikes against the ear of the hearer.[23] Philemon Holland uses similar language in his translation of Plutarch's *Moralia* (1603):

> for voice is a *stroake* or *percussion* by the aire of that which the eare doth heare; for as the aire is smitten by motion, so it striketh againe the auditorie organ forcibly, if the motion be quicke; and gently, if the same be slow.[24]

Shakespeare uses these terms in Titus Lartius's tribute to Coriolanus as a warrior:

Thou wast a soldier
Even to Cato's wish, not fierce, and terrible
Only in *strokes*; but with thy grim looks and
The thunder-like *percussion* of thy sounds,
Thou mad'st thine enemies shake, as if the world
Were feverous and did tremble. (I.iv.56–61)

Coriolanus's "sounds" included both his battle cry and the clashing of his sword. He seemed almost an elemental force, such as an earthquake.

In *Cymbeline* the queen describes Imogen as "so tender of rebuke that *words are strokes* And strokes death to her" (III.v.40–41). Earlier Imogen spoke of her husband's accusation against her: "I have heard I am a strumpet, and mine *ear*, Therein false *struck*, can take no greater wound" (III.iv.116–117). In *The Tempest* Sebastian pretends that a great roaring noise "*struck my ear* most terribly" (II.i.313).

Sometimes the image of air percussion is one of piercing rather than of striking. Mercutio jestingly says of Romeo, "he is already dead; stabb'd with a white wench's black eye; run through the ear with a love song" (II.iv.13–14). But in *Othello* Brabantio says,

> But words are words; I never yet did hear
> That the bruised heart was *pierced through the ear*.
>
> (I.iii.218– 219)

This negates Mercutio's account of Romeo's being "run through the ear." Brabantio thinks that the heart is wounded only through the eyes, as is most commonly the case.

Shakespeare shows a keen interest in the sense of sight.[25] In *Troilus and Cressida* Achilles discourses to Ulysses on the necessity of a "mirror," if one is to see himself as others see him:

> The beauty that is borne here in the face
> The bearer knows not, but commends itself
> To others' eyes; nor doth the *eye* itself,
> That most pure *spirit of sense*, behold itself,
> Not going from itself; but eye to eye oppos'd
> Salutes each other with each other's form;
> For *speculation* turns not to itself
> Till it hath travell'd and is mirror'd there
> Where it may see itself. (III.iii.103–111)

This is a rather complicated way of saying that one may see his reflection in the eyes of another person but that he cannot see it without those opposite eyes or some other kind of mirror (Lat. *speculum*). Speculation, the mirroring power, shows what is before the mirror, not what is behind it; hence, one's own eyes may serve as

a mirror to reflect the image of another person but cannot reflect one's own image.[26]
The speculative or mirroring power of the eye is associated with vigorous life, its absence with death. Batman writes of it:

> Phisitions say, that the Images that we see in eyen, bee not seene in the eyen of them, that shal die, three dayes afore. And if the sayd Images bee not seene, it is a certeine token of death.[27]

He makes clear that the "Images" are reflections normally mirrored by the eye. He adds to this another sign of approaching death:

> And therefore if the nosethrilles waxe sharpe, and the eyen deepe, in sharpe features, it is a token of death.[28]

Batman also writes that the eye reflects all emotions felt in the soul. The "spirit of sight" originates in the crystalline humour of the eye.[29] The "spirit of feeling" (spiritus sensibilis) has more mastery in the eye than in the other sense organs, and therefore the eye is more tender and easily wounded.[30]

Shakespeare seems to have been impressed by these ideas. In King John Salisbury says to Melun, "But I do see the cruel pangs of death Right in thine eye" (V.iv.59–60). Macbeth at the banquet cries out to the ghost of Banquo, "Thou hast no speculation in those eyes That thou dost glare with" (III.iv.95–96); because Banquo is dead, his eyes do not mirror the objects before them. And Mistress Quickly recognized Falstaff's approaching death because "his nose was as sharp as a pen" (Henry V, II.iii.17).

Shakespeare appears to have confused the spiritus sensibilis or "spirit of sense," which is most strongly evident in the eye, with the membranes of the eye itself. The phrase reappears in Troilus's description of Cressida's soft hands "to whose soft seizure The cygnet's down is harsh and spirit of sense Hard as the palm of ploughman" (I.i.57–59). Here the membranes of the eye are contrasted with the coarse and calloused hand of the workman, and the hands of Cressida were even softer than the eye. Soft hands are more sensitive than hard hands; in Hamlet's words, "The hand of little employment hath the daintier sense" (V.i.77).

Batman argues that the greater sensitivity of the eye is evidence of its greater "nobility" among the other sense organs and members of the body.[31] In this he directly follows Aquinas, who draws the same conclusion in his treatise on light[32] and again in his commentary on Aristotle's *De Anima*.[33] Aquinas also argues that the eye is noblest because it is the most "spiritual" of the sense organs. Touch and taste are applied directly from the objects perceived, hearing results from a local motion of the air, smell results from a "fumal evaporation" that is sensed by the nose. But what enters the eye is an image or "intention" of the object perceived and made possible by means of light, more subtle and less grossly physical than the action of the other sense organs. One sometimes speaks of intellectual light or the light of reason. But this is possible only by analogy, for a corporeal sense can perceive only corporeal things. Still, sight seems closer to the incorporeal world of ideas than the other external senses do.[34]

When *spirit* is used metaphorically to represent the soul, it cannot be perceived by any corporeal sense. But spirit is basically a corporeal substance and serves as a vehicle for the senses. The spirit of sight is employed in a manner unlike that of the other senses. Macrobius states that the eyes actually emit rays, while the other four senses are receptive only.[35] In Ficino's commentary on Plato's *Symposium*, he elaborates on this theory at length in discussing how people fall in love. The spirits of the body are the strongest and purest (most volatile) in the sense of sight. The eyes emit rays as if through glass windows, and these rays draw with them a "spiritual vapour" of corrupted blood that "infects" the eye of the person beheld. As evidence for this ray, he quotes Aristotle to the effect that women, during their menstrual periods when blood predominates in their bodies, sometimes notice on their mirrors tiny drops of blood that have been ejected through their eyes; at other times the drops are too small to be noticed. This ray and dart of spirit enters the eye of the opposite person, descends to the heart, and wounds the heart. Ficino quotes Apuleius as saying, "For those your eyes, having descended through my eyes to my inmost heart, produce in my vitals a most violent flame."[36] Several succeeding chapters explain how persons are ensnared (*irretiamur*) by love in this fashion. "Physical (*vulgaris*) love is a perturbation of the blood" is the chapter heading of VII.vii, reminding us of Iago's definition of love: "It is merely a lust of the blood and a permission of the will" (*Othello*, I.iii.339).

In the writings of poets and others, this invisible ray of the eye speedily became identified with Cupid's arrow. George Turbervile, writing in 1567, declared that his wits were "intrapt" as he gazed on his lady's face:

> Downe by mine eyes the stroke
> descended to the hart:
> Which *Cupid* neuer crazde before
> by force of golden dart.

My notes to this passage show similar passages from Publius Syrus's *Sententiae* (Latin), Tottel's *Miscellany* (1547), *A Petite Pallace of Pettie His Pleasure* (1576), and *Alcilia* (1595).[37] I am sure that I have not exhausted the supply of examples.

When one projects his eye beam into another person's eye, he may receive a return stroke from that person's eye. But in seeing an inanimate object, no such return stroke is possible. The action of the sight may be compared to a rescue in a stormy sea by means of the breeches buoy. An arrow with an attached cord is fired into the doomed vessel, a heavier cord is drawn over and made fast, the crewmen are brought back one by one along the cord by means of a sling above the waves. So the eye darts its beam to the object, makes fast, and then relays impressions back to the sender. A better understanding of light rays would have made such a theory unnecessary.

John Donne has invented a clever variation of this theory. In *The Ecstasy* as he and his beloved sit, holding each other's hands,

> Our eye-beams twisted, and did thread
> Our eyes upon one double string. (lines 7-8)

As the lovers dart their eye beams into each other's eyes, the parallel beams twist around each other, forming a single bond of double strength.

In Shakespeare the eye beam is pictured as an arrow, an eye dart, or an eye shot. When Juliet's mother asks her to view Paris as a possible husband, Juliet agrees,

> But no more deep will I *endart mine eye*
> Than your consent gives strength to make it fly. (I.iii.98-99)

She will not fall in love without her mother's permission, an ironical comment in the light of her later experience.

In *Cymbeline* Imogen bids farewell to her husband Posthumus:

> You must be gone;
> And I shall here abide the hourly *shot*
> Of angry *eyes*. (I.i.89–90)

In *All's Well* Helena says of herself and Bertram:

> And is it I
> That drive thee from the sportive court, where thou
> *Wast shot at with fair eyes?* (III.ii.108–110)

This concept of the eye shot gives new meaning to a puzzling line in *Romeo and Juliet*. Juliet asks the nurse:

> Hath Romeo slain himself? Say thou but ay,
> And that bare vowel I shall poison more
> Than the death-darting eye of cockatrice.
> I am not I, if there be such an ay,
> Or those *eyes' shot* that makes the answer ay. (III.ii.45–49)

The original text reads "eyes shot." Most editors have adopted Capell's emendation of *shut* for *shot*, referring to Romeo's eyes supposedly closed in death. In my edition of the play,[38] I retain *shot* and add the apostrophe to *eyes*. The reference is then to the nurse's eyes. Her voice announcing Romeo's death would kill Juliet through the ear or her hesitant eye glance revealing the same news would kill Juliet through the eyes, in the same manner as the cockatrice (basilisk) can kill by shooting poison from its eyes. Shakespeare thus repeats his double-death theme from Mercutio's jesting remark that Romeo was dead, "stabb'd with a white wench's black eye, run through the ear with a love song" (above, p. 85). Both passages demonstrate the methods of perception by sight and by hearing, the two most eminent of the five external senses.[39]

2. The Internal Senses

I have already noted that the internal senses, or five wits, are common sense, phantasy, imagination, judgment, and memory.

Batman and Allott have omitted memory and substituted intellect or understanding (above, p. 73). This involves an attempt to distinguish between intelligence and intellect, as already explained (above, p. 74). But Shakespeare uses the usual classification, with memory as the fifth internal sense. In a number of passages he shows a close observation of the process of perception as explained by Aquinas and La Primaudaye, among others.

La Primaudaye recognizes three ventricles in the brain. In the front ventricle reside common sense, phantasy, and imagination; in the middle ventricle, the judgment or reason or estimative power; in the rear ventricle, the memory.[40] The order of perception is as follows: The five external senses present to the common sense impressions of things exactly as they are sensed, in the same manner as a camera or tape recorder. These impressions are then submitted to the phantasy (fantasy, fancy) and the imagination for interpretation. These two add to the impression such qualities as beautiful, ugly, dangerous, fortunate, pleasant, unpleasant, and these constitute the phantasmata submitted to the judgment. The judgment draws upon past experience and knowledge as recorded in the memory to determine whether the phantasmata are correctly formed or are in error. Since many phantasmata of the same object may be submitted, the judgment's task may be to select the correct one, which is then stored in the memory for future use. The judgment must constantly restrain the activity of phantasy and imagination, which can lead to confusion and madness if completely unrestrained.[41]

Aquinas explains the ways in which this can happen:

> Thence, when the intellect is not dominant, animals act after phantasy. Some indeed because they entirely lack intellect, such as beasts. And some because they have the intellect veiled, such as men. This veiling of the intellect happens in three ways. First, from a certain passion of wrath, or concupiscence, or fear, or anything of that kind. Second, it results from a certain infirmity, such as occurs in frenzied or furious persons. And third, in a dream, as happens in sleeping persons. For from these causes it happens that the intellect does not prevail over the phantasy, whence the person follows the phantastic apprehension as if it were true.[42]

Aquinas rather agreed with Averroes that phantasy and imagination are so much alike that they need not be viewed as different senses. But he did explain what the supposed difference is. Phantasy is completely uncontrolled, flitting skittishly from one impression to another, giving a multitude of different conceptions of an object presented to it by the common sense. Imagination involves a more orderly sequence of impressions and has a collecting and combining power not present in the phantasy. For example, it has an impression of *gold* and an impression of *mountain*; by combining these it creates a phantasm of a golden mountain, though no such object ever existed.[43] In the same manner poets created centaurs, satyrs, and harpies by combining images of human beings with images of horses, goats, and vultures; the Minotaur, or bull-man, is a case in point. None of these creatures ever existed but were formed by the imagination. The phantasy lacks this combining power, though sometimes phantasmata can remain in the mind after the object from which they were drawn has disappeared. For this reason La Primaudaye considered that phantasy and imagination are really the same. They seem to be different degrees of the same power rather than separate and distinct mental powers.[44]

Shakespeare discusses both phantasy and imagination in Theseus's comment on the story told by the four lovers in *A Midsummer Night's Dream*:

> I never may believe
> These antique fables, nor these fairy toys.
> Lovers and madmen have such seething brains,
> Such shaping fantasies, that apprehend
> More than cool reason ever comprehends.
> The lunatic, the lover, and the poet
> Are of imagination all compact.
> One sees more devils than vast hell can hold;
> That is, the madman. The lover, all as frantic,
> Sees Helen's beauty in a brow of Egypt.
> The poet's eye, in a fine frenzy rolling,
> Doth glance from heaven to earth, from earth to heaven;
> And as imagination bodies forth
> The forms of things unknown, the poet's pen
> Turns them to shapes and gives to airy nothing

> A local habitation and a name.
> Such tricks hath strong imagination,
> That, if it would but apprehend some joy,
> It comprehends some bringer of that joy;
> Or in the night, imagining some fear,
> How easy is a bush suppos'd a bear! (V.i.2–22)

This is a systematic exposition of the functioning of the phantasy and the imagination. The "shaping fantasies" alter the realistic impressions transmitted by the common sense. To the madman other persons or objects appear as devils, for his hallucinations are not dispelled by the critical judgment. To the lover a swarthy, homely girl seems to be a great beauty; as Montaigne says, "An amorous passion addeth beauties, and lendeth graces to the subject it embraceth."[45] To the poet the phantasmata are controlled by the imagination, which "bodies forth The forms of things unknown." This is exactly the action of the imagination as stated by Aquinas.

The poet's pen gives a place and a name to "airy nothing." To Shakespeare the word *nothing* does not mean non-existent but non-tangible; it is literally "no thing." To Mercutio's account of Queen Mab, Romeo says, "Thou talk'st of *nothing*," to which Mercutio replies,

> True, I talk of *dreams*,
> Which are the children of an idle brain,
> Begot of nothing but vain *fantasy*,
> Which is as thin of substance as the air
> And more inconstant than the wind. (I.iv.96–100)

As Aquinas pointed out, in dreams the intellect does not control the phantasy, which can fill the slumbering mind with vain and unreal images.

The image-forming power of the phantasy is illustrated in the last two lines of Theseus's speech. If one already fears the presence of bears in the forest, the phantasy turns the vague image of a bush into that of a bear. The common sense presents the outline of a bush, but the phantasy—or the imagination—sees a bear, attaching to the bush an image already in the mind.

In this speech Shakespeare twice stresses the antithesis between *apprehend* and *comprehend*. Phantasy apprehends and reason comprehends. Imagination apprehends a joy—for example, of love—and then comprehends a particular person as a lover who will bring such joy.

Apprehend means to gather or lay hold upon impressions. Aquinas uses *comprehend* to mean "include" or "understand," very much in its modern usage. Two significant examples will illustrate this. A chapter heading in his *De Spiritualibus Creaturis* reads;

> Although a spiritual substance cannot be *comprehended* by the body, it yet can communicate its being to the body, and on account of this can be united to the body as form.[46]

A passage on *ecstasy* also illustrates the use of *comprehend;* this is from the *Summa Theologica:*

> To suffer ecstasy means to be placed outside oneself. This happens as to the apprehensive power and as to the appetitive power. As to the apprehensive power, a man is said to be placed outside himself, when he is placed outside the knowledge proper to him. This may be due to his being raised to a higher knowledge; thus, a man is said to suffer ecstasy, inasmuch as he is placed outside the connatural apprehension of his sense and reason, when he is raised up so as to *comprehend* things that surpass sense and reason: or it may be due to his being cast down into a state of debasement; thus a man may be said to suffer ecstasy, when he is overcome by violent passion or madness. As to the appetitive power, a man is said to suffer ecstasy when that power is borne towards something else, so that it goes forth out from itself, as it were.[47]

As I have already noted, both the external and the internal senses are said to apprehend; but only the reason or judgment can be said to comprehend, for comprehension involves a critical faculty that is not present in apprehension.

The passage just quoted on ecstasy suggests that it is possessed by those who rise above or sink below the normal limits of rational comprehension. To surpass sense and reason is to experience the kind of inspiration that is felt by prophets and poets;[48] St. Bruno calls it "that ecstasy and excess of mind into which we can ascend on no other than spiritual feet."[49] The "poet's eye in a fine frenzy rolling" illustrates this type of ecstasy. When one sinks below sense and reason into a state of debasement, then his ecstasy is that of madness. The madman plagued by visions of devils illustrates this form of ecstasy. Theseus's third instance is that of the lover. This corresponds to the ecstasy of the appetitive power mentioned by Aquinas and discussed at length in the two preceding articles of the *Summa Theologica*, concerning the "apprehensions" of love.[50]

Thus ecstasy is a form of excessive feeling including madness but is not limited to madness. Hamlet and his mother suspect each other of temporary madness. Hamlet declares that her sense must have been enthralled to ecstasy to allow her to choose Claudius in preference to her first husband. A few minutes later, when Hamlet sees the ghost that his mother cannot see, she says, "This bodiless creation ecstasy Is very cunning in" (III.iv.74, 138).

Portia experiences the ecstasy of love when Bassanio chooses the leaden casket:

> O love, be moderate; allay thy *ecstasy;*
> In measure rein thy joy; scant this excess.
> I feel too much thy blessing; make it less
> For fear I surfeit. (*Merchant of Venice*, III.ii.111–114)

Troilus feels a similar excitement before his first sexual experience with Cressida:

> I am giddy; expectation whirls me round.
> Th'*imaginary* relish is so sweet
> That it enchants my *sense.* (III.ii.19–21)

Like Portia, he fears that his joy of anticipation is so great that it may injure him physically.

In *The Tempest* Prospero rises to the level of inspired prophecy in his vision of the world's transiency: "We are such stuff as dreams are made on." Before he spoke, Ferdinand noted that he felt strongly moved, and afterward Prospero felt faint: "A turn or two I'll walk To still my beating mind" (IV.i.143–163). Though the word *ecstasy* is not used, Shakespeare is illustrating the elevation of mind described by Aquinas and ascribed to the poet in Theseus's speech.

94

This elevation of mind may reveal flashes of insight beyond the ordinary perceptions of reason and sense. Sometimes it functions much like the instincts of animals, but on a higher plane. In *Richard III* a citizen, fearing the advent of civil strife, remarks;

> By a *divine instinct* men's minds mistrust
> Ensuing dangers; as by proof we see
> *The waters swell before a boist'rous storm.* (II.iii.42–44)

These words seem to be drawn directly from Cicero's *De Divinatione* in two separate passages:

> Indeed there is a certain force and nature, which now by means of signs observed over a long period of time, and again by some *divine instinct* and inspiration, foretells the future.[51]
> Come, let us view those things which, although they are of another kind, yet are very much like divination:
> "And likewise the heaving *sea* often gives warning of future *storms* when suddenly and from its very depths it begins to *swell.*"[52]

This "divine instinct and inspiration" is an intellectual power and is not the same in its action as ordinary reason, which proceeds logically and gradually from one point to another until a conclusion is reached. This logical process is called by Aquinas the *discursio rationis*,[53] by La Primaudaye and Holland, the "discourse of reason."[54]

Hamlet declares that a beast "that wants discourse of reason" would have mourned its dead mate longer than his mother has done (I.II.150). Again he reproaches himself for failing to use his "large discourse . . . and god-like reason" and succumbing to "bestial oblivion" (IV.iv.36–40). Hector accuses Troilus of using "no discourse of reason" in wishing to continue the war (II.ii.116), and Troilus accuses himself of "madness of discourse" in debating with himself as to Cressida's unfaithfulness when it is all too evident to his eyes (V.ii.142). And Desdemona protests that she has not been unfaithful to Othello "either in *discourse of thought* or actual deed" (IV.ii.153). These uses of "discourse" are quite different from those that represent speech and conversation.

To assure true perceptions and reject false perceptions, the judgment must constantly supervise the images presented by phantasy
and imagination. If judgment abdicates this function, the mind will
sink into madness through its uncritical acceptance of false images. In
Hamlet the king describes Ophelia as "divided from herself and her
fair *judgment*, Without the which we are pictures or mere beasts"
(IV.v.85–86). He hesitates to punish Hamlet for Polonius's death
because "he's lov'd of the distracted multitude, Who like not in their
judgment, but their eyes" (IV.ii.4–5). In *Julius Caesar* Antony cries
out against the applause given to Brutus's speech justifying Caesar's
death: "O *judgment*, thou art fled to brutish beasts, And men have
lost their reason" (III.ii.109–110). And Lear adjures his own hands
to strike his head: "Beat at this gate that let thy folly in And thy dear
judgment out" (I.iv.293–294).

Judgment can abdicate its power by eventual acquiescence in what
it at first considers to be improper. This constitutes a surrender to
habit, or custom. La Primaudaye writes;

> In the meane time we may learn this, that if *custome* be of so great
> force, that (as we saie) it *ouercommeth nature*, it is chiefelie to be
> seene in vice and dissolutenes, which is a gulfe wherein a man
> may verie easilie cast himselfe headlong, but it is a verie difficult
> matter, yea vnpossible to withdrawe himselfe againe. And (as a
> wise Romane said) most horrible & execrable offences through
> *vse* and *custome* are made small faults, and are commonlie
> practised.[55]

In the prologue to *Pericles* Gower comments on the incest of
Antiochus with his daughter:

> By *custom* what they did begin
> Was with long *use* account'd no sin. (lines 29–30)

In Hamlet's conversation with his mother (II.iv) he repeatedly
uses this theme. He will wring her heart

> If damned *custom* have not braz'd it so
> That it is proof and bulwark against *sense*. (lines 37–38)

And again:

> That monster, *custom,* who all *sense* doth eat,
> Of habits [d]evil, is angel yet in this,
> That to the use of actions fair and good
> He likewise gives a frock or livery,
> That aptly is put on. . . .
> For *use almost can change the stamp of nature.* (III.iv.161-168)

Here *custom* and *use* are pictured as serving to corrupt a good disposition if the habits are evil and likewise to improve an evil disposition if the habits are good. This stems from Aristotle's discussion of habits in *Nicomachean Ethics* (III.ii). In Aquinas's commentary on this work, he states that incontinence through custom is more easily changed than incontinence through nature; but custom, through long study and practice, may come to be one's nature.[56] Shakespeare probably knew this comment, but his words reflect those of La Primaudaye.

Violent passion or "affection" is usually aroused by faulty perceptions. Othello, angry at the brawl between Cassio and Montano, describes his own state of mind:

> My blood begins my safer guides to rule;
> And passion, having my best *judgment* collied [darkened],
> Assays to lead the way. (II.iii.205-207)

Blood or "hot blood" is here used as the source of anger and passion and therefore as the opponent of judgment. Hamlet congratulates Horatio on his ability to keep a proper balance between "blood and judgment"; that is, between the rational and the irascible faculties of the soul. The seat of the latter is in the heart and is therefore represented by blood (*Hamlet,* III.ii.74).

Iago, secretly hating Othello, plots to put him "into a jealousy so strong That *judgment* cannot cure" (II.i.310-311). When Othello is "eaten up with passion" (III.iii.391) at the false picture of Desdemona in Cassio's arms, Iago's plot is on the way to success. But Othello's susceptibility to the passion of anger, which may overcome his judgment, is indicated in his earlier speech.

This theme is repeated in *The Winter's Tale.* Hermione, instructed by her husband, playfully takes and holds Polixenes's hand to persuade him to prolong his visit by a week. As Leontes watches, his perception of them suddenly changes from a picture of good friends to a picture of guilty lovers. They hold hands too long and ardently and are "too hot." It seems to him that "to mingle friendship far is mingling bloods" (I.ii.109); fornication is a natural sequel to hand-holding. This false suspicion grows to an unshakable conviction that ends only with the loss of his children and his wife.

As Leontes feels his suspicions develop, he analyzes his state of mind in a remarkable speech, which employs the psychological terms found in the Latin of Aquinas:

> *Affection,* thy *intention* stabs the *center.*
> Thou dost make possible things not so held,
> *Communicat'st* with dreams; how can this be?—
> With what's unreal thou *co-active* art,
> And fellow'st *nothing.* Then 'tis very credent
> Thou mayst *co-join* with something; and thou dost,
> And that beyond *commission,* and I *find* it,
> And that to the *infection* of my brains
> And hardening of my brows. (I.ii.138–146)

Since these terms are used somewhat differently from their usual meanings, it is necessary to examine them in detail.

Affection. Hallet Smith cites Cooper's *Thesaurus* (1582) as defining *affectio:* "a disposition or mutation happening to bodie or minde: trouble of minde. Impetus, commotio."[57] In this scene affection refers to Leontes's own mind, not to the friendly conduct of Polixenes and Hermione. Its basic meaning is "a state of mind" or "an inclination of the mind." It came to mean an emotional impulse that opposes the governance of reason. We have frequent references in Shakespeare to the war of reason (or conscience) and the affections, most notably in *Lucrece* when Tarquin overrules his reason and exclaims, "Affection is my captain" (line 271) and "nothing can affection's course control" (line 500).Affection is stimulated to action by the images from phantasy and imagination unchecked by reason or judgment. Its action in the soul is essentially that which responds to a too vivid imagination.[58]

Intention is the term used by Aquinas, Albertus Magnus, and

Ficino for an image presented to the mind by the apprehensive senses.[59] Aquinas lists a first intention and a second intention. The first intention is the actual image presented by the external senses to the common sense. The second intention is the image formed by the phantasy or imagination on the basis of the first intention.[60] Thus in Theseus's line, "How easy is a bush suppos'd a bear," the first intention or actual image is a bush; the second intention or imagined image is a bear. When the type of intention is not specified, the second or imagined image is nearly always meant, as it is in Leontes's speech.

Center refers to Leontes's own soul or heart; the terms are often used interchangeably (below, p. 114). Shakespeare is quoting from himself: "Poor *soul*, the *center* of my sinful *earth*" (sonnet 146) and "Turn back, dull *earth*, and find thy *center* out" (*Romeo and Juliet*, II.i.2). The soul or heart in the body is like the center of the earth "drawing all things to it" (*Troilus and Cressida*, IV.ii.110). Leontes uses metaphorically the image of being stabbed to the heart; he is wounded by the "intention" or picture of guilty lovers, which his "affection" causes him to see in his wife and friend.

Communicat'st does not signify an oral or written message. It is a formal term in psychology, used in its original sense of "impart, share, hold in common." Affection, with the imagination, can "make possible things not so held," such as the golden mountain, the centaurs, the satyrs, and the harpies (above, p. 91). It holds this image-making power in common with dreams, which also can present impossibilities from phantasmata remaining in the mind after their original source is no longer perceived.

Aquinas writes, "With friends and brothers, a man ought to have trust and a *communication* of things," stressing the idea of sharing.[61] He also uses the term in expressing the relationship of the spiritual form to the material body (above, p. 93) and of lower bodies to heavenly bodies.[62] Albertus Magnus thinks that in "true" dreams the imagination receives impulses from heavenly powers and that these are "communicated" back to the common sense to be presented again to the mind.[63]

Co-active refers to the joint action of affection, through imagination, with the unreal things already mentioned: the golden mountain and others; these are "no thing" (nontangible) but are mental images only. Likewise, dreams are "no thing," as I have already stated (above, p. 92). Aquinas uses the terms *coactio* and *coactus* in his commentary upon the *Nicomachean Ethics*.[64]

Co-join repeats the action of affection in imagining unreal images. Since affection can do this, it can certainly cojoin with a real image of a real thing, a "some thing" as distinguished from the "no thing" of phantasies and dreams. This "some thing" is the physical presence of Hermione and Polixenes holding hands. *Co-join* is the same as Aquinas's *conjungere* (or *coniungere*). In *De Unitate Intellectus* Aquinas states that Aristotle sought to "cojoin" those things that are of the intellect with those things that are of the sense. Intellect functions by "cojoining" with the phantasm presented to it.[65]

As affection "cojoins" with the first intention from the common sense to form a second and false intention of "guilty lovers," the next stage should be for the intellect or judgment to cojoin with this false intention to discover or "find" its falsity. But Leontes's intellect is not up to the task. Affection sweeps him on; he "finds" the phantasm of "guilty lovers" and can go no farther.

Commission does not seem to be a technical term in the psychology of Aquinas. It may be explained as follows: Leontes had "commissioned" Hermione to speak to Polixenes in friendly fashion and to invite his continued presence. But the warmth of Hermione's greeting exceeds her husband's "commission," and by watching them he "finds" or detects a sexual attachment beyond ordinary friendliness.

Infection is the term already quoted from Ficino for the action of a lover's eyebeam upon the eye and soul of the beloved (above, p. 87). Leontes metaphorically speaks of his brain as being infected by his view of Hermione and Polixenes when he really means that his mind has been infected by the intention of "guilty lovers" formed in his imagination. The hardening of his brows uses the current jest of the cuckold's horns sprouting invisibly from the forehead of a deceived husband.

Such "infection" is variously applied by Shakespeare to the brain, the external senses, and the reason or judgment itself. In *Coriolanus* Menenius exclaims scornfully to the tribunes, "More of your conversation would *infect* my *brain*" (II.i.103). In *Cymbeline* Pisanio receives Posthumus's letter ordering Imogen's death because of adultery:

O master, what a strange *infection*
Is fall'n into thy *ear*! What false Italian,

As poison-tongu'd as handed, hath prevail'd
On thy too ready *hearing?* (III.ii.3–6)

In *Richard III* Lady Anne says to Richard, "Out of my sight! Thou dost *infect* mine *eyes*," to which he replies, "Thine *eyes*, sweet lady, have *infected* mine" (I.ii.149–150). Anne's use of the word suggests the infection of disease, but Richard's use suggests the infection of love. Similarly Benvolio would have Romeo overcome his hopeless love for Rosaline:

Take thou some new *infection* to thy *eye*,
And the rank poison of the old will die. (I.ii.50–51)

In *The Tempest*, after the violent storm caused by Ariel, Prospero asks him. "Who was so firm, so constant, that this coil would not *infect* his *reason?*" Ariel's answer is, no one (I.ii.207–208).

Leontes's technical analysis of the onset of his own jealousy even while he is experiencing it illustrates the dictum of Aristotle and Aquinas that the human intellect can not only reason but can observe itself in the process of reasoning; it apprehends images and at the same time can analyze the method by which it apprehends them.[66] This ability of self-observation is one mark that distinguishes men from beasts.

3. *The Perceptive Soul*

The ability of the rational soul to debate with itself, to entertain two contrary points of view at the same time, led some observers to question its unity. Were not two different entities required to consider opposite conclusions at the same moment? The answer was in the negative. Macrobius writes that the soul, alien from any contagion of earthly matter, infuses the immensity of the universe yet undergoes no divorce of its unity.[67] He is presumably speaking of the world-soul, which is the model for the individual souls of men.

Aquinas discusses Aristotle's *De Anima* (III.ii) on unity and/or divisibility of the soul. Perception through the several external senses might seem to indicate divisibility, but perception through several senses at the same time (as when we notice the color and

101

fragrance of a rose, the plumage and music of a songbird, the clarity and coldness of an icicle) indicates one common sense, itself undivided though its functions may seem divisible. Likewise, the perceptive soul is one and undivided.[68] Again he illustrates the internal struggle between the sensitive appetite, which may judge a particular pleasure to be good, and reason, which may judge it to be evil. This makes the soul seem divided, but it is not.[69]

Shakespeare gives to Troilus a speech on this subject when he sees the amorous meeting of Cressida and Diomedes; Troilus can hardly believe the testimony of his own eyes and ears:

> This is, and is not, Cressid.
> Within my soul there doth conduce a fight
> Of this strange nature, that a thing inseparate
> Divides more wider than the sky and earth,
> And yet the spacious breadth of this division
> Admits no orifex for a point as subtle
> As Ariachne's broken woof to enter. (V.ii.146–152)

"Ariachne's broken woof" is a filament of a spider's web. The soul, "a thing inseparate," seems divided by its two contrary impressions of Cressida's character; but the soul endures no separation of its substance, not even enough to admit one filament of a spider's web. Like Aquinas, Troilus is asserting the apparent division and real unity of the perceptive soul.

St. Augustine makes this same point in his *De Quantitate Animae*, using the illustration of a spider's web. The soul is incorporeal and admits nothing having solidity. One can imagine length, or a line, as being incorporeal; but the thinnest thread, the filament of a spider's web, is three-dimensional, having length, breadth, and depth. Therefore it has solidity, is corporeal, and cannot be thought of as penetrating an incorporeal entity such as the soul.[70]

In *Twelfth Night* Sebastian is similarly puzzled after Olivia proposes marriage, mistaking him for Cesario (Viola):

> For though *my soul disputes well with my sense,*
> That this may be some error, but no madness,
> Yet doth this accident and flood of fortune
> So far exceed all instance, all *discourse,*
> That I am ready to distrust mine eyes

> And *wrangle with my reason* that persuades me
> To any other trust but that I am mad
> Or else the lady's mad. (IV.iii.9–16)

Sebastian's rational soul and its judgment correctly perceive that some error of identification is involved; yet the whole circumstance is so wildly improbable, so completely outside any "discourse of reason," that his judgment also concludes that one of the parties must be mad. This debate is repeated in Troilus's speech as he watches Cressida with Diomedes:

> O *madness of discourse,*
> That cause sets up with and against thyself,
> Bi-fold authority, where reason can revolt
> Without perdition, and loss assume all reason
> Without revolt. (V.iii.142–146)

His speech on the soul's inseparability immediately follows. The "revolt" of reason would seem to divide the soul against itself, into two factions fighting each other; but actually the perceptive soul is not divided.

This struggle between two contradictory perceptions within the soul is reflected in Hamlet's scene with his mother (III.iv). She has accepted the public's view of her marriage to Claudius as a necessary move for the safety of the state, one that incidentally agrees with her own inclinations.[71] As Hamlet bitterly taxes her with infidelity and adulterous lust, she perceives her conduct in a different light and the two perceptions violently clash with each other. She begs Hamlet to stop, for "these words like daggers enter in my ears" and she may be slain through her sense of hearing (above, pp. 85, 89). The ghost recognizes her distress and says to Hamlet:

> But, look, amazement on thy mother sits.
> O, step between her and *her fighting soul.*
> Conceit in weakest bodies strongest works.
> Speak to her, Hamlet. (lines 112–115)

The fight in Gertrude's soul is a civil war in which her aroused conscience is overcoming her former complacency; the struggle is so violent as to threaten her life or her sanity. To "step between" her and her soul is metaphorically to distract her attention from the revised image of her conduct and hence to make the struggle less violent. But Hamlet does not wish to banish the struggle entirely until Gertrude has repented:

> Mother, for love of grace,
> Lay not that flattering unction to your soul,
> That not your trespass, but my madness, speaks.
>
> (lines 144–146)

It is necessary that she continue to perceive her conduct as guilty but to feel it with reduced intensity, so that she may be brought to repentance without endangering life or sanity.[72]

Pericles, discovering his lost child, Marina, whom he believed dead, exclaims;

> I will believe thee,
> And *make my senses* credit thy relation
> To points that seem impossible. (V.i.123–125)

Here the struggle is between the view of Marina as dead, as recorded in his memory, and the new possibility that she is alive, which presents itself to his mind. Both his external and his internal senses are involved in this conflict.

The conflicts we have here listed are those in which the soul questions its own perceptions when it develops rival "intentions" of the same perceived object. Troilus, Sebastian, and Pericles repeat Leontes's device of analyzing the process of his own thoughts even while he is thinking them (above, p. 101).

The more usual conflict within the soul is that between reason and the affections for control of the will. I have already treated the topic at length in *Shakespeare's Derived Imagery* (chapters 5–7), but it may be useful to study further the sources of this conflict.

The soul has two basic powers: to perceive and to act. Aquinas and Acciaiolus call these two powers the *speculative* or image-making power and the *active* or *practical* power.[73] La Primaudave explains them in these words:

Therefore we sayde before, that there was a double discourse of reason in man: whereof the one is *Theor[et]icall* and *Speculatiue,* which hath *Trueth* for his ende, and hauing found it goeth no farther. The other is *Practical,* hauing *Good* for his end, which being found it stayeth not there, but passeth forward to the *Will,* which God hath ioyned vnto it, to the end it should loue, desire and follow after the Good, and contrariwise hate, eschew, and turne away from euill.[74]

Therefore it is no difficult matter to iudge that the Vnderstanding differeth from the Will and affections, and that they are distinct *offices,* and seuerall properties and vertues of the soule: which haue also their diuers seates and *instrumentes.* For the internall senses are ioyned with that *power* which the Soule hath to knowe: and the heart with the *power* of the Will and Affections.[75]

He adds that reason and knowledge should control the will and the affections but do not always do so, for the latter frequently follow baser appetites.[76]

Again La Primaudaye compares the soul to a workman, the senses and faculties to the workman's instruments.[77] He also writes;

Let us consider how God hath distributed the powers, vertues, and *offices* of the soule in the body, and in euery part therof.[78]

When Othello asks the Venetian Senate to allow Desdemona to accompany him to Cyprus, he protests that he will never allow lovemaking to dull "my speculative and offic'd instruments" (I.iii.271). This line seems to reflect La Primaudaye's words. The understanding, or speculative power, has as its "instruments" the five internal senses. The will, itself an instrument of the active or practical power, uses the heart as a physical instrument. Understanding and will are distinct "offices" of the soul and their instruments are described as "offic'd."

In *Julius Caesar* Brutus says,

> Since Cassius first did whet me against Caesar,
> I have not slept.

Between the acting of a dreadful thing
And the first motion, all the interim is
Like a *phantasma* or a hideous *dream*.
The Genius and the *mortal instruments*
Are then in council; and the state of man,
Like to a little kingdom, suffers then
The nature of an insurrection. (II.i.61-69)

Here "acting" means to enact, or to decide to act, a decision made by the will. The "first motion" begins the actual carrying out of that decision. The "Genius" is the guardian spirit accompanying man through life and advising him through the intellect. The "mortal instruments" are all the powers of the soul except the intellect itself. Aristotle wrote that the active part of the intellectual soul is separable from the body and is all that is incorruptible and immortal. The passive part, including sense perception and reminiscence, receives impressions through the organs of the body, hence it is inseparable from the body and is corruptible and mortal.[79] The "mortal instruments" therefore include the will, the affections, and all the internal senses except judgment, besides the animal spirits, which are the soul's messengers within the body. Other physical "instruments" are not included in the "council" that represents the working of Brutus's mind. The organs of the body and the external senses are "instruments" of a lower order. In *Coriolanus* Menenius so describes them in his fable of the belly and the members (I.i.104-105).

In *The Tempest* Prospero further illustrates the person who can analyze his own thought processes even as he is thinking. Deciding to forgive the noblemen who had wronged him, he says,

Though with their high wrongs I am struck to th' quick,
Yet with my nobler reason 'gainst my fury
Do I take part. The rarer action is
In virtue than in vengeance. (V.i.25-28)

Here the "I" seems to be a third entity that takes sides with reason (from the rational faculty) against fury (from the irascible faculty). The "I" represents the will as an instrument of the active intellect; in this case the will follows its natural allegiance to the intellect.

Eleanor Prosser has discovered the probable source of Prospero's speech in Montaigne's essay "Of Crueltie" in Florio's translation:

> He that through a naturall facilitie, and genuine mildnesse, should neglect or contemne injuries received, should no doubt performe a *rare action*, and worthy commendation: But he who being toucht and *stung to the quicke, with* any *wrong* or offence received, should arme himselfe with *reason* against this *furiously-*blind desire of *revenge*, and in the end after a great conflict, yeeld himselfe master over-it, should doubtlesse doe much more. The first should do well, the other *vertuously*. The one *action* might be termed goodnesse, the other *vertue*.[80]

Both Prospero's speech and Montaigne's words represent the triumph of the rational faculty in controlling the irascible faculty. A third faculty of the soul is the concupiscible faculty, from which stem the desires for food, drink, and sexual experience, desires of the sensitive appetite. These desires are good if regulated by will according to reason. But sometimes reason does not assert its control in time and the will is controlled by the "affections," which lead the person into sin.

In *Troilus and Cressida* Ulysses praises "degree," the proper respect for one's superiors and tolerance for one's inferiors. To him it is the symbol of order,[81] and when it is "shak'd" all justice, all sense of right and wrong, will disappear:

> Then everything includes itself in power,
> Power into will, will into appetite,
> And appetite, an universal wolf,
> So doubly seconded with will and power,
> Must make perforce an universal prey,
> And last eat up himself. (I.iii.119–124)

Aquinas names four powers of the soul that are conducive to the apprehension of things. These are intellect, knowledge, opinion, and sense.[82] The will is an "appetite" of the intellect and is normally guided by the intellect, which draws its conclusions from the other three powers just named.[83] As Ulysses envisions the process of surrender to destruction, the power of the soul surrenders to the will instead of instructing it, the will surrenders to the affections of the sensitive appetite, and uncontrolled appetite finally destroys itself and the person in whom it resides. This destruction of the individual is parallel with the cosmic destruction of the universe and with the internal destruction of a state.

On this topic Ficino observes that mind cannot exist as power (*potentia*) alone "because through power confusion and chaos reign; an orderly distinction is made through an act of the mind."[84] This distinguishes between the perceptive function of the intellect and its active function, which instructs the will. (Some speak of the passive intellect and the active intellect, but it is really one intellect with two functions.) It is failure to assert its active function strongly enough that leads to chaos and confusion through the unguided will and the unrestrained appetite (below, pp. 185–186).[85]

4. Figurative Uses

Shakespeare has numerous figurative uses of the organs and processes of perception, and he also had abundant precedent for these in the sources he may have read. One example is the parallel between the human mind and a commonwealth or state, already noticed in Brutus's comparison of himself to a "little kingdom" threatened with "insurrection," to which the "council" of his internal senses is seeking a solution (above, p. 106).

In this instance Shakespeare probably recalled a passage from *The French Academie*. La Primaudaye says that Plato called the *council* of magistrates the anchor, head, and *soul* of the city:

> It is certain that the Magistrat is the same thing in the common wealth, which the *heart* is in the body of a liuing creature. If the heart be sound and pure, it giueth life vnto the whole body, because it is the *fountain* of the blood, and of the spirits: but being corrupted, it bringeth death and destruction to al the members. So fareth it with the Magistrate, who is the *soule of the people*, their glas, and the white whereat his subiects aime[86]. . . . as Plato saith, hee holdeth the same place in the common wealth, that *reason* doth in the *soule*, which guideth the other parts by wisedome.[87]

Seneca, in *De Clementia,* uses a similar comparison:

So this immense multitude surrounding one *soul* is ruled by its *spirit,* is guided by its *reason,* which will be pressed and broken by their powers unless it is sustained by counsel. . . . The *ruler* is indeed that *bond* (*vinculum*) through which the state coheres, that *vital spirit* which so many thousands draw upon, who would receive nothing by themselves except burdens and pillage if that *commander's* mind should be withdrawn.[88]

Here the commander among his people is compared to the heart, soul, and spirit within the human organism.[89]

In the council of Greek leaders in *Troilus and Cressida,* Ulysses addresses Agamemnon:

Thou great *commander,* nerve and bone of Greece,
Heart of our numbers, soul and only *spirit,*
In whom the tempers and the minds of all
Should be shut up. (I.iii.55–58)

Here a ruler in the state is compared to the heart, the soul, and the spirit in the human body, as in the examples just quoted. Seneca's *vinculum* by which the populace coheres may have suggested the "shutting up" of all their tempers and minds in the leader. *Heart* and *soul* are used interchangeably as the "center" of the body.

Ulysses later explains to Achilles how his attachment to one of Priam's daughters had become known:

There is a mystery . . . in the soul of state
Which hath an operation more divine
Than breath or pen can give expressure to. (III.iii.201–204)

Here the "soul of state," including the commander, has occult powers of perception for the protection of the people, a power granted by divine permission (below, p. 220).

Believing Hamlet's madness a danger to King Claudius's life, Guildenstern and Rosencrantz agree to escort him to England:

> *Guil.* Most holy and religious fear it is
> To keep those many many bodies safe
> That *live* and *feed* upon your Majesty.
> *Ros.* The single and peculiar life is bound
> With all the strength and armour of the mind
> To keep itself from noyance, but much more
> That *spirit* upon whose weal depends and rests
> The lives of many. (III.iii.8–15)

This passage repeats the sentiments of Seneca's lines without using his image of the "soul of state." The "live and feed" of Guildenstern's line and the "spirit" upon which so many lives depend may echo Seneca's "vital spirit which so many thousands draw upon," provided by the leader.

As might be expected, discussions of beauty and love draw heavily upon the language of perception, and much of this language is figurative. Not all of it is attributable to the poets. For example, in Plato's *Symposium* Aristophanes' grotesque account of divided human bodies, each half seeking its other half, is designed to illustrate the desire for union with one's beloved (188–193). Such figurative elements are elaborated in Ficino's *Commentarium in Convivium* and in some instances have become commonplaces of poetic language.

As Ficino writes, the soul of man is his true "being," of which the body is a shadow or a garment.[90] Beauty of form and feature reflects the beauty of the inward soul. Beauty is a *ray (radius)* of God appearing in four ways: in the divine mind as ideas, in the world-soul as reasons, in nature as seeds, and in matter as forms.[91] Beauty, coming from God, shines in three mirrors: the angels, the world-soul, and the world-body.[92] This divine and universal beauty is reflected in the beauty of individual souls and forms. True love, aroused by the sight of corporeal beauty, perceives in it this element of divine and absolute beauty; otherwise, love becomes lust.[93] Ficino describes the beauty of individual persons as follows:

> Beauty is a certain living and spiritual *grace, infused* first by a shining *angel-ray* of God, and thence into men's souls, the forms of their bodies, and their voices; a ray which moves our souls through reason, sight, and hearing, and delights us, ravishes *(rapit)* by delighting, and by ravishing inflames us with burning love.[94]

110

In *1 Henry VI* Joan of Arc, in her first interview with the dauphin, explains the source of her personal beauty:

Dauphin, I am by birth a shepherd's daughter,
My wit untrain'd in any kind of art.
Heaven and our Lady *gracious* hath it pleas'd
To shine on my contemptible estate.
Lo, whilst I waited on my tender lambs,
And to sun's parching heat display'd my cheeks,
God's mother deigned to appear to me,
And in a vision full of majesty
Will'd me to leave my base vocation
And free my country from calamity.
Her aid she promis'd and assur'd success;
In complete glory she reveal'd herself;
And whereas I was black and swart before,
With those *clear rays* which she *infus'd* on me
That *beauty* I am bless'd with which you see. (I.ii.72–86)

The appearance of the Virgin Mary to Joan of Arc was drawn from historical sources, but the language of the last two lines resembles the words of Ficino.

In *Measure for Measure* the disguised duke comments on Isabella's beauty:

The hand [of God] that hath made you fair hath made you good; the goodness that is cheap in *beauty* makes *beauty* brief in goodness; but *grace,* being the *soul* of your complexion, shall keep the *body* of it ever fair. (III.i.184–188)

Here appears Ficino's "grace," which is the beauty infused into souls and bodies by God. The "complexion" of the soul and body refers to the general state of their health and well-being, not only to the coloration of the face.

In *Othello* Cassio refers more casually to the divinity of beauty in explaining to Montano why the ship bearing Desdemona came safely through the storm:

111

> Tempests themselves, high seas, and howling winds,
> The gutter'd rocks and congregated sands,
> Traitors ensteep'd to enclog the guiltless keel,
> As having *sense of beauty*, do omit
> Their mortal natures, letting go safely by
> The *divine* Desdemona. (II.i.68–73)

In this hyperbole the beauty of "divine" Desdemona is so great that inanimate objects seem to perceive it and to avoid doing her an injury.

When Troilus sees Cressida with Diomedes and doubts the evidence of his own eyes, he says,

> If *beauty* have a *soul*, this is not she.
> If *souls* guide *vows*, if *vows* be *sanctimonies*,
> *If sanctimony be the gods' delight*,
> If there be rule in *unity* itself,
> This is not she. (V.ii.138–142)

Here Ficino's comments on beauty and the soul seem to have been supplemented by a chapter on vows, drawn from his *Compendium in Timaeum* (chapter vi):

> Most Choice Precepts concerning Vows and Prayers.
> Thus all things are from God, so that nowhere are the least of these severed from God. For everywhere there flourishes the divine unity, through which these things exist. And by a certain perpetual and internal circle they are most wonderfully revolved to God himself, from whom and in whom they are; otherwise, they would run hastily into nothingness. From *divine unity* all things go out; and, having gone out, they retain in themselves a certain imprinted *unity*, an image of the divine unity, by which they are recalled to it and, having been recalled, are made perfect. This *unity* itself prompts souls to *vows*, by which union with God is inwardly implored for us. . . . Indeed, five principal things pertain to the setting forth of a *vow*. First is a certain notion of what is to be adored and by what reason it is to be united. Second is a certain resemblance of our life to the divine life, proceeding from purity, chastity, *sanctimony*, disci-

pline, order, striving for divine benevolence and subjecting souls to the divine dispensation. Third is a certain contact through which we now almost touch the divine essence and verge upon it by a certain elevation of soul. Fourth is a certain entrance into the court of divine light. Fifth is a union inwardly entering and connecting the individual unity of a soul to the divine unity, and now one and the same action uniting the soul and God; moreover, this is not beyond our right, for we are of God, covered and surrounded with divine splendour. But of this adoration, which is to be performed without intermission, the supreme end is that it cojoin the evident alteration of the soul with its own permanence; and whatever has proceeded from *divine unity,* it again firmly restores the same to *unity* and surrounds our light with a supernal light. Accordingly, only right adoration restores souls to the blessed country. Only *sanctimony* is a full virtue. Only the good man, as Plato writes in *Laws,* addresses God decently and fortunately. Only the habit of prayer makes us blessed with the superior beings.[95]

I have already shown how *unitas* is mathematically used to represent God (above, p. 70). Here *vows,* equivalent to daily prayer, are *sanctimonies* to the heavenly ones and admit us to the *divine unity.* Shakespeare has combined these with the *soul of beauty* found in the *Commentarium in Convivium.* A further use of this last phrase is found in *Troilus and Cressida* when Paris's servant describes Helen as "the mortal Venus, the heartblood of beauty, love's invisible soul" (III.i.34–35). Helen is here viewed as an apotheosis of beauty and is compared to the inward soul from which beauty of form emanates.

As the individual soul seeks to become one with God, to rejoin the divine unity, it may also seek unity with another human soul, and this seeking for unity through union is an act of love. The beginning of love is a perception and "infection," usually through the eyes, from which grows the desire for union. Plato had said that what lovers really desire is to become one, and this is felt in friendship as well as in romantic love.[96] Friendship is more frequently expressed as one soul in two bodies, romantic love as an exchange of souls between two lovers, though this is not uniformly so.

Donatus Acciaiolus writes that "a true friend is as if another self."[97] He also comments that "Two friends have one soul between them" is a common proverb.[98] Montaigne repeats the statement in his essay "Of Friendship."[99] Similar sentiments are stated by La Primaudaye.[100]

In *Julius Caesar*, after the quarrel of Brutus and Cassius, the latter says,

> O my dear brother,
> This is an ill beginning of the night.
> Never come such *division 'tween our souls*.
> Let it not, Brutus. (IV.iii.233–236)

The avoidance of division implies that the souls of friends are united.[101] In *As You Like It* Celia decides to accompany her cousin Rosalind into banishment, since "thou and I am one" (I.iii.99). In *Two Gentlemen of Verona* Valentine commends his friend Proteus by saying, "I knew him *as myself*, for from our infancy We have convers'd and spent our hours together" (II.iv. 62–63). In a more extended passage from *A Midsummer Night's Dream*, Helena reminds Hermia of their former friendship:

> We, Hermia, like two artificial gods,
> Have with our needles created both one flower,
> Both on one sampler, sitting on one cushion,
> Both warbling of one song, both in one key,
> As if our hands, our sides, voices and minds
> Had been incorporate. So we grew together,
> Like to a double cherry, seeming parted,
> But yet an *union* in partition.
> Two lovely berries moulded on one stem;
> So, with *two* seeming *bodies* but *one heart*. (III.ii.203–212)

In the figurative language of love, *heart* and *soul* are used interchangeably.[102]

Aquinas, in the *Summa Theologica*, discusses the sharing of souls between friends and between lovers. In each instance love is a unitive force. A man wishes good to his friend as he does to himself, for he "apprehends" the friend as his "other self." Hence Augustine in *Confessions* (ch. iv) says, "well did one say to his friend: Thou half of my soul."[103]

Aquinas notes scriptural authority in Philemon 1:7, "For that I have you in my heart," a phrase that seems to suggest one person dwells in the body of another. This is true in apprehension, though not in fact. The lover is not satisfied with a superficial apprehension of the beloved but seeks to possess the beloved perfectly, by penetrating into his or her heart and soul. Thus the imagination may envision a mutual indwelling of souls between lovers, but this is figurative rather than factual.[104]

Ficino, in his *Commentarium in Convivium,* explains further the indwelling of souls. When one loves, his soul dies in his own body and lives in the body of the beloved; if the beloved does not return his love, the soul of the lover is dead, with nowhere to live.[105] In mutual love there is a double death and a double revivification within each other. Whoever is loved ought to love in return; otherwise he or she is a murderer. The soul of the lover is a mirror in which shines the image of the beloved.[106] Again Ficino remarks that the soul of a lover may desert its domicile to cross over into the body of the beloved.[107]

Chaucer, in *Troilus and Criseyde,* portrays lovers' exchange of hearts in Criseyde's dream (II.931). Shakespeare makes effective use of the exchange of hearts and souls. He applies it to friendship in sonnet 22:

> For all that beauty that doth cover thee
> Is but the seemly raiment of my heart,
> Which in thy breast doth live, as thine in me.

In sonnet 24 he varies the "mirror" image mentioned by Ficino to make his friend's likeness a painted image:

> Mine eye hath play'd the painter and hath stell'd
> Thy beauty's form in table of my heart;
> My body is the frame wherein 'tis held.

The "table" is a tablet on which the picture is painted in the lover's heart; his body is the surrounding picture frame.

Sonnet 31 involves a complicated use of the indwelling heart or soul:

115

> Thy bosom is endeared with all hearts
> Which I by lacking have supposed dead. . . .
> Thou art the grave where buried love doth lie. . . .
> Their images I lov'd I view in thee,
> And thou, all they, hast all the all of me.

The lover's heart, with the full force of all his love, dwells in his friend's breast. This love revives the memory of his past loves, all of which now reinforce his present passion; the hearts of others that had dwelt in his breast now accompany his own heart to dwell in the breast of his beloved.

In sonnet 42 the poet, who has lost his mistress to his friend, says that since "my friend and I are *one*. . . . she loves but me alone." In sonnet 46 the poet's eye and heart debate as to which shall house the image or "picture" of the beloved; the eye will house his outward appearance, and the poet's heart will house the friend's "inward love of heart."

These instances serve to show how the "conceit" of soul exchange and soul sharing influenced Shakespeare's poetic imagination. Other instances occur in his plays.

After Romeo leaves the ball at Capulet's house, he says to himself:

> Can I go forward when *my heart is here?*
> Turn back, dull earth, and find thy center out. (II.i.1–2)

By analogy, the earth is his body; its center is his heart or soul (above, p. 99). But this heart now dwells in Juliet's body. A few minutes later, when Juliet calls to him, he says, "It is my soul, that calls upon my name" (II.ii.165), that is, his soul now dwells in Juliet's breast.

In *Two Gentlemen of Verona*, when Valentine is banished from court, he says of Silvia:

> To die is to be banish'd from myself,
> And Silvia *is myself*. Banish'd from her
> Is self from self, a deadly banishment. . . .
> She is my essence, and I leave to be
> If I be not by her fair influence
> Foster'd, illumin'd, cherish'd, kept alive. (III.i.171–184)

116

Some weeks later, in the forest, Valentine soliloquizes,

> O thou that dost *inhabit in my breast,*
> Leave not the mansion so long tenantless. . . .
> Repair me with thy presence, Silvia. (V.iv.7–11)

Valentine's first speech reflects Ficino's statement that the lover's soul that is rejected by the beloved must die, for it has nowhere to go. Both passages may be indebted to *The French Academie*:

> And againe, loue causeth him that doth loue to engraue & imprint in his heart, that face and image which he loueth: so that the *heart* of him that loueth is made like to a *looking glasse,* in which the image of the party beloued shineth and is represented. Therefore when hee that is loued and beholdeth and acknowledgeth himself in him that loueth him, he is mooued and whetted on to loue him againe, as one within whome he knoweth himselfe to be as it were *Inhabitant,* yea, as *a second self.*[108]

La Primaudaye has repeated the mirror image used by Ficino. His reference to the beloved as an "inhabitant" of the lover's breast seems to have influenced Valentine's language.

The theme occurs again in Othello's meditation upon Desdemona's supposed infidelity:

> But there, where I have *garner'd* up my *heart,*
> Where either I must live or bear no life,
> The *fountain* from the which *my current runs*
> Or else dries up; to be discarded thence! (IV.ii.57–60)

The meaning is clear. His heart and soul now dwell in Desdemona's breast and must die if they are discarded therefrom.

Shakespeare's imagery in Othello's speech draws upon several sources. La Primaudaye writes,

> The *heart* also is like to a seller [cellar] or *garner,* wherein counsels and thoughts are locked and closed vp.[109]

The "garner" of Othello's heart is stored in Desdemona's breast. Levinus Lemnius twice identifies the heart as "the fountaine of life.[110] On one page La Primaudaye identifies this fountain as the heart,[111] on another page as the soul:

> For that thing is the fountaine and original of life, which first mooueth a liuing creature to the works belonging vnto life. So that when wee inquire what this *fountaine* and spring is, then doe we seeke to know what the soule is.[112]

Macrobius uses the fountain image, stressing the soul as a fountain of motion and the current or stream proceeding from it. The current corresponds to the thoughts, joys, hopes, and fears that are the motions of the soul. If one seeks to know the origins of human motions and actions, one's mind runs backward to the soul as if to a fountain.[113]

* * *

Shakespeare's numerous references to the external and internal senses, the perceptive soul, and the popular conceits based upon them betoken an active interest in, and perhaps a considerable study of, the psychology of perception.

V

The Unsettled Humours

IN *King John* (II.i.66) Chatillon's figurative reference to "th'unsettled humours of the land" is also an accurate description of the humours within the human body, for these are constantly flowing and are never completely stable. Any one of the four may become dominant for brief periods of time until a balance is restored or for a longer time if the balance is completely upset. The four humours—blood, phlegm, choler, and melancholy—are physical substances that have a large share in determining the temperament of the individual and demonstrate the interaction of the body and the mind (above, p. 81). Consequently, they play some share in Shakespeare's presentation of temperamental characteristics. He himself was an actor in Ben Jonson's early comedy *Every Man in His Humour*, which stresses humours as individual oddities or extremes of temperament rather than as physical substances in the body.

Any discussion of this topic must cover ground that has been often traversed before. Books by Ruth Anderson, Lily B. Campbell, John W. Draper, Lawrence Babb, William I. D. Scott, and Bridget Gellert Lyons have treated the subject extensively[1] and so have numerous shorter articles. Still it seems to me that there is something more to say, particularly in the classification of Shakespearean characters by their dominant humours. The subject does not lend itself to precise answers and some conclusions must be tentative, but additional background and opinion may be of assistance to the reader. The authors whose works Shakespeare read in English—including Bright, Batman, Lemnius, and La Primaudaye—appear to be in-

119

debted to Latin commentaries by Aquinas and Acciaiolus on the *Nicomachean Ethics* of Aristotle and also to Ficino in works Shakespeare may have read for himself.

1. The Well-Balanced Man

Both Aquinas and Acciaiolus praise the *neutri*, neutral or well-balanced persons who maintain a proper balance of the humours and hearken carefully to the voice of reason.[2] One must not confuse them with the phlegmatic men, who cannot be aroused to anger at all because of the sluggishness and dullness of their temperaments. The *neutri* experience wrath and desire, but always under the control of reason.

Timothy Bright, whose *Treatise of Melancholy* (1586) presents some of the explanations from Ficino and Acciaiolus, sensibly observes that we should not automatically call a cheerful man sanguine, a sad one melancholy, an angry one choleric, or a dull one phlegmatic, since such dispositions may be temporarily caused in a well-ordered body by outward occurrences. Only when no external cause is present can we use these dispositions as evidence of a particular temperament. Also it must be a chronic "complexion," not a temporary one.[3]

Bright's reference to a "well-ordered body" indicates a proper balance of the humours, when a person is in good health physically and mentally and is capable of exercising self-control. Persons of this stamp are the *neutri* of Acciaiolus and Aquinas. Imperturbable, they are sometimes mistakenly called phlegmatic. Likewise, a well-balanced person is sometimes called sanguine simply because he is not agitated by anger, grief, or fearful imaginings. This is equally a mistake. Or perhaps we should say that a well-balanced person may have slight leanings toward one humour or another, but only when one humour is clearly predominant over the others for a considerable period of time should we characterize the person by that particular temperament.

While various treatises in English and in Latin discuss the four humours at some length, I have nowhere else found them summed up so concisely as in the *De Imagine Mundi* of Honorius of Autun. Honorius equates the four elements, the four qualities of the elements, the four seasons of the year, the four humours of the body, and the four stages in a person's life: childhood, youth, adulthood, old age. He then gives the qualities of the four temperaments based on the humours:

Sanguine: merry, sympathetic, laughing, talkative
Choleric: lean, greedy, swift, bold, wrathful, agile
Melancholy: stable, grave, deliberate, cunning
Phlegmatic: slow, somnolent, forgetful[4]

Most authors agree substantially with this classification.

2. *The Phlegmatic Man*

It is difficult to find uses of the phlegmatic temperament in Shakespeare. Most authorities agree that the phlegmatic temperament is naturally sluggish, slow, drowsy, and forgetful, just as Honorius has described it. Phlegm is a watery humour evident in the watery eyes of old and senile persons and in the dull minds of younger ones. In this view Miss Campbell's suggestion that Fortinbras is phlegmatic is quite mistaken.[5] He is well-balanced; his constancy of purpose arises from self-control, not from a deficiency of the more active humours. Goneril accuses Albany of such a deficiency in *King Lear* (IV.ii), of being a "moral fool," too preoccupied with the mistreatment of Lear and Gloucester to respond vigorously to the French invasion; but hers is a prejudiced view.[6]

Shakespeare uses the term *phlegmatic* only once, when Mistress Quickly mistakenly applies it to the choleric Dr. Caius (*Merry Wives*, I.iv.79). In the same play Ford thinks Page "a secure fool" for not believing that his wife may be seduced by Falstaff (III.i.241), and this complacency might be considered phlegmatic; but this is Ford's view, and Page is actually well-balanced. It is Ford who is unbalanced, choleric, and prone to jealousy.

Perhaps we should look for phlegmatic characters among Shakespeare's simpletons. My first choices are William and Audrey in *As You Like It*. These two seem completely lacking in any strong impulses of their own and are content to do Touchstone's bidding. Other possible examples are Dull, the constable in *Love's Labour's Lost;* Peter, the nurse's servant in *Romeo and Juliet;* and Francis, the drawer in *1 Henry IV.* A different instance is Barnardine in *Measure for Measure*, a man whose faculties have been so obscured by chronic drunkenness tnat he has almost lost all human sensibility.

3. The Sanguine Man

Sanguine men, says Bright, are more than ordinarily cheerful and are seldom anything else. They enjoy life, have an abundant flow of high spirits, and are boon companions. They may drink wine, but they also have a natural "wine" in their bodies that keeps them in a constant state of exhilaration.[7] They laugh at things not ordinarily amusing because of the free-flowing spirits in their veins. Constant laughter sometimes makes them appear ridiculous. Melancholy, on the other hand, checks the free flow of spirits by shutting up some of them in the heart.[8] King John, in talking to Hubert, describes this contrast:

> Or if that surly spirit, melancholy,
> Had bak'd thy blood and made it heavy, thick,
> Which else runs tickling up and down the veins,
> Making that idiot, laughter, keep men's eyes
> And strain their cheeks to idle merriment. (III.iii. 42–46)

The last three lines state the internal action in the sanguine man; the first two lines envision the blood as thickened by natural melancholy. If it were "adust" melancholy, part of the blood would have burned and left a residue like cinders or ashes.

Miss Campbell quotes Thomas Walkington's *Optick Glasse of Humours* (1607), which idealizes the sanguine man, confessing only that he is excessively fond of sexual indulgence.[9] She also quotes King James's *Demonologie* (1597), describing two opposite types of men who practiced witchcraft. One group was made up of melancholy men. The opposite group were for the most part "fatte or corpulent in their bodies, and most part of them altogether given over to pleasures of the flesh, continual haunting of companie, and all kind of merrines, both lawfull and unlawfull, which are thinges directly contrary to the symptomes of Melancholie."[10]

James is apparently contrasting the sanguine man with the melancholy man; and he has given an almost perfect description of the only character to whom Shakespeare attributes a sanguine temperament, that is, to Falstaff. In the contest of epithets in *1 Henry IV* (II.iv), Prince Hal calls Falstaff "this *sanguine* coward, this bed-presser, this horseback-breaker, this huge hill of flesh" (lines 267–269). In other instances Shakespeare uses the term to mean bloody or bloodthirsty, not referring to the sanguine temperament.

Othello refers to the sanguine temperament when he tells Desdemona that her hand is "hot and moist," betokening too great aptness toward sexual indulgence (above, p. 83). But he is fitting her temperament into a preconceived pattern suggested by Iago. Actually, Desdemona has a well-balanced temperament.

It thus appears that there is a considerable range in the portrayals of sanguine persons. That other Falstaffian carouser, Sir Toby Belch in *Twelfth Night*, must certainly be included (below, p. 133). Perhaps Autolycus, the tuneful peddler in *The Winter's Tale*, should be named also. Walkington's view of the sanguine man as affable, friendly, and brave but strongly given to "venery" is clearly exemplified in Edward IV before illness makes him melancholy (*Richard III*, I.i.136); in Othello's Lieutenant Cassio, whose "daily beauty" of life is marred by his amour with Bianca;[11] and above all in Mark Antony, whose bravery and generalship are brought to naught by the overindulgence of his lusts. Cleopatra shows similar marks of the sanguine temperament. Sanguine characters marked by laughter and a great flow of witty language are Biron in *Love's Labour's Lost*, Mercutio in *Romeo and Juliet*, Benedick and Beatrice in *Much Ado*, and Gratiano in *The Merchant of Venice*. Most of these characters also have a "touch" of choler and become angry upon occasion.

In sanguine characters the flow of high spirits must sometimes be modified in order to give them better balanced temperaments. In *Love's Labour's Lost* Rosaline loves Biron but urges that he use his wit to entertain invalids in a hospital for a year before their marriage. His jesting wit needs humanizing and must be divested of the contempt he sometimes expresses; he must develop more of the sympathy that is to be found in the ideal sanguine man. Rosaline does not wish to destroy but to modify Biron's sanguine temperament (V.ii.851–881).

A similar change develops in Faulconbridge, the bastard son of Richard the Lion-heart, in *King John*. He jauntily exults in his bastardy, is amused by the maneuvers of statecraft, and regards war as a laughable, exciting adventure. But the death of Arthur, apparently a murder, brings him up short; war and politics are no longer a big joke:

> I am amaz'd, methinks, and lose my way
> Among the thorns and dangers of this world. (IV.iii.140–141)

He develops a much needed seriousness while retaining the vigour of his sanguine temperament, becomes a true patriot instead of a clever intriguer, and saves his country from invasion by the French.

In *King Lear* a similar jauntiness concerning his bastardy is displayed by Edmund, who uses his birth to justify a departure from all moral restraints.[12] He seems to feel that he is evil by "nature" (I.ii.1) and cannot be blamed for his natural disposition towards treachery. At the end of his life he tries "to do some good . . . despite of mine own nature" by saving Lear and Cordelia (V.iii.243–244). This marks the first arousal of his conscience. Throughout the play his manner and appearance are those of a sanguine man, but his jealousy and dark plotting are more like the cunning melancholy of Iago (below, p. 221).[13]

Perhaps a sanguine temperament also explains the character of Richard II. He is gay, laughing, and careless of consequences. Even in the abdication scene he appears more like an actor playing a tragic role with relish than like a tragic figure himself. I am not sure that he ever gets really angry, even when he speaks angrily. His queen reproaches him for not getting angry:

> The lion dying thrusteth forth his paw
> And wounds the earth, if nothing else, with rage
> To be o'erpower'd; and wilt thou, pupil-like,
> Take the correction, mildly kiss the rod,
> And fawn on rage with base humility? (V.i.29–33)

In Pomfret Castle, before his death, he continues his role playing in his own mind but has the wisdom to recognize that his woes proceed from his own gay carelessness and negligence. He is like a boy who has at last grown up.

124

4. The Choleric Man

In *Nicomachean Ethics* (VII.vi [149a]) Aristotle makes some observations on the absence of self-control when anger or lust overcomes a person's reason. Aquinas considers this as applied to the choleric man who wishes to take revenge:

> Wrath seems in a measure to listen to reason, especially in so far as the wrathful man reasons in such fashion that on account of an injury done him he ought to take revenge. But he half-listens—that is, he listens to reason imperfectly—because he cares not to await the judgment of reason as to the extent and manner of revenge.[14] [He is like a messenger who rushes away before he has received all his instructions.] And so it is concerning wrath: for one may hear reason in something but, because of natural heat and swiftness of choler moving him to wrath, before he hears the whole advice of reason he moves to punish the offender.[15]

This tendency of the choleric man "to go off half-cocked," as it were, is clearly used by Shakespeare: Titus Andronicus's stabbing of his son Mutius, Hotspur's anger at Henry IV's remarks about Mortimer, Laertes's violent threats against King Claudius, Capulet's harshness to Juliet when she refuses to wed Paris, Lear's disinheritance of Cordelia, Coriolanus's angry denunciations of the Roman tribunes and later of Aufidius.

Shakespeare even uses the phrase "humours of revenge." In *Merry Wives* a source of comedy is the repeated errors in reference to the humours by Nym and Mistress Quickly. After Falstaff reveals his plan to seduce Mrs. Page and Mrs. Ford, Nym says,

> I have operations which be *humours of revenge.* . . . My humour shall not cool. I will incense Page to deal with poison; I will possess him with *yellowness,* for the revolt of mine is dangerous. That is my true *humour.* (I.iii.98–112)

He will cause Page to be angry, governed by yellow bile or choler, which is also Nym's own humour at the moment.

A physical reaction to aroused choler is felt by Tybalt in *Romeo and Juliet* when Capulet restrains him from challenging Romeo at the dance:

Patience perforce with wilful *choler* meeting
Makes my flesh tremble in their different greeting. (I.v.91–92)

The swift onset of the choleric humour makes it difficult for Tybalt to assert his self-control, but he succeeds in doing so, overawed by the choleric scolding of his uncle, Capulet.

Other Shakespearean characters who are described as choleric are Dr. Caius, the peppery Frenchman in *Merry Wives* (II.iii.89); Pistol, Falstaff's blustering follower (*2 Henry IV*, II.iv.175); and the duke of Buckingham in *Henry VIII* (I.i.130, 152). Those whose natural disposition seems to be choleric, though not called so, are Petruchio and Katherine in *The Taming of the Shrew*, Master Ford in *Merry Wives*, the usurping duke Frederick in *As You Like It*, Othello, the duke of Cornwall in *King Lear*, and Leontes in *The Winter's Tale*.

5. The Choleric-Melancholic Man

Acciaiolus expands Aquinas's discussion of the men who desire revenge to include melancholy men and a third group that he calls choleric-melancholic men because of the equal mixture of yellow bile with black bile in their bodies. The men of cold and moist complexion, the phlegmatic, cannot be aroused to anger because their bodies lack both yellow bile and black bile. Sanguine men can be aroused "because wrath is born from an ebullition of blood around the heart."[16]

Choleric men, says Acciaiolus, are quick to anger and equally quick to desist when the angry fit is over. In one way this is a virtue, since the psalmist says "Let not the sun go down upon your wrath," but the habit of oft-repeated angry outbursts is a vicious habit. In choleric-melancholic men the mixture of yellow and black bile is viscous, not easily resolved and digested; but it gradually is digested and one's wrath slowly fades. The melancholy men are dominated by black bile alone and should not be called choleric. Their humour is cold, dry, and heavy, most difficult of all to dissolve; hence their anger, once aroused, is not easily placated and lasts the longest of all.[17]

In these discussions the authors are referring to the natural humours of the body, not to burnt or "adust" humours. Miss Campbell was the first observer to make a sharp distinction between natural melancholy and "adust" melancholy, as all the humours are called after they are "burned" in the heat of violent passion.[18] It is sometimes difficult to know which kind of melancholy is mentioned, whether a choleric character suffers from adust melancholy (burnt choler) or is a choleric-melancholic type in his natural humours. For instance, in *Julius Caesar* Cassius is described as choleric (IV.iii.30–43), but he commits suicide because of an error in judgment caused by melancholy (V.iii.67). Since he does not seem to be at or near the point of madness just before his death, as he might be if suffering from adust melancholy, I judge that he is a choleric-melancholic type. Acciaiolus explains the actions of the two humours:

> But the bold and swift who are acute [choleric] and melancholy mostly act incontinently after that incontinence which they call temerity [rashness]. The acute men act quickly because of the swiftness of choler. But the melancholy men act quickly because they have vehement imaginations caused by black humour and are led by vehement phantasy rather than by reason, whereas the *neutri* [balanced men] await reason.[19]

Cassius's imagination causes him to think that the horsemen surrounding Titinius are the enemy, and in that mistaken belief he dies. As the messenger says,

> Mistrust of good success hath done this deed.
> O hateful error, *melancholy's* child,
> Why dost thou show to the apt thoughts of men
> The things that are not? (V.iii.66–69)

Early in the play Julius Caesar analyzes Cassius's character in terms that show him to be a choleric-melancholic type as contrasted with the sanguine type:

> Let me have men about me that are fat,
> Sleek-headed men and such as sleep o' nights.

127

Yond Cassius has a lean and hungry look,
He thinks too much; such men are dangerous.
          . . . . He reads much,
He is a great observer, and he looks
Quite through the deeds of men. He loves no plays
As thou dost, Antony; he hears no music;
Seldom he smiles, and smiles in such a sort
As if he mock'd himself and scorn'd his spirit
That could be mov'd to smile at anything.
Such men as he be never at heart's ease
Whiles they behold a greater than themselves,
And therefore are they very dangerous. (I.ii.192–210)

Cassius's leanness and greediness (IV.iii.10) are characteristics of the choleric man; his deep thought, wakefulness, and extensive reading are characteristics of the melancholy man. In contrast, Antony is the sanguine man and Brutus, the well-balanced man in this play.

Shakespeare applies the terms *choleric* and *melancholy* together to another character, Timon in *Timon of Athens*. After Timon's angry retreat to the woods to avoid mankind, Apemantus reproaches him with yielding to "a poor unmanly melancholy" and the banditti describe his condition as melancholy (IV.iii.203, 402). Yet in the same scene Timon says to Apemantus, "Choler does kill me that thou art alive" (line 372).

The lasting and almost irrational quality of Timon's rage suggests that he suffers from adust melancholy from the "burning" of his natural humour. His conduct may give us the clue to what that natural humour was. Ficino describes the effect of burnt humour upon persons of differing temperaments, producing a state of violent passion or even insanity. If the natural humour burned was yellow bile, or choler, the person becomes furiously angry, talks loudly, rushes back and forth, and strikes himself and others. If the natural humour was blood, the sanguine person breaks out into violent laughter, throws himself about beyond all custom, speaks of marvelous and unreal things, and exults in songs and in dances. If the natural humour was black bile, or melancholy, the person weeps perpetually and fashions dreams or visions that terrify the present and make fearful the future.[20]

Since Timon's conduct in his rage resembles the one first described by Ficino, we see that his natural dispositon was choleric or "acute." Such men are impulsive as well as easily angered. Timon's disillusionment with his "friends" is so great that his natural choler is burned into adust melancholy and therefore cannot be easily purged, as natural choler could be. His passion of anger endures until his death. Bright says that sufferers from adust melancholy frequently seek death or "seeke to auoide the societie of men, and betake them to wildernesses, and deserts, finding matter of feare in euery thing they beholde, and best at ease, when alone they may digest these fancies without new prouocations, which they apprehende in humane societie."[21] Timon's conduct resembles that described in this passage.

Violent anger causes a congestion in the face and body. La Primaudaye writes that when a choleric man's rage can find no outlet in action "it vexeth and closeth vp as it were the heart, bringing great griefe and great torment to the whole body, so that a man so affected is as if *his heart and body were ready to burst asunder.*"[22] Timon apparently gives this impression when expressing his choler, for Apemantus replies, "Would thou wouldst *burst!*" (line 373). Cassius gives the same appearance in his choleric outburst against Brutus, who says, "You shall digest the venom of your spleen Though it do *split* you" (*Julius Caesar*, IV.iii.47–48).

Three other characters whose tempers are haughty and quick to anger, hence choleric, are described as lapsing into melancholy. In *All's Well* Bertram becomes melancholy after his unwished marriage to Helena (III.ii.4–9). In *Troilus and Cressida* Achilles sulking in his tent is described by Ajax as "lion-sick, sick of proud heart. You may call it *melancholy* if you will favour the man, but, by my head, it is pride" (II.iii.93–96). In *The Winter's Tale* Polixenes, after his choleric outburst against Florizel and Perdita for falling in love, is full of grief and seeks to purge his melancholy (IV.iv.781–791). These are all instances of natural choler and natural melancholy in combination.

The choleric temperament is very clearly illustrated in the duke of York, father of Edward IV and Richard III. In him choler does not burn to adust melancholy, but it frequently boils or seethes, fogging his mind and choking his voice. When he meets with the French to treat of peace, he says,

129

Speak, Winchester; for *boiling choler* chokes
The hollow passage of my poison'd voice,
By sight of these our baleful enemies.
                              (*1 Henry VI*, V.iv.120-122)

Later, explaining to Buckingham why he has raised an army against
Henry VI, he soliloquizes, "Scarce can I speak, my *choler* is so
great," and then explains his delay in speaking by saying that "My
mind was troubled with deep *melancholy*" (*2 Henry VI*, V.i.23, 34).
He thus proclaims himself to be of the choleric-melancholic temperament and shows that a person may be influenced by these two
humours at the same time or in quick succession.

6. The Melancholy Man

The effects of melancholy are most interesting of all because they are
so varied. When a well-balanced person has a slight tendency toward
natural melancholy, he is sober and takes life seriously. Scholars and
wise men almost always have a slightly melancholy complexion and
enjoy the pleasures of contemplation.[23] Students are likely to be
troubled with excessive melancholy through too much application
to their books.[24] In moderate proportions melancholy is conducive
to wisdom, though Ficino assures us that this is true only of natural
melancholy, not of adust melancholy.[25] Melancholy of this degree is
the subject of Milton's *Il Penseroso*, just as the pleasures of the
moderately sanguine man are the subject of *L'Allegro;* both poems
could apply to the same man in two different moods.

When natural melancholy grows to excess in the human body, it
may produce varied effects. Bright writes of it:

> The perturbations of Melancholie are for the most parte, sadde
> and fearefull, and such as rise of them: as distrust, doubt,
> diffidence, or dispaire; sometimes furious, and sometimes merry
> in apparaunce, through a kind of Sardonian, and false laughter,
> as the humour is disposed that procureth these diuersities.[26]

Sadness, fear, fury, and sardonic laughter are all possible reactions
caused by natural melancholy. Fury would seem to betoken the
choleric-melancholic type, which I have already discussed.

Bright names the most common external causes of melancholy:

> Melancholicke men are not all of one nature passionate this way:
> the one taking his dolorous passion from his loue, another from
> his wealth, the other from his pleasures.[27]

Rather, he becomes melancholy from the present or expected loss of
these things. Sometimes, however, there seems to be no external
cause:

> We doe see by experience certaine persons which enjoy all the
> comforts of this life whatsoeuer wealth can procure, and what-
> soeuer friendship offereth of kindnes, and whatsoeuer securitie
> may assure them: yet to bee ouerwhelmed with heauines and
> dismaide with such feare, as they can neither receiue consolation
> nor hope of assurance, notwithstanding there be neither matter
> of feare, or discontentment, nor yet cause of daunger, but
> contrarily of great comfort, and gratulation. This passion being
> not mooued by any aduersity present or imminent, is attributed
> to melancholy the grossest part of all the bloud.[28]

Shakespeare probably had in mind this very passage when he
wrote the opening lines of *The Merchant of Venice*. Antonio speaks to
Salarino and Salanio:

> In sooth, I know not why I am so *sad*.
> It wearies me; you say it wearies you;
> But how I caught it, found it, or came by it,
> What stuff 'tis made of, whereof it is born,
> I am to learn;
> And such a Want-wit *sadness* makes of me,
> That I have much ado to know myself. (I.i.1–7)

His friends immediately assume that he is worried over the safety of
his wealth, then that he is in love. These are two of the three causes of
melancholy given by Bright. When Antonio denies both causes,
Salarino assumes that it is a freak of nature, which produces some
men who laugh at anything, others who will laugh at nothing. When
Antonio expresses his mood of sadness to Gratiano, that sanguine

friend states his preference for mirth and laughter and jestingly suggests that Antonio is affecting an air of grave solemnity in order to be reputed wise:

> There are a sort of men whose visages
> Do cream and mantle like a standing pond,
> And do a wilful stillness entertain,
> With purpose to be dress'd in an opinion
> Of wisdom, gravity, profound conceit,
> As who should say, "I am sir Oracle,
> And when I ope my lips let no dog bark!" . . .
> But fish not with this *melancholy* bait
> For this fool gudgeon, this opinion. (I.i.88–102)

Here Shakespeare uses a dramatic contrast between two temperaments, the melancholy and sanguine. The other friends of Antonio represent the well-balanced men against whom the melancholy man and the sanguine man can be measured. Gratiano continues his antic behaviour and is warned by Bassanio that in Belmont he must control his "skipping spirit" and speak more modestly, to which Gratiano mockingly agrees (II.iii.189–206). Antonio's sad mood endures to the end of the play, when news of his ships' safe arrival seems to dispel his melancholy despondency (V.i.286). Shakespeare has used similar contrasts of temperaments in several other plays.

Gratiano's speech quoted above does not apply to Antonio, but it is strikingly accurate if applied to Malvolio in *Twelfth Night*. So is Salarino's description of the melancholy men "of such vinegar aspect That they'll not show their teeth in way of smile Though Nestor swear the jest be laughable" (*Merchant of Venice*, I.i.54–56). Malvolio's pompous gravity and unsmiling countenance proceed partly from a melancholy complexion of humours and partly from his notion of the dignity required by his position as chief steward in a noble house. His refusal to laugh at Feste's jokes illustrates the point (I.v.89–96). He finds it impossible to laugh at himself and at the practical joke played upon him (V.i.386). This contrasts with the conduct of Falstaff, the sanguine man in *Merry Wives*, who accepts the joke upon himself with good grace and genially sits down to drink with his tormentors (V.v.170–180).

Twelfth Night, it seems to me, presents a contrast between sanguine and melancholy characters, five of each. The sanguine characters are Sir Toby Belch, Sir Andrew Aguecheek, Feste, Fabian, and Maria, the five involved in the practical joke on Malvolio. These differ widely from each other but all display a merry temperament, at least temporarily. The five melancholy characters are Malvolio, Olivia, Orsino, Viola, and Sebastian. Again they differ widely from each other, but all have a melancholy complexion for the time being. Olivia is grieving for the loss of her brother; Sebastian is grieving for the loss of his sister. Orsino suffers melancholy for the love of Olivia, Viola, for the love of Orsino.

Orsino expresses his love in the messages conveyed by Viola (Cesario) to Olivia. Viola expresses her love in her account of her hypothetical sister who suffered from a green-and-yellow melancholy and sat like Patience on a monument (II.iv). It is difficult to say whether their original temperaments were melancholy or not.

Olivia surprises herself by the suddenness of her passion for Cesario even while she is mourning her brother. Likewise, Sebastian finds his grief for Viola's "death" swept away by his passion for Olivia after she mistakes him for Cesario and proposes marriage. Aquinas explains how this can happen:

> And he [Aristotle] says that those who are melancholy by natural disposition always lack medicine against sadnesses, because their bodies suffer corrosion on account of a certain dryness of complexion. And so they have a vehement desire for a delight through which sadness of this kind may be repelled. . . . And because melancholy people vehemently desire delights, thence it is that frequently they become intemperate and depraved.[29]

The natural appetite for love is reinforced by the unconscious wish to dispel grief. Hence the onset of passionate love is more vigorous when it has the added merit of dispelling sadness from the mind. One may love in order to forget. Aquinas's final sentence helps to explain the pleasure seeking of Dr. Faustus in Marlowe's play about him.

The sudden onset of passionate love in a person melancholy with grief is again illustrated in Romeo. His unrequited love for Rosaline has left him sad, heavy in spirit, and secretive, avoiding the society of his friends. Ficino says that love madness arises when the humours are retained in the heart and that it characterizes those persons who love "with loss" (*perdite*).[30] The impetuosity of Romeo's aroused love for Juliet is accelerated by the grief it helps him to overcome.

In *Romeo and Juliet* Shakespeare has illustrated four different temperaments in the four young men of the play. Romeo is melancholy, and his love melancholy has endured for some time. Mercutio is sanguine, with a lively flow of animal spirits, talkative, and merry. Tybalt is choleric, taking offense from slight causes and seeking an occasion to fight. Benvolio is the well-balanced man who seeks to calm the aroused passions of the other young men. In addition I have already suggested Peter as a man of phlegmatic temperament.

In *Love's Labour's Lost* Shakespeare contrasts the sanguine man, Biron, with the melancholy lover, Don Armado. There is some evidence that Longaville is choleric (II.i.49, II.i.206) and that Dumain is well-balanced (II.i.56–60), but their characters are not developed sufficiently for purposes of comparison.

Don Armado's love melancholy has elements that are repeated in later plays. His self-conscious love for a "base wench," Jaquenetta, resembles Touchstone's attraction to Audrey, "a poor thing but mine own," in *As You Like It*; and Touchstone parodies Armado's euphuistic language in his expressions of love for Audrey. Armado's exchange of love confidences with his page Moth may have furnished the pattern for Orsino's conversations with Cesario (Viola) in *Twelfth Night*.

In *Much Ado* a minor instance of love melancholy is displayed by Claudio after he first falls in love with Hero (II.i.221). After Richard II's departure for Ireland, his queen suffers from a "heavy sadness" that she cannot explain. It is more than grief at her husband's departure, for she feels a premonition of oncoming danger (II.ii.1–40). This is not love melancholy but is more like the inexplicable melancholy of Antonio in *The Merchant of Venice*.

A sardonic temperament represents another aspect of melancholy. Its possessor indulges in Sardonian or false laughter, according to Bright. This is not true merriment or enjoyment of life but is an ironic criticism of life. Jaques, in *As You Like It*, is an example of this temperament. He wishes to "cleanse the foul body of th'infected world" by his sarcasm and protests that he never attacks "any private party"(II.vii.60, 71). The duke thinks that Jaques's hatred of the world stems from his former licentiousness, or his "pleasures," the third cause of melancholy mentioned by Bright (above, p. 130):

For thou thyself hast been a libertine,
As sensual as the brutish sting itself;
And all th'embossed sores and headed evils
That thou with license of free foot hast caught,
Wouldst thou discharge into the general world. (II.vii.64–69)

The duke may be suggesting that Jaques has suffered from venereal disease contracted by his "license of free foot" and that he extends his personal grievances to the generality of mankind. It is he, not the world, that is warped.[31]

A similar example of sardonic melancholy is Apemantus, in *Timon of Athens*. He has the same gift of irony, though not of laughter, that is found in Jaques. Early in the play Timon will not listen to him "rail on society" (I.ii.250). After Timon's loss of wealth, Apemantus reminds him of his former warnings. It is difficult to trace the origins of Apemantus's melancholy. He is lowly born and has always been extremely poor; so he professes indifference to what he cannot have and comes to believe that beasts are actually superior creatures to men (IV.iii). His melancholy has produced confirmed misanthropy.[32]

Pericles is a man made melancholy by successive blows of fortune. As a young man, he becomes melancholy when he knows that Antiochus seeks his life (I.ii.2). He remains melancholy during his wanderings (II.iii.54). After his happy marriage his wife dies in childbirth; some years later his daughter reportedly dies. Finally in his melancholy state of illness (V.i.222) his daughter is restored to him, bringing him extreme joy. The scene is somewhat like the reunion of Lear and Cordelia. But Pericles, while blaming the individuals who cause his troubles, never extends his resentment to the world at large. He remains philosophic rather than misanthropic.

Another type of melancholy temperament is suggested by Honorius's list of qualities: men who are cunning and crafty (above, p. 121). Since melancholy men tend to be secretive and somewhat withdrawn from their fellows, they find it easy to conceal their true motives and to use their talents for secret purposes. When they have a real or fancied grievance, their purposes may become villainous. They compensate for their grievances through action, where the sardonic men compensate through talk.

An example of cunning melancholy is Don John in *Much Ado*. He has the "vinegar aspect" mentioned by Salarino and is melancholy:

Beatrice. How tartly that gentleman looks! I never can see him
but I am heart-burn'd an hour after.
Hero. He is of a very melancholy disposition. (II.i.4–6)

He is a bastard brother of Don Pedro, prince of Aragon, and knows
he is barred from succession to the throne by his illegitimacy.
Through some unnamed misdeed he has fallen out of favour with his
brother, but they are now outwardly reconciled. Still he is jealous of
Claudio, since "that young start-up hath all the glory of my over-
throw" (I.iii.68). From this jealousy develops his plot to strike at
Claudio by blackening the reputation of his beloved Hero. We
should also notice in the play the contrast of temperaments. Benedick
and Beatrice are sanguine, Don John is melancholy, Leonato is
choleric, and perhaps Don Pedro represents the well-balanced man.
    In *Titus Andronicus* Aaron the Moor describes himself as melan-
choly:

> What signifies my deadly-standing eye,
> My silence and my cloudy *melancholy,*
> My fleece of woolly hair that now uncurls?
>
> (II.iii.32–34)

These lines suggest that Aaron's love of villainy is a form of revenge
on the world for its contemptuous treatment of him because of his
race. He is black. Though he is Tamora's lover, he was formerly her
prisoner and now is a prisoner of the Romans. But whatever the
origin of his temperament, it is a form of melancholy. As he plans the
murder of Bassianus, he declares that his desires are governed by
Saturn (II.iii.31). Noel Taillepied, in *A Treatise of Ghosts* (1588),
describes violently melancholy men as Saturnians.[33] Aaron is in
dramatic contrast to Titus, who is choleric.
    That Don John and Aaron are both designated as melancholy
leads us to name Iago as melancholy also, for he displays the same
type of villainy. He takes pride in his secretiveness (I.i.61–65) and in
his ability to deceive Othello, Cassio, Desdemona, and Roderigo.
They believe him honest because he seems so and thus reveal their
simplemindedness. Yet he recognizes that in another sense their
frankness is superior to his treachery and is a quality he cannot
emulate. Since Coleridge's dictum of "motiveless malignity,"[34]

much good ink has been spent in discussing Iago's motivation.[35] Here it is sufficient to show that his temperament is recognized as cunning melancholy. He is in dramatic contrast to Othello, who is choleric, and to Cassio, who is sanguine.

Perhaps to this group of cunning men should be added Richard III. Richard's technique of tyranny is more like that of the choleric man, for he openly and arrogantly commits crimes, relying on trumped-up excuses and quick timing for success in his coups. Yet these were not spur-of-the moment decisions; most of them were carefully and secretly planned in advance. He sometimes uses sardonic jesting. Also, his villainy stems largely from a gnawing consciousness of his physical deformities. The cunning-melancholy temperament is certainly a part of Richard's disposition, though possibly he should be listed as the choleric-melancholic type explained by Acciaiolus (above, p. 126).

Before the final battle Richard awakes from a dream of his slain victims and exclaims, "O coward conscience, how dost thou afflict me!" (V.iii.179). This introduces a new problem, for Bright warns us that we must not confuse the operations of conscience with the operations of melancholy humour. Humour is a product of the body. Conscience is wholly of the mind and has nothing to do with any humour. He names Saul, Judas Iscariot, and Esau—after the sale of his birthright—as examples of tormented conscience.[36]

This consideration inhibits us in seeking to determine the dominant humours of Macbeth and Lady Macbeth, for example, and of king Claudius in *Hamlet,* unless we can use their conduct before they are afflicted with torments of conscience. Such persons must make their peace with God; medicine cannot help them.

After Lady Macbeth's sleepwalking scene, the doctor decides, "More needs she the divine than the physician" (V.i.82). When he reports to Macbeth that Lady Macbeth is not sick so much as "troubled with thick-coming fancies," Macbeth asks,

> Canst thou not minister to a mind diseas'd,
> Pluck from the memory a rooted sorrow,
> Raze out the written troubles of the brain,
> And with some sweet oblivious antidote
> Cleanse the stuff'd bosom of the perilous stuff
> Which weighs upon the heart? (V.iii.40–45)

The doctor replies, "Therein the patient Must minister to himself" (lines 45-46).

The "perilous stuff" Macbeth mentions is the dregs of adust melancholy, which can sometimes be purged from the system by drugs such as hellebore; but the doctor recognizes that Lady Macbeth's difficulty lies elsewhere, in the tormentings of her conscience. He states accurately Bright's conclusions about it.

The most interesting—and confusing—study of melancholy is the temperament of Hamlet. Hamlet shows the signs of melancholy grief: sadness, occasional sardonic laughter, bad dreams. He speaks of "my weakness and my melancholy," which the devil may use to deceive him with illusions and so imperil his soul (II.ii.630). Before sending him to England, the king tells Polonius, "There's something in his soul O'er which his melancholy sits on brood" (III.i.173). By this time the king suspects what that "something" is, but Polonius still thinks that the whole problem is one of unrequited love.

Miss Campbell thinks that Hamlet is melancholy during the play but that this is adust melancholy caused by the shock of his father's death and that his natural temperament is sanguine. As conclusive evidence she quotes Hamlet's words to Laertes as they struggle in Ophelia's grave:

> I prithee, take thy fingers from my throat.
> Sir, though I am not *splenitive and rash,*
> Yet have I something in me dangerous,
> Which let thy wiseness fear. (V.i.283-286)

La Primaudaye, among others, states that melancholy is engendered in the spleen, choler in the gall.[37] Therefore, Miss Campbell reasons, if Hamlet is not splenitive, he is not naturally melancholy.[38]

Unfortunately for this argument, Shakespeare himself refutes it. In *Julius Caesar,* when Cassius and Brutus quarrel, the latter says,

> Must I give way and room to your *rash choler*? . . .
> Go show your slaves how *choleric* you are . . .
> You shall digest the venom of your *spleen*
> Though it do split you. (IV.iii.39-48)

At this time Shakespeare's knowledge of physiology was simply mistaken, for he thought the spleen to be the source of choler, or yellow bile. Since *Hamlet* was written shortly after *Julius Caesar,* we may assume the same background of information. Hamlet's statement that he is not splenitive means that he is not choleric, as he suggests that Laertes is. Cassius's "rash choler" came from the spleen; if Laertes is "splenitive and rash," he is thereby termed choleric. This leaves open the question of Hamlet's natural temper: he is naturally melancholy or sanguine or well-balanced, but not choleric.

A dozen years later, in *Henry VIII,* Shakespeare had corrected his knowledge of physiology. The duke of Buckingham plans to denounce Wolsey to the king. Norfolk warns him, "Stay, my lord, And let your reason with your *choler* question What 'tis you go about" (I.i.129–131). A few moments later Buckingham thanks Norfolk and agrees to follow his counsel of prudence, "but this topproud fellow, Whom from *flow of gall* I name not" (lines 151–152). He is so choleric that he cannot even speak Wolsey's name. And here choler is definitely attributed to the gall.

Whatever Hamlet's temperament may have been in former years, he is melancholy throughout the course of the play and, for dramatic purposes, exemplifies the melancholy man. Just as he implies that Laertes is choleric—"splenitive and rash"—so he names Horatio as the well-balanced man:

> for thou hast been
> As one, in suffering all, that suffers nothing,
> A man that Fortune's buffets and rewards
> Hath ta'en with equal thanks; and blest are those
> Whose blood and judgment are so well commingled,
> That they are not a pipe for Fortune's finger
> To sound what stop she please. Give me that man
> That is not passion's slave. (III.ii.70–77)

Another bit of evidence adduced by Miss Campbell to prove that Hamlet's natural temperament is not melancholy is his mother's words in the duel scene: "He's *fat,* and scant of breath. Here, Hamlet, take my napkin, rub thy brows" (V.ii.298–299). Miss Campbell quotes King James to the effect that no fat man is melancholy by nature; he is usually sanguine.[39]

These words by Hamlet's mother have troubled many a reader, for a corpulent Hamlet seems dramatically inappropriate, even though some stout actors have successfully played the role. But Shakespeare also uses *fat* to mean greasy or oily, and he describes sweat as an oily substance. Gertrude offers her napkin for Hamlet to wipe the sweat from his face; consequently, she may mean that he is sweaty and scant of breath, not that he is unusually corpulent.

This suggestion can be supported by a few quotations. In the *Oxford English Dictionary* under *sweat* we find, "The Cedar *sweateth* out Rozen and Pitche," from Barnabe Googe's translation of Heresbach's *Husbandrie* (1577); under *fat* we find resinous wood described as "fat" in both England and America. In a short note in *American Speech,* Robert Withington quotes an American survival of this usage:

> When we were motoring through Michigan, we stopped at a farmhouse—it was a very warm day, and the perspiration was pouring down our faces. The farmer's wife came out and exclaimed, "How *fat* you are!"[40]

In *1 Henry IV* Prince Hal is hugely amused that Falstaff sweats so profusely from unaccustomed exercise:

> Falstaff *sweats* to death
> And *lards* the *lean earth* as he walks along. (II.ii.115–116)

Here Falstaff's "sweat" will grease or "fatten" the lean earth to make it fertile. Again Prince Hal humourously likens sweaty Falstaff to a dish of butter melting in the sun (II.iv.134); his sweat is the fat that has melted.

In the New Cambridge Shakespeare edition of *Hamlet,* J. Dover Wilson suggests that "fat and scant of breath" means "sweaty and scant of breath." He cites Prince Hal's reference to a "fat room"— hot enough to cause perspiration (*1 Henry IV,* II.iv.1)—and Doll Tearsheet's words after Falstaff's swordplay with Pistol: "Alas, poor ape, how thou sweat'st. Come, let me wipe thy face" (*2 Henry IV,* II.iv.234). Doll's action is almost the same as that of Hamlet's mother.

Perhaps these quotations, coupled with Gertrude's action in

offering her napkin, afford an alternative to a corpulent Hamlet; instead, he is a sweaty Hamlet. As such, his "fatness" cannot be used to disprove his melancholy disposition.

Miss Campbell's—and Shakespeare's—unfortunate mistakes in interpreting Hamlet's word *splenitive* have caused her to assume that his actions during the play are a result of adust melancholy, not of natural melancholy. Yet this conclusion is highly questionable. One's natural humour is not fixed from birth. Each person has all the humours, and different ones may predominate at different times and under different circumstances. Even if Hamlet's earlier temperament was sanguine, as Miss Campbell thinks, it could easily change to natural melancholy through grief at his father's death. Lemnius explains how this could happen:

> By many and sundrye wayes do men fall into this ill case and habiting [of natural melancholy], who afore were cleare & free enough from it. . . . Some be brought into it, through long sorrow and heauynesse for the death of their Parentes, or some greate losse of worldly wealth, or finally by myssing and beyng disappointed of some great desyre and expectation, which they hoped & had, of some thing to come to passe.[41]

Hamlet has two of these motives for melancholy: the death of a parent and his failure to be named as his father's successor to the throne, a post he seems to have expected. This second motive has never been sufficiently stressed; Hamlet repeatedly mentions it (III.ii.354, V.ii.65), and his disappointment is aggravated by his feeling that his mother has taken part with Claudius against him.[42]

Lemnius writes further:

> If it [melancholy humour] be immoderatelye or too much enflamed, it bringeth the mynde into furious fitts, phrenticke rages, and brainsicke madnesse: Contrarylye, when all thinges consiste wythin mediocritye [the mean], it causeth and bringeth forth sharpenesse of witte, excellency of learning, subtility of inuention, eloquence of tongue & right skilful vtteraunce, with knowledge howe to speake.[43]

The furious fits, frantic rages, and brainsick madness are the marks of adust melancholy and involve a loss of control by the sufferer of a

141

violent passion. Ficino and Timothy Bright agree as to the loss of control; Bright says that the burning of any humour to make adust melancholy simply forces the natural traits of that humour to greater extremes.[44] The result is madness or near-madness, over which it is difficult to assert control. La Primaudaye remarks that from adust melancholy "there are many sorts of melancholike persons, of mad, senselesse and furious people."[45]

Lemnius's account of the moderately melancholy man sounds like a description of Hamlet's character, though his natural melancholy has been deepened by his grief. But, though intensified, does it ever reach the stage of adust melancholy? Does Hamlet suffer the loss of control that is a mark of madness? We know that he feigns madness, but how much is feigning and how much is real? The king, overhearing his talk with Ophelia, thinks that he is not mad but that his melancholy is approaching the danger point when he may commit some violence in a frenzied rage. As the messenger warns Christopher Sly in *The Taming of the Shrew:*

> Seeing too much sadness hath congeal'd your blood,
> And melancholy is the nurse of frenzy. (Ind. ii.134–135)

King Claudius decides to send Hamlet to England before that danger point is reached (III.i.170–183), but he waits too long and Polonius dies.

Hamlet is an intelligent, well-read man who can recognize his own condition and seeks to keep his emotions under control. Several times he almost loses control. One occasion comes after his first encounter with the ghost. Hamlet fears his own physical collapse and writes in his notebook that one may smile and yet be a villain (I.v.92–112). This conduct is not stupid or silly; his troubled mind seeks relief in some kind of physical action.

Another crisis comes after the players' performance and before his interview with his mother. He is now convinced of her and Claudius's guilt, but he does not wish to kill her; he "will speak daggers to her, but use none" (III.ii.414). This is a conscious effort at self-control. A third crisis comes at Ophelia's grave when he first learns that she is dead and that Laertes holds him responsible. He suffers a temporary loss of control; in his later apology, he excuses this and Polonius's death by his "madness," which seems real enough to those about him. In all these instances it seems to me that Hamlet verges upon but never quite reaches the point of frenzy or madness, with its attendant "adustion" of his natural humour. He quickly returns to his state of normal intelligence after each crisis is past; a quick recovery is not possible after the humour is actually burned. Harry Levin makes an accurate distinction, saying that Hamlet is "thought-sick" but not "brainsick."[46] Bridget Gellert Lyons agrees that Hamlet's actions do not proceed from adust melancholy.[47] We may contrast Hamlet with King Lear, who tries to exert self-control of his choleric humour (III.iv.21) but fails and does go over the edge into madness.[48]

As I have already pointed out (above, p. 66), there are really two Hamlets coalesced into one. The first is the nineteen-year-old youth of Shakespeare's first conception; the other is the thirty-year-old man of his later conception. To the first attaches those evidences of a former sanguine temperament that Miss Campbell finds in the character. To the second belongs the natural melancholy of the mature scholar who seeks to view himself and his problems with judicious detachment, who has attained the stability of the philosophic man.

7. The Union of Temperaments

Ficino, in his *Commentarium in Convivium,* studies the compatibility in wedlock of persons having the several temperaments. In discussing these for dramatic purposes, we should not forget to include the *neutri,* or well-balanced persons, against whom the others can be measured. In Jonson's *Every Man in His Humour* (London version), this role is taken by Edward Knowell and by Mrs. Bridget, whom he loves. In Shakespeare's first comedy, *The Comedy of Errors,* the well-balanced person is Luciana, who seeks to soothe the choleric temper of her sister Adriana. Adriana's husband, Antipholus of Ephesus, with his love of pleasure and his roving eye, seems to represent the sanguine temperament, while Antipholus of Syracuse is melancholy from his long and fruitless search for his mother and brother (I.ii.20–40); the sudden onset of his love for Luciana is a rebound from melancholy (above, p. 133). But most interesting is the abbess' reprimand to Adriana, purporting to show how her choleric scolding has driven her husband into "moody and dull melancholy" and finally into madness (V.i.68–86). This speech seems to be almost a parody of sixteenth-century writing about the four humours.

The wedding of Antipholus of Ephesus to Adriana united the sanguine and the choleric temperaments. According to Ficino, they will continue to live in alternate periods of anger and happiness. If sanguine weds sanguine, the harmony of temperaments will produce happiness. If sanguine weds melancholy, the two will live in reasonable content, the cheerfulness of one humour offsetting the gloominess and bitterness of the other. If choleric weds melancholy, the result is misery, with wrath and violence on one side, tears and continual complaints on the other. For choleric to wed choleric is intolerable, since likeness of complexion is offset by the wrath in each one. The phlegmatic and the melancholy seldom take the initiative in love but may be "captured" by persons of other temperaments. A melancholy person is not easily won but, once captured, is never afterward free.[49] Ficino does not say what happens when two persons of melancholy temperament or two persons of phlegmatic temperament wed each other.

In *The Taming of the Shrew* Petruchio devises his own formula for making the choleric-to-choleric union work with himself and Katherine: "he kills her in her own humour" (IV.i.183) by being violently choleric toward everyone and everything except Katherine. He thus modifies both her and his own choleric temperaments to achieve a better balance of the humours and greater happiness in marriage. To some extent Petruchio's choler is a pretense, for he also demonstrates qualities of a sanguine temperament.[50]

* * *

In this chapter I have tried to base my observations on Shakespeare's own references to characters as being choleric, melancholy, or in one instance sanguine; and I have then extended the list to include others who display the same temperaments. I have tried to avoid the temptation to assign every character a dominant humour and have named only those whom the author clearly intended to illustrate the several humours. I have also supplemented the treatises in English with Latin authors whom Shakespeare may have read, believing that we thereby obtain more complete information on his knowledge of the humours. These have clearly played an important part in his conceptions and portrayals of many characters.

VI

The Human Condition

IN ADDITION to the four humours, other physical elements of the body have a strong influence upon man's personality and his social relationships. Shakespeare shows an awareness of this influence in a variety of ways, usually in single phrases or bits of dialogue. The more essential physical organs are correlated with the several faculties of the soul, and the disruptive effects of bodily disease upon the mind are carefully noted. The origin of man, his prenatal life, and his place in the family and in larger social units are all of interest to the poet. He also perceives that man's body of corruptible flesh may house an immortal soul, and he further realizes that the body itself is not annihilated by death but survives in a different form. We cannot expect from his casual references a systematic presentation of the human condition, but we do get a surprisingly large number of sidelights upon the life of man while he inhabits the earth. In this chapter I am primarily concerned with items that can be traced to Shakespeare's reading.

1. Those Sovereign Thrones

In *Twelfth Night,* when Duke Orsino's messenger reports that Olivia will not entertain his proposals of marriage because she has vowed to mourn her brother's death for seven years, the duke exclaims,

146

O, she that hath a heart of that fine frame
To pay this debt of love but to a brother,
How will she love when the rich golden shaft
Hath kill'd the flock of all affections else
That live in her; when *liver, brain,* and *heart,*
Those sovereign thrones are all supplied and fill'd
Her sweet perfections with one self king! (I.i.33-39)

He obviously hopes that the "one self king" will be himself.

In this quotation Shakespeare has used *thrones* instead of its more common synonym *seats.* Latin *sedes* means both *seat* and *throne.* In II.iv.22 Viola says that a song played at Orsino's command "gives a very echo to the *seat* where love is *thron'd,*" that is, to the heart.

The brain, the liver, and the heart are recognized as the three vital organs most essential to a continuance of life. La Primaudaye calls them "seats,"[1] as does Timothy Bright.[2] Aquinas quotes Plato's *Timaeus* (70-72) as placing the rational soul in the brain, the nutritive soul in the liver, the appetite in the heart.[3] Acciaiolus varies this explanation:

Plato said those powers of the soul are distinguished not only according to reason, but according to substance also. So he stated that one is in the heart, one in the brain, and one in the liver. That is, he placed reason in the brain, the irascible faculty in the heart, the concupiscible faculty in the liver, as Cicero also says in his *Tusculan Disputations.*[4]

Aquinas refers to the threefold soul—vegetal, sensible, rational— as I have already discussed it (above, p. 71). Acciaiolus refers to the three faculties of the soul and to the organs in which these faculties supposedly operate. We have noted that the three kinds of spirit are also divided among the three vital organs: natural spirit in the liver, vital spirit in the heart, and animal spirit in the brain (above, p. 82).[5]

Timothy Bright writes of the three organs as follows:

The *braine* is the chiefe instrument of sense, and motion, which it dryueth by the Spirit before mentioned, into all the partes of the bodie, as also of thoughtes, and cogitations, perfourmed by common sense, and fantasie: and storing vp as it were, that

147

which it hath conceaued in the chest of memorie: all which the braine it selfe with farther communication exerciseth alone. The *hart* is the *seate* of life, and of affections, and perturbations, of loue, or hate, like, or dislike, of such thinges as fall within the compasse of sense, either outward, or inward [external or internal], in effect, or imagination onely. The *liver* is the instrument of nourishment, and groweth, and is serued of the stomach by appetite of meats and drinkes, and of other parts, with lust of propagation.[6]

Montaigne writes in "An Apologie of Raymond Sebond":

But to returne unto our soule, where *Plato* hath *seated* reason in the braine; anger in the heart; lust in the liver.[7]

The three faculties of the soul—rational (in the brain), irascible (in the heart), and concupiscible (in the liver)—are the major combatants in the internal warfare or *psychomachia* of the individual person. From the concupiscible faculty arise those emotions, passions, and perturbations associated with food, drink, and sexual desire. These are controlled by the irascible faculty under the direction of the rational faculty, except at such times as the former succumbs to uncontrollable passions of anger, grief, nonsexual love, and so forth and rejects the control of reason.[8]

Orsino, then, looks forward to the time when Olivia, struck by Cupid's arrow, will love him with all three faculties of her soul. Her liver, or concupiscible faculty, will feel strong sexual desire. Her heart, or irascible faculty, will experience a passionate devotion over and beyond the demands of sex. Her brain, or rational faculty, will judge him an admirable man, in every way worthy of her love. Hers will be the perfect romantic love.

Figuratively referring to the three vital organs as essential to life, king Cymbeline compliments the three men whose valiant fighting had done most to defeat the Romans: "To you, the *liver, heart,* and *brain* of Britain, By whom I grant she lives" (V.v.13–14). These are Belarius, Guiderius, and Arviragus.

An understanding of the three faculties of the soul and their seats in the three vital organs gives meaning to various Shakespearean passages. In *Merry Wives* Pistol says that Falstaff loves Mistress

Ford "with liver burning hot," that is, with strong sexual desire (II.i.121). In *Love's Labour's Lost*, when Biron overhears Long-aville's justification for breaking his vow by falling in love with Maria, he calls that line of reasoning "the *liver-vein*, which makes flesh a deity, A green goose a goddess" (IV.iii.74–75). "Goose" was slang for a prostitute. The "liver-vein" argues for sexual indulgence.

The heart and brain also receive attention. In *3 Henry VI* Westmoreland exclaims, "My heart for anger burns" (I.i.60), and Queen Margaret mocks the captive duke of York and his "fiery heart" (I.iv.87). King John's brain is termed "the soul's frail dwelling house" in reference to the rational soul (V.vii.3).

Shakespeare has several references to the internal struggle of the soul's faculties. In *The Tempest*, after Ferdinand is accepted as Miranda's suitor, Prospero warns him not to take advantage of her innocence by seducing her. Ferdinand replies,

> I warrant you, sir;
> The white cold virgin snow upon my heart
> Abates the ardor of my liver. (IV.i.54–56)

The concupiscible faculty in the liver has selfish love, seeking to gratify one's sexual appetite. But the heart and the irascible faculty generate an unselfish love, which seeks the welfare of the beloved. Hence the heart's chaste love will overcome the liver's unchaste love.

A similar opposition between liver and heart occurs in Gratiano's speech in *The Merchant of Venice*, already mentioned (above, p. 132):

> And let my liver rather heat with wine
> Than my heart cool with mortifying groans. (I.i.81–82)

To "mortify the flesh" is to weaken one's appetites by fasting or self-castigation of various kinds. This is opposed to the self-indulgence of the convivial man. The opposition is between the heart and the liver.

An opposition between brain and heart is shown in *Antony and Cleopatra* when Antony plans a night of revelry before his most crucial battle. Enobarbus comments,

149

And I see still
A diminution in our captain's *brain*
Restores his *heart*. When valour preys on reason,
It eats the sword it fights with. (III.xiii.197-200)

When Antony's brain is weakened, his heart develops a foolish rashness. He refuses to recognize the true facts of his situation and substitutes unthinking bravery for rational courage.

The coordination of the three major physical organs of the body with the three faculties of the soul is an attempt to express in some detail that interrelationship of the soul and body that is the most significant feature of the human condition.

2. A Distemper'd Appetite

In *Twelfth Night* Malvolio spitefully describes Feste as a barren fool, lacking in wit. Olivia says,

Oh, you are sick of self-love, Malvolio, and *taste with a distemper'd appetite.* (I.v.97-98)

This figurative use of the sense of taste draws an analogy between the state of the mind and the state of the body, in which sickness is likely to alter the taste of certain foods to the taster. In *A Midsummer Night's Dream* Demetrius uses the same image in describing his temporary aversion to Helena, whom he now loves:

But, like in sickness, did I loathe this food;
But, as in health, come to my natural taste,
Now do I wish it, love it, long for it. (IV.i.177-179)

This analogy is drawn from two brief references in Aristotle's *Nicomachean Ethics* (III.iv; 1113a and VII.viii; 1150b). These references are made more explicit in the commentary of Donatus Acciaiolus. In the first instance he says that a vicious man cannot judge accurately because he has a corrupt judgment from a bad habit, just as happens in the taste of a sick man *(in gustu aegrotantis).*[9] The second instance reads,

Illa ratio declaratur, quia intemperans habet vitium et rationem corruptam, sicut *febricitans habet corruptum gustum,* et putat illud esse bonum quod ab eo *appetitur.* (That reason is stated, because the intemperate person has vice and corrupt reason, just as *a fever-patient has a corrupt taste* and thinks that to be good which is desired by it.)[10]

The similar meanings are readily apparent. Shakespeare's use of *appetite* and Acciaiolus's use of *appetitur* point up the resemblance even more. This passage may also be reflected in Coriolanus's words to the Roman citizens:

> Your affections are
> *A sick man's appetite,* who desires most that
> Which would increase his evil. (I.i.181–183)

The fever patient appears again in lines from Lucretius deploring the vain love of wealth and high position:

Nec *calidae* citius decedunt corpore *febres,*
Textilibus si in picturis ostroque rubenti
Iacteris, quam si in plebeia veste cubandum est.
Quaepropter quoniam nil nostro in corpore gazae
Proficiunt neque nobilitas nec gloria *regni,*
Quod superest, animo quoque nil prodesse putandum.
(Nor do *hot fevers* sooner quit the body, if you toss about on pictured tapestry and blushing purple, than if you must lie under a poor man's blanket. Wherefore since treasures avail nothing in respect of our body nor birth nor the glory of *kingly power*, advancing farther you must hold that they are of no service to the mind as well.—trans. Munro)[11]

In Henry V's nocturnal soliloquy before the Battle of Agincourt, he compares the lot of a king unfavourably with that of a labourer:

Think'st thou the *fiery fever* will go out
With titles blown from adulation?
Will it give place to flexure and low bending? . . .
I am a *king* that find thee, and I know . . .
Not all these, laid *in bed majestical,*
Can sleep so soundly as the wretched slave. (IV.i.270–285)

A passage of similar intent, with no reference to fevers, appears in *3 Henry VI* (II.v.1–54). Both Shakespearean speeches express sentiments similar to those given by Lucretius.

Montaigne quotes the first three lines of the above quotation from Lucretius, with a comparison of the king and the common man:

> Doth the ague, the megrim, or the gout spare him more than us?
> ... will our *lowting-curtzies, or putting-off of hats*, bring him in tune againe? His *bedstead enchased with gold and pearles hath no vertue to allay the pinching pangues of the cholicke.*[12]

Montaigne also cites lines from Horace's *Epistulae* (I.ii.47):

> Non domus et fundus, non aeris acervus et auri,
> Aegroto domini deduxit corpore *febres*,
> Non animo curas.
> (Not house and land, and heapes of coine, and gold
> Rid agues, which their sicke Lords body hold,
> Or cares from minde—trans. Florio)[13]

The repetition of *febres* relates the two passages to Henry V's speech; Montaigne's comments have supplied or reinforced the "flexure and low-bending," and the "bed majestical" of Shakespeare's lines.

Finally, the fever appears in Macbeth's figurative usage:

> Duncan is in his grave;
> After *life's fitful fever* he sleeps well. (III.ii.22–23)

The distemper that agitates and upsets the body or mind has become an expression of disillusionment with life itself.

3. The Natural Touch

In *Macbeth*, when Lady Macduff hears that her husband has fled the kingdom, she resents Ross's suggestion that wisdom may have caused Macduff's flight:

> Wisdom! to leave his wife, to leave his babes,
> His mansion and his titles, in a place
> From whence himself does fly? He loves us not,
> He wants *the natural touch*; for the poor wren,
> The most diminutive of birds, will fight,
> Her young ones in her nest, against the owl. (IV.ii.6–11)

Here the "natural touch" is identified as the devotion of a man to his family, especially to his children. The word *touch* is used to mean a quality or characteristic, a quality of sensitiveness.

In *Troilus and Cressida,* when Cressida is exchanged for Antenor and is told that she must go to her father in the Grecian camp, she says,

> I will not, uncle. I have forgot my father;
> I know no *touch of consanguinity*;
> No kin, no love, no blood, no soul so near me
> As the sweet Troilus. (IV.ii.102–105)

Her consanguinity, or blood relationship, is to her father and is described as a "touch" she no longer feels.

In *The Tempest,* when Ariel expresses pity for the shipwrecked Italian noblemen, Prospero replies,

> Hast thou, which art but air, a *touch*, a feeling
> Of their afflictions? (V.i.21–22)

Here the "touch" is extended beyond the feeling for one's relatives. In *Troilus and Cressida,* when Ulysses warns Achilles that the Greeks will soon forget him in favor of some new warrior if he takes no part in the battle against Troy, he says,

> One *touch of nature* makes the whole world kin,
> And all with one consent praise newborn gauds.
> (III.iii.175–176)

Here the universal feeling of kinship is asserted as a "touch of nature," one example of which is a touch of novelty, a fondness for new and unfamiliar things.

153

La Primaudaye describes men as being "touched with honesty"[14] and "touched with couetousnesse."[15] The *Oxford English Dictionary* under "touch" quotes from Richard Taverner's *Proverbs of Erasmus* (1539): "maners . . . qualities, *touches*, condicions, and procedynges"; and a later instance from 1679: "as if men had forgon all *touches* of humanity." Shakespeare's "one touch of nature" is cited under the same heading.

The naturalness of the child-parent relationship, without the word *touch*, is found in the prologue to act II of *Henry V* as a comment on the plot to murder the king:

> O England! model to thy inward greatness,
> Like little body with a mighty heart,
> What might'st thou do, that honour would thee do,
> Were all thy *children kind and natural*! (lines 16-19)

The three unnatural children are the conspirators who would murder the king.

Shakespeare's conception of the "natural touch" seems to be drawn directly from a passage in Cicero's *De Finibus:*

> Again, it is held by the Stoics to be important to understand that *nature* creates in parents an affection for their children; and parental affection is the germ of that social community of the human race to which we afterwards attain. This cannot but be clear in the first place from the conformation of the body and its members, which by themselves are enough to show that nature's scheme included the procreation of offspring. Yet it could not be consistent that nature should at once intend offspring to be born and make no provision for that offspring when born to be loved and cherished. Even in the lower animals the *touch of nature* (*vis naturae*) can be clearly discerned; when we observe the labour that they spend on bearing and rearing their young, we seem to be listening to the actual voice of nature. Hence, as it is manifest that it is natural for us to shrink from pain, so it is clear that we derive from nature herself the impulse to love those to whom we have given birth. From this impulse is developed the sense of mutual attraction which unites human beings as

such, this also is bestowed by nature. The mere fact of their common humanity requires that one man should feel another man to be akin to him. (trans. Rackham, slightly altered)[16]

Cicero's phrase *vis naturae* is a fairly close equivalent of Shakespeare's "touch of nature." Ficino, for example, regularly uses *vis* to mean a quality in the same way that Shakespeare uses *touch* in these phrases.

Thomas Aquinas, in his commentary on the *Nicomachean Ethics*, gives an order of priorities to the claims of nature. A man should have trust and a sharing of goods first with friends and brothers, then with other relatives, then with members of his own tribe or clan, then with fellow citizens of his city or state.[17] This involves the same extension of the *vis naturae* to include the whole of humanity that Cicero had already described. Shakespeare's several uses of the *touch of nature* illustrate the same point, at last including "the whole world."

When Hamlet seeks to restrain himself lest he should kill his mother, he exclaims, "Let me be cruel, not *unnatural*" (III.ii.413). Gloucester says of Lear, "The king falls from the *bias of nature*; there's father against child" (I.ii.121). When Coriolanus tries to remain obdurate in his determination to destroy Rome, he says,

> All *bond and privilege of nature*, break!
> Let it be virtuous to be obstinate.
>   . . . and my young boy
> Hath an aspect of intercession which
> Great *nature* cries, "Deny not." . . .I'll never
> Be such a gosling to obey *instinct*, but stand
> As if a man were author of himself
> And knew no other kin. (V.iii.25–37)

But he cannot hold to this resolution; nature and instinct prevail.

Finally, the extension of this "natural" affection to the whole human race is eloquently stated in John Donne's "No man is an island" essay, which supplied Ernest Hemingway's title *For Whom the Bell Tolls*.

4. Kin *and* Kind

In the second scene of *Hamlet*, the first words that Hamlet speaks during the play have caused considerable puzzlement. The king, having dismissed Laertes, turns to Hamlet:

> *King.* But now, my *cousin* Hamlet, and my *son,*—
> *Ham.* A little more than *kin*, and less than *kind*.
> *King.* How is it that the clouds still hang on you?
> *Ham.* Not so, my lord; I am too much i' th' *sun*. (I.ii.64–67)

Hamlet's first line seems to be an aside, heard only by himself, while his second is an ironic reply to the king's words, with a pun on the similar sounds of *son* and *sun*. He is suggesting that he is more of a "son" than he wishes to be and that he is too much exposed to the "sun" of Denmark, that is, to the presence of the king. The queen speaks next, allowing Claudius to disregard what might be taken as a veiled insult by Hamlet. Claudius's later uses of "son" in lines 111 and 117 follow his formal declaration that Hamlet is now the next heir to the Danish throne.

The word *cousin* was frequently used for any degree of kinship beyond that of parent-child, husband-wife, brother-brother, brother-sister, or sister-sister. (In Dutch *neef* is still used to mean both a nephew and a cousin.) As a "cousin" Hamlet is of Claudius's kin, but as a stepson he is "a little more than kin," in a closer relationship than that of a nephew. His annoyance at this double kinship is later expressed in his reference to "my uncle-father and aunt-mother" (II.ii.393).

In Hamlet's first line, of whom is he speaking: of himself, of Claudius, or of them both? If *kind* is taken as an adjective meaning sympathetic and friendly, Hamlet may mean that "there is no love lost between us"; and this is the usual interpretation. If he uses *kind* to mean natural, then he is saying that Claudius's marriage is unnatural; and this interpretation has met with some favor. But there is in Shakespeare a parallel use of *kin* and *kind* that cannot possibly be interpreted with these meanings. In *Richard II* the bishop of Carlisle predicts disaster for the kingdom if Richard is forced to abdicate in favour of Bolingbroke:

I speak to subjects, and a subject speaks,
Stirr'd up by God, thus boldly for his king.
My Lord of Hereford here, whom you call king,
Is a foul traitor to proud Hereford's king;
And if you crown him, let me prophesy,
The blood of English shall manure the ground,
And future ages groan for this foul act.
Peace shall go sleep with Turks and infidels,
And in this seat of peace tumultuous wars
Shall *kin with kin* and *kind with kind* confound. . . .
O, if you raise this house against this house,
It will the woefullest division prove
That ever fell upon this cursed earth.
Prevent it, resist it, let it not be so,
Lest child, child's children, cry against you "woe!"

(IV.i.132– 149)

Since Richard and Bolingbroke (Hereford) are both grandsons of
Edward III, the latter is revolting against his own royal house in
deposing the lineal heir, Richard. By the sentence structure *kin* and
kind must be nouns, and *kind* cannot be an adjective signifying
kindness. There is a strong possibility that the combination of words
from *Richard II* was repeated in *Hamlet* with the same meanings. I
shall seek to determine what those meanings can be.

There is little difficulty with *kin,* which signifies relatives or
kindred. But *kind* should then have a different or more limited
meaning than *kin* or the terms are merely redundant. One might
interpret *kind* as *sort.* Hamlet would then be saying, "The king and I
are not the same sort of person." The bishop would be saying, "War
turns kinsmen against each other and different classes of persons
against each other." This would make sense in both quotations after
a fashion.

The *Oxford English Dictionary,* under *kind,* gives "family, an-
cestral race, or stock from which one springs" (12). This usage
would merely duplicate the meaning of *kin.* But the dictionary also
gives "offspring, brood, progeny, descendants," citing the Rheims
(Catholic) version of Acts 17:28, "Of his *kinde* also we are" (11 b).
Using this meaning of lineal descendants, the bishop's speech means,

157

"Wars shall set kinsman against kinsman and child against child," that is, brothers will oppose each other in battle. This usage makes *kind* a more specific and limited form of *kin*, referring to sibling offspring instead of to the larger circle of kinsmen; it would also include grandchildren as well as children. The last line of the bishop's speech may underscore this usage: "Lest *child, child's children*, cry against you 'woe!'' "

Applying this meaning to Hamlet's line, he says, "A little more than a nephew and less than a child or offspring." He is only a stepson and not really of Claudius's "kind" or progeny. *Cousin* and *kin, son* and *kind*, have essentially the same meanings. Hamlet comments to himself that both of Claudius's terms are inaccurate; Hamlet is somewhere between a cousin and a son to him. This seems to me the most likely explanation of Hamlet's line.

Since Hamlet is punning on the similar sounds of *son* and *sun*, another pun may be involved in *kin* and *kind*, with the second word having a short *i*, as in "kinn'd'" and "kindred." We cannot be sure enough of Elizabethan pronunciation to know whether the word *kind* had a double pronunciation.[18] But another element may have influence here. Hamlet has just returned from Germany; and the word for *child* in German and in Dutch is *kind*, pronounced with a short *i* and with the final *d* sounded as *t*. Since Hamlet is talking to himself, he may have made the pun by recalling the German pronunciation of *kind*, which has the same meaning in English.[19] In *All's Well* La Feu uses a foreign word in commenting on the king's renewed health: "*Lustig*, as the Dutchman says" (II.iii.47). Hamlet may also be using a foreign word, or a foreign pronunciation of an English word, in order to make his pun.

5. A Thing of Nothing

After the death of Polonius, Hamlet is sought out by Rosencrantz and Guildenstern and the following exchange takes place:

> *Ros.* My lord, you must tell us where the body is and go with us to the king.
> *Ham.* The body is with the king, but the king is not with the body. The king is a thing—

Guil. A thing, my lord!
Ham. Of nothing: bring me to him. (IV.ii.27–32)

I take this riddling utterance of Hamlet to mean that the body of man is adjunct to and dependent upon the soul, while the soul is not dependent upon the body for life but is living of itself. In Claudius the body is still joined with its king, the soul; but in Polonius the kingly soul is no longer joined with the body.

Macrobius quotes Plotinus's observation upon what constitutes the essential man, concluding that the passions pertain to the animal and perishable nature of man but that the "true man" is the rational soul, which is imperishable:

Sed nec hoc neglectum vel non quaesitum relinquit, quo animae beneficio, quave via societatis animetur. Has ergo omnes quas praediximus, passiones adsignat animali, verum autem hominem ipsam animam esse testatur. Ergo qui *videtur,* non ipse *verus homo* est, sed verus ille est, a quo regitur quod *videtur.* Sic cum morte animalis discesserit animatio, *cadit corpus regente viduatum,* et hoc est, quod *videtur* in homine mortale, anima autem, qui *verus homo* est, ab omni condicione mortalitatis aliena est, adeo ut in imitationem dei mundum regentis regat et ipsa corpus, dum a se animatur. (But neither does he neglect or fail to seek out by what benefit of soul or by what manner of association a person is animated. All these passions which we have before mentioned, he assigns to the animal nature; but he witnesses that the *true man* is the soul itself. Therefore, the one who *is seen* is not himself the *true man,* but the true man is that by which what *is seen* is ruled. So when by death the animal animation has been cut off, *the body falls emptied of its king,* and this body is what *is seen* in mortal man; but the soul, which is the *true man,* is alien from every condition of mortality; even as, in imitation of God ruling the world, it itself rules the body, while it has life of itself.)[20]

This passage expresses the meaning of Hamlet's first sentence, "The body is with the king, but the king is not with the body."

Hamlet's second phrase, "a thing of nothing," is indebted to two possible sources. In the Prayer-Book version of Psalm 144:4, we read, "Man is like a thing of nought" (below, p. 189). In Montaigne's "An Apologie of Raymond Sebond," we read,

> God had made man like unto a shadowe, of which who shall judge, when the light being gone, it shall vanish away? Man is *a thing of nothing*.[21]

Montaigne seems to refer to man's ephemeral body, which shall vanish and leave no trace. But there is another meaning, based upon Shakespeare's use of *nothing* as meaning "no thing" (above, p. 234).

Rosencrantz's use of *king* refers to Claudius, but his words "the body" recall to Hamlet the image of the rational soul as the "king" of the body. This "king" is immortal, immaterial, intangible, and invisible, literally "no thing." In Polonius this "king" is no longer associated with his fleshly body; so will it ultimately be with all men. Hamlet then returns to Rosencrantz's use of *king* and says, "bring me to him." His mind fluctuates between the general and the particular, between the soul as *king* of the body and Claudius as *king* of Denmark.

Macrobius's distinction between inward reality and outward appearance is used in Hamlet's speech to his mother when she seeks to comfort him after his father's death:

> *Seems*, madam! Nay, it *is*; I know not "seems."
> 'Tis not alone my inky cloak, good mother,
> Nor customary suits of solemn black,
> Nor windy suspiration of forc'd breath,
> No, nor the fruitful river of the eye,
> Nor the dejected haviour of the visage,
> Together with all forms, moods, shows of grief,
> That can *denote me truly*. These indeed *seem*,
> For they are actions that a man might play;
> But I have that *within* which passeth show,
> These but the trappings and the suits of woe. (I.ii.76–86)

The fact that Latin *videtur* means both "is seen" and "seems" has apparently suggested this passage. The manifestations of grief denote the passions that belong to the animal nature of man and may be observed by external signs. But the *true* man is the rational soul that

160

is hidden *within,* not visible to human eyes.[22] It *is,* while one's outward manner only *seems.* Its preëminence in and separability from the body are characteristic of the human condition.

6. *The Generation of Life*[23]

In the Quarto and Folio versions of *Hamlet* (II.ii) occurs the following bit of byplay during Hamlet's conversation with Polonius:

> *Ham.* For if the sun breed maggots in a dead dog, being a good kissing carrion—Have you a daughter?
> *Pol.* I have, my lord.
> *Ham.* Let her not walk in the sun. Conception is a blessing, but not as your daughter may conceive. (lines 181–187)

The alternative reading, "a god kissing carrion," results from an emendation by William Warburton, which was greatly admired by Dr. Johnson and has met with a varying reception from editors ever since. To make his meaning perfectly clear, Warburton inserted a comma between "god" and "kissing." Otherwise it is possible to read the two words as though hyphenated, which would have then the effect of making the carrion kiss the god. Warburton assumed that "being" modifies "sun" rather than "dog"; the sun is the god, the dead dog is the carrion, and the god kisses the carrion, thereby breeding life within it. Warburton's moralistic interpretation of the passage has met with less favour than the emendation itself. He considered it to mean the saving power of God for a mankind sunk in original sin.

More important, however, than the precise word used is the question of logical sequence in the passage as a whole. Why does Hamlet suddenly leap from his discussion of the carrion to a comment upon Ophelia? Is the succeeding remark amusingly irrelevant or does it have a logical relation to what precedes it? Hamlet's use of "conception" and "conceive" involves, of course, a fairly obvious pun: here "conception" means "quickness of understanding" and "conceive" means "become pregnant." As has often been pointed out, Shakespeare used the same *double entendre* in *King Lear*: Kent, failing to understand Gloucester's reference to Edmund's illegitimate birth, says, "I cannot conceive you," to which Gloucester replies, "Sir, this young fellow's mother could" (I.i.12). Adopting these meanings, we find that Hamlet's words imply that pregnancy will not be a blessing to Ophelia, perhaps because it is not a blessing to women in general. This interpretation is strengthened by his words to her in a later scene: "Get thee to a nunnery. Why wouldst thou be a breeder of sinners? . . . I say we will have no more marriages" (III.i.122-123, 155).

We have yet to explain the words, "Let her not walk in the sun." The implication seems to be that walking in the sun will cause pregnancy in women. The sun also forms a connecting link with the earlier words, "if the sun breed maggots in a dead dog." Are we to consider that these are two functions of the sun and that the two functions are somehow similar? If so, the speech will have a logical consistency it otherwise lacks. To answer the question will lead us into theories of the generation of life, material of which Shakespeare clearly had some knowledge.

The breeding of maggots in a dead dog by the sun's influence is an obvious instance of spontaneous generation. Shakespeare's interest in this phenomenon is further made evident by his reference in *Antony and Cleopatra* to "the fire that quickens Nilus' slime" (I.iii.69) and by Lepidus's speech to Antony: "Your serpent of Egypt is bred now of your mud by the operation of your sun; so is your crocodile" (II.vii.29). The reference to the Nile suggests Ovid's *Metamorphoses* as the probable immediate source, though the idea had become a commonplace. The interested reader may consult C. W. Lemmi's "Monster-Spawning Nile-Mud in Spenser," where there is mention of similar passages by Strabo, Herodotus, Aelian, Diodorus Siculus, and Albertus Magnus.[24] Closely analogous to such generation of life in moist earth is its generation in rotting wood, dungheaps, and decayed flesh. In reading ancient theories of these phenomena, we realize how tremendously the microscope (perfected 17th c.) has changed our ways of thinking. Lucretius, for instance, attempts to disprove the immortality of the soul by the appearance of maggots in a dead body. He reasons that the soul is the entire life force of the human body, that to be immortal it must be indivisible and on departing from the body at death must leave none of itself behind. But obviously some of the life force is left behind, since shortly new living creatures appear in the dead body without any way they could have entered from the outside. Accordingly, the soul is divisible and cannot be immortal.[25] Lucretius did not know the elementary fact that maggots are born from the eggs of flies, that their life force does come from without into the dead human body, which merely serves them as food, not as a source of generation.

I should devote particular attention to Aristotle's views on generation: first, because he treated the subject extensively and systematically; and, second, because his work had such great influence on later writers. In his *History of Animals* and *On the Generation of Animals* he acknowledges the existence of spontaneous generation among both plants and animals: among certain parasitic plants, such as the mistletoe, which seem to have no seed,[26] and among a wide variety of animals that proceed from putrid matter through the application of heat.[27] It must be animal heat or heat from the sun's rays—the heat of fire will not have a generative effect.[28] He also mentions, but does not support, a common belief that originally all creatures, including men, were produced directly from the earth by a similar spontaneous generation.[29] Prominent among Aristotle's assumptions is his belief that basically all generation of life has the same cause. Whether birth proceeds from the seed, the egg, or the womb or spontaneously from putrid matter, it is really the same process, subject to local variations. He develops the thesis that all change in the region of mutability below the moon is caused by the sun, particularly by means of the ecliptic, or path of the sun around the earth, which results in the succession of the seasons.[30] All things are subject to corruption and decay, which are a necessary prelude to any new generation of existence. Hence all generation of life has a common cause and consists of analogous processes.

This theory held by Aristotle received support both before and after his own time. Hippocrates compares the generation of plants with that of human beings:

> I judge that all things born of the earth live from the moisture of the earth, and such moisture as the earth has within herself, such also will her offspring have from her. So also the child lives from its mother in the womb; and by whatever state of health the mother is affected, such also will the child have. For if one will consider what is said of these things, from the beginning even to

163

the end, he will find that all natures are alike, both of things born from the earth, and of men.[31]

Galen, near the beginning of his work *On the Natural Faculties*, remarks, "The seed having been cast into the womb or into the earth (for there is no difference)," thus stressing the similarity of all generation.[32] Pico della Mirandola quotes Avicenna as believing it possible for even a man to be generated from putrefaction, in the manner of the smaller creatures.[33] Perhaps the essential likeness of all generation is most cogently presented by Julius Caesar Scaliger in his commentary upon Aristotle's *History of Animals*. He writes,

> The generation of man has indeed something in common with all generations of animals, in such a manner as the imperfect by a certain power is contained by the perfect. For if from seed an egg is made, and from the egg an animal, therefore in that seed from which an animal is made directly the quality (*vis*) of the egg is contained. If from putrefied wood or other bodies an animal is made, in the same way [an animal born in the usual manner] is made from food changed [by putrefaction] into seed. And what particular quality is in a certain genus that like may procreate through a like form, the same quality is in the common round of Nature's power, so that from a dunghill she may generate a mouse like to an [ordinary] mouse, whose species is in the mind of this same Nature. God has all things present before him, and he is all things; nor does he place more effort in animating seed that a man may be made, than in animating dung that he may fashion a mouse. For who gave to man the form through which a like form is contained in the power of his seed? All must indeed derive from one beginning, which is God, whose will is called Fortune and whose power is Nature.[34]

We may now examine more closely the process of human generation. Here Aristotle's authority was generally accepted. According to him, the embryonic child is formed from "seed," consisting of the seminal fluid of the father and the menstrual fluid of the mother. Neither of the two fluids possesses active life of itself, but each has potentialities of life.[35] The seed, after being properly mingled, lies

motionless in the womb for seven days,[36] at the end of which time it
begins to "work": to ferment or putrefy or coagulate, to use terms
employed by several commentators.[37] Aristotle compares the process to the curdling of milk and makes clear that it is a form of
corruption that is followed by generation.[38] Paracelsus lists seven
stages in corruption and generation: calcination, sublimation, solution, putrefaction, distillation, coagulation, and tincture.[39] As the
central one of these, putrefaction represents the end of corruption
and the beginning of generation; it thus marks the transition from
death to birth. To Paracelsus it seems a great gift of God, enabling
the old to perish and to reappear in new forms. He writes,

> For putrefaction brings forth great things, of which we have a
> beautiful example in the holy Evangelist, where Christ says,
> "Unless a grain of wheat be buried in the earth and putrefy, it
> cannot bear fruit a hundredfold." From this we are to know that
> many things are multiplied in putrefaction so that they may bear
> a noble fruit. For putrefaction is the mutation and death of all
> things, the destruction of the former essence of all natural
> things, whence there may come forth to us regeneration and a
> new generation a thousand times better.[40]

The pattern of human generation may be stated in more detail.
The individual takes food in order to generate nourishing blood, but
the food must undergo corruption, that is, be digested, before the
blood is generated.[41] In turn, elements of the blood are concocted in
order to form the genital fluids in both male and female.[42] When these
fluids are mingled in the womb, they are only potentially alive and
must undergo corruption before the embryonic child can be generated.[43] Thus all life proceeds from corruption, the necessary beginning of generation. The mysterious process of conception in the
mother's womb is the same in kind as the sprouting of a plant from
the decay of its seed, the breeding of a chick from the decay of its egg,
the breeding of maggots in a dead dog from the decay of its flesh.

I should note here that this theory of human generation was still
quite generally held in Shakespeare's day and was not effectively
refuted until a report made by William Harvey in 1651. Harvey,
observing the dismemberment of pregnant does by the king's hunts-
men, looked in vain for the mass of "seed" from which the embryo

was supposed to have sprouted. Since he could not find it, he concluded that Aristotle must be mistaken, though he himself could not furnish the true explanation. He assumed the similarity of animal and human generation.[44]

The function of the sun in human generation is now to be considered. While Aristotle thought the sun the ultimate source of all generation and corruption, he did not make it an immediate agent of human generation in his works devoted to that subject. But in *Physics* (II.ii) he dropped almost at random the remark, "Man and the sun generate man." This was eagerly seized upon by later commentators. Thomas Aquinas quotes it in three different works to explain human generation.[45] It is similarly used by Duns Scotus[46] and by Vincent de Beauvais.[47] The Greek neo-Platonist Hermeias repeats it,[48] as does Marsilio Ficino, the Florentine Platonist. Ficino explains that "the universal virtue of the sun produces man only through the medium of another man as the particular and proper cause."[49] The Variorum *Hamlet* lists the phrase as coming from Giordano Bruno.[50] Obviously its popularity was widespread. It helped to explain why oftentimes conception did not take place after sexual contacts. If the influence of the sun were not present, there could be no generation of life.

Brief mention should be made of the influence of the mythographers upon this complex of ideas. As early as the fifth century, Macrobius sought to prove, in his *Saturnalia*,[51] that the whole body of Greek myth proceeded from allegorical representations of the sun and its generative powers. His ideas were in part reproduced in two popular handbooks of mythology, Boccaccio's *De Genealogia Deorum* and Natalis Comes's *Mythologiae*. In each of these works the generative powers of the sun are frequently mentioned. Boccaccio, for instance, interprets the Jupiter-Io myth as the union of the sun with human semen, illustrating Aristotle's words, "Man and the sun generate man."[52]

In *Hamlet,* however, the jesting remark, "Let her not walk in the sun," seems to imply that woman could actually become pregnant from the sun's rays alone, that man is not an indispensable agent in the generation of his own kind. We find at once that such a belief has been widely held in different places and periods of the world. Sir James Frazer, in *The Golden Bough,*[53] and E. S. Hartland, in *Primitive Paternity,*[54] list supernatural pregnancy, without masculine agency,

166

as one of the commonest superstitions of primitive peoples. One of the methods of inducing such pregnancy is by the sun's rays. They record a number of instances in which girls upon first reaching the age of puberty were shut up in darkness for several weeks lest the sun's rays should impregnate them. A Sicilian folktale tells of a maiden who was warned against exposure to the sun and who became pregnant from a single beam of sunlight that penetrated a cranny in her castle wall.[55] Possibly such an idea is the basis of many of the Greek myths, but there the sun god is nearly always represented as visiting his human mistress in the guise of a man or of an animal. Boccaccio, however, quotes one legend that exactly illustrates the superstition. It concerns the birth of Branchus, known as a son of Apollo. His mother, shortly after her marriage to Sucron, was resting one day when she beheld the rays of the sun come into her chamber, enter her mouth, and penetrate to her womb, after which they emerged again. Shortly thereafter she realized that she was pregnant and in time bore Branchus as the fruit of this union with the sun. Boccaccio distrusts the accuracy of the myth, expressing his belief that the miraculous conception was actually a dream signifying the gift of prophecy her offspring was to possess.[56]

The clearest statement of all occurs in *The Faerie Queene*, in Spenser's account of the miraculous conception of Belphoebe and Amoret from the influence of the sun's rays. Their mother, the nymph Chrysogone, after bathing in a fountain lay nude in the sunlight and incautiously fell asleep. Spenser writes,

The sunbeames bright upon her body playd,
Being through former bathing mollifide,
And pierst into her wombe, where they embayd
With so sweet sence and secret power unspide,
That in her pregnant flesh they shortly fructifide.

Miraculous may seeme to him that reades
So straunge ensample of conception;
But reason teacheth that the fruitfull seades
Of all things living, through impression
Of the sunbeames in moyst complexion,
Doe life conceive and quickned are by kynd:
So, after Nilus inundation,

167

Infinite shapes of creatures men doe fynd,
Informed in the mud, on which the sunne hath shynd.
(III.vi.7–8)

Here we have spontaneous generation from the earth used to explain spontaneous generation in the womb, in each case through the agency of the sun. We need not suppose, however, that because Spenser and Shakespeare used such a theory for literary purposes they actually believed in human impregnation from the sun's rays alone. Both of them have consciously pursued a train of thought from generally accepted facts into the realm of semi-mythical theory. Hamlet is fond of quaint veins of speculation, of which this is one.

To return to the question of logical sequence in Hamlet's speech, let us reconsider the alternative readings "good kissing" and "god kissing" in the light of the material just presented. I should note that elsewhere Shakespeare refers to the sun's kiss: "Didst thou never see Titan kiss a dish of butter?" (*1 Henry IV*, IV.iv.133). Assuming first that he wrote "good kissing," my analysis must run somewhat as follows: Since the "carrion" cannot refer to the sun except by an extreme distortion of figurative language, it must refer to the dead dog. Since the dog is dead and unable to do any kissing itself, it must be the recipient of the kissing, and the phrase means "good for the purposes of being kissed." Who then is the kisser? A person, according to the usual interpretation, which makes of the phrase a morbidly ironic comment to the effect that "a rotten carcass is surely a sweet object!" But there is a satisfactory alternative explanation. If the sun is the kisser, then the phrase means "good for receiving the sun's kiss"; that is, the corrupted flesh is already predisposed to the breeding of life from the impulse of the sun's rays and for that purpose is superior to living flesh. The "kiss" suggests the nuptial union of the sun with matter for the generation of life, in this case life in the form of maggots.

Why then should Ophelia not walk in the sun? Here Hamlet is pursuing the same pseudoscientific train of thought involved in the first part of his speech. Ophelia, like all women, is made of corruptible flesh and blood; and within her yet living flesh one portion, the menses, already undergoes the corruption that prepares it for the generation of life This but anticipates that corruption to which her entire body must in time arrive. So, speculates Hamlet, if the sun's kiss breeds life in one form of corrupt matter, it is likely to breed it in another, and Ophelia may unexpectedly find herself pregnant. His whole speech is an ingenious bit of ratiocination that serves quite well to confuse Polonius while allowing Hamlet to pursue the current of his own thoughts.

I may now turn to Warburton's emendation and read the phrase as "a god kissing carrion." With this reading most of what I have just said will still apply. The dead dog is still the carrion or object kissed, the sun is again the kisser, and the verbal logic that makes them so is clearer and simpler than with the first reading. Ophelia's walking in the sun retains the same hazards. But the reference to the sun as a god introduces a profound philosophical concept. It suggests the divine agency in a world of mortality, the pure immutable essence that, changeless itself, touches all matter in a world of change and from the corruption of death brings the regeneration of life.[57] This is a miracle of the physical world that may also have moral implications. Warburton's suggestion that the carrion may represent original sin recalls Calvin's comparison of the man unredeemed from sin to a carrion carcass[58] and also finds a striking medieval analogy in Alanus de Insulis's *Distinctions of Theological Terms*. In explaining the various uses of the word "worm" in the scriptures, Alanus writes,

Worm signifies Christ in David's words, "I am a worm and not a man." A worm is born from the earth without seed and without show; it is trodden on, despised, and considered vile. So Christ was born of the Virgin without masculine seed; he lived humbly among men; . . . condemned and despised by the Jews, he was put to death. Again, *worm* signifies Sin in Job's words, "I have said to putridity, You are my father; to the worms, You are my mother and my sister." In the phrase "I have said to putridity, You are my father," he has insinuated that every man descends from a tainted origin; and he adds "to the worms, You are my mother and my sister," because plainly both from putridity itself and with it we come into this world; and in so much as pertains to the material of corruptible flesh worms are my mother and my sister, because we have proceeded from putridity and with putridity we bring whatever we bear. . . . Again, *worm* signifies carnal delight in Job's words concerning the lustful man, "the sweetness of that worm," because he who stews in desire of carnal corruption breathes forth the stench of putridity.[59]

In the first usage here quoted, as in the passages already given from Scaliger and Spenser, spontaneous generation from the earth is made analogous to human generation; it particularly resembles the generation of Christ, who had no human father. In the second usage quoted the putridity or putrefied "seed" from which human generation begins represents the weakness of the flesh, the source of original sin. In the third usage quoted sexual lust is a desire for fleshly corruption and is a yielding to the "worm" of sin.

It should now be apparent that whatever reading of Hamlet's speech is adopted its sequence of thought is based upon a theory of the generation of life. One's preference between the two readings is likely to reflect one's opinion of the value of textual authority. Certainly the fact that "good kissing" appears in all the textual sources is a powerful argument in its favour. Still, we know that errors do appear in the textual sources of Shakespeare's plays, and this may be one of them. The verbal logic of the speech is definitely more strained than it is with Warburton's emendation. Furthermore, "god kissing" seems almost necessary if we make the "carrion" represent the flesh as a source of original sin. This is a favourite idea with Shakespeare. Images of decay appear in sonnets 71, 74, and 81; in sonnet 146 he describes his flesh as "my *sinful* earth," which shall become the inheritance of worms. Likewise, Hamlet's remarks upon Polonius's corpse and Yorick's skull, with his reference to "my Lady Worm" (V.i.96), show an ironic contemplation of corruption and decay as the necessary and unpleasant ending of all mortal life; his words to Ophelia, "Virtue cannot so inoculate *our old stock* but we shall relish of it," are a clear reference to the "old Adam" within us, or original sin, the ineradicable taint accompanying man's body of corruptible flesh. One can make a strong argument for Warburton's reading as the expression of a sentiment found elsewhere in Shakespeare and clearly present in this particular play.

For those who believe that Shakespeare's plays present moods that he himself had experienced, there is satisfaction in the sequel to these images of corruption and decay. In *The Tempest* Ariel sings to Ferdinand:

Full fathom five thy father lies,
Of his bones are coral made,
Those are pearls that were his eyes,
Nothing of him that doth fade
But doth suffer a sea-change
Into something rich and strange. (I.ii.396–401)

The "sea-change" can be nothing else than the putrefaction of the human body and its transformation into other forms. The process is the same as with the "carrion," yet here it is viewed as a process of strange and wonderful beauty. The material body dies but its substance lives, ever perishing and ever revivified in new existences. The lines of Ariel's song may be the comment of a man who has come to terms with himself, who has learned to accept without regret the conditions of his mortal nature, who can face life without flinching and see in death itself the prelude to a fresh adventure.

*　*　*

According to Carlyle, Shakespeare was "world-wide" in his observation and understanding of people.[60] His study of the human condition included not only individual characters but also more general inquiries into man's origin, physical qualities, family loyalties, and divine attributes. His general conclusions lend strength and substance to his portrayals of persons.

VII

The Ascent of Man

SHAKESPEARE FURTHER ILLUSTRATES the nature of man by a comparison with the beasts. Both beasts and men are animals, or animated beings, but men are not beasts. Men are the "higher" animals; beasts are the "lower" animals. Physically the two orders seem much the same, but the human race has a capacity for improvement that beasts do not share to the same degree. Civilized man did not emerge full-armed, like Pallas Athene from the head of Zeus. Only by gradual stages did he develop the "arts" of civilization. To the practical arts of daily living were eventually added the "fine" arts: music, literature, and the plastic arts of painting, sculpture, and architecture. These are evidences of man's superior intellect, which elevates him above the beasts. Through the arts he has the opportunity to project his name and influence into the future, and in this way he may survive in the memories of men after his own physical death.

1. Caliban the Bestial Man[1]

The character of Caliban continues to be a source of speculation to readers of *The Tempest*, but gradually we are learning those elements of sixteenth-century thought that suggested him to Shakespeare. Some years ago Morton Luce pointed out that Caliban can be viewed in three distinct ways: (1) as a hag-born monstrosity, (2) as a slave, and (3) as a savage, or dispossessed Indian.[2] The second of

172

these ways may be explained by the third, since the English could read many accounts of the manner in which the Spaniards had reduced the Indians to slavery. But while Caliban worships a Patagonian god (below, p. 175), he is the child of an African witch from Argier (Algiers). This would seem to indicate that Shakespeare is not trying to represent primarily a red Indian from the New World but has broadened the conception to represent primitive man as a type. The name *Caliban,* a metathesis of *canibal,* supports this view; for contemporary voyagers, as well as early travelers from Homer and Herodotus to Mandeville, had found cannibals in many different quarters of the world.

Caliban's birth furnishes an explanation of his appearance and character. He was "got by the devil himself" upon the witch Sycorax, and Prospero refers to him as "hag-seed," "demi-devil," and "a born devil." These references stamp him as the offspring of an incubus. In sixteenth-century demonology the incubus is sometimes *the* devil, sometimes *a* devil, who takes the form of a man in order to seduce women to illicit sexual relations. When he takes the form of a woman in order to seduce men, he is known as a succubus.[3]

The offspring born to such unnatural unions are usually deformed in shape or possess some other singularity that makes them unlike normal human beings. R. R. Cawley quotes evidence to this effect from Sir John Mandeville, Pierre Le Loyer, and Reginald Scot.[4] Caliban's parentage would thus account for his monstrous appearance. It is also possible that Shakespeare thought of such parentage as explaining the more debased tribes of savages. The fact that Caliban "didst gabble like A thing most brutish" before learning Prospero's language is highly suggestive of a passage added to the 1665 edition of Reginald Scot's *A Discourse concerning Devils and Spirits* (II.iv):

> Another sort are the Incubi, and Succubi, of whom it is reported that the Hunns have the original, being begotten betwixt the Incubi, and certain Magical women whom *Philimer* the King of the *Goths* banished into the deserts, whence arose that savage and untamed Nation, whose speech seemed rather the mute attempts of brute Beasts, than any articulate sound and well distinguished words.[5]

173

While Shakespeare may not have read this passage, he may have read its original in Jornandes's *History of the Goths* (chapter xxiv).[6] It would account very neatly for his having combined into one individual the incubus-begotten monster and the debased savage or type of primitive man.

While Caliban's deformity makes him look like a fish, he is not like the ordinary conception of a merman, for he is "legged like a man! and his fins like arms!" (II.ii.34). Some monster of this kind had clearly been in Shakespeare's mind for a considerable period before he wrote *The Tempest*, as we gather from Thersites' jesting characterization of Ajax in *Troilus and Cressida* (III.iii.265): "He's grown a very land-fish, languageless, a monster." Caliban is a fishlike monster who dwells on land and was languageless until Prospero taught him speech.

It is entirely probable that Caliban's physical appearance is derived from some freak of nature brought back or described by returning voyagers. The early travelers give many descriptions of curious creatures, and Shakespeare shows a strong interest in them.[7] J. W. Cunliffe has noted a passage in Purchas, describing the voyage of Friar Joanno dos Sanctos in 1597. As the passage seems to have escaped general notice, I include it here:

> Heere I may mention also a Sea monster, which we saw neere the River Tendanculo, killed by the Cafres, found by Fishermen on the Shoalds. Hee was ash-coloured on the backe, and white on the belly, hayrie like an Oxe but rougher: his head and mouth lyke a Tygre, with great teeth, white Mustachos a span long, as bigge as bristles which Shoomakers use. He was ten spans long, thicker then a man; his tayle thick, a span long, *eares of a Dog, armes like a Man without haire, and at the elbowes great Finnes like a fish;* two short feet nigh his tayle, plaine like a great Apes, without legs, with five fingers a span long on each foot and hand, covered with skin like a Goose foot, the hinder feet having clawes like a Tygres; neere his tayle were the signes of a Male, his Liver, Lights and Guts like a Hogs. The Cafres seeing our Slaves slay him, fell upon him and eate him; which they which spare nothing had not done before, because they thought him (they said) *the sonne of the Devill* (having never seene the like) the rather, because *hee made a noyse which might be heard halfe a league off.*[8]

The monster here described has certain features in common with Caliban. He is thought to be a son of the devil, he is found in the country of the cannibals, he has fins on his arms, he has dog's ears like "puppy-headed Caliban,"[9] he has a roaring voice. Shakespeare could not have read Purchas but may have read this account in manuscript, since the voyage took place thirteen years before the composition of *The Tempest*.

The influence of the voyagers is evident not only in Caliban's appearance but in the "un-inhabited island" where he dwells. While the island is supposedly in the Mediterranean, it draws certain features from accounts of the New World. Caliban's deity is Setebos, the "great devil" of the Patagonians.[10] The storm is brewed with dew brought by Ariel from "the still-vex'd Bermoothes" and is patterned after the storm in the several accounts of Sir George Somers' shipwreck among the Bermuda Islands.[11] The presence of spirits in the island has been attributed to the same accounts, which refer to Bermuda as "the isle of devils."

While these narratives were almost certainly in Shakespeare's mind, I suggest that the appearance of spirits in conjunction with Caliban may have been developed from two passages in another book he had read, Ludwig Lavater's *Of Ghosts and Spirites Walking by Nyght* (1572):

> Ludouicus Viues, saythe in his firste booke *De veritate fidei* that in the newe world lately found out, there is nothing more common, than, not only in the night time but also at noone in the midday, to see spirits apparantly, in the cities & fields, which speake, commaund, forbyd, assault men, feare them & strike them. . . .
>
> They whiche sayle on the greate Ocean sea, make reporte, that in certayne places, where the *Anthropophagi* doo inhabite, are many spirites, whiche doo the people there very muche harme.[12]

Lavater gives as a marginal note to *Anthropophagi:* "Which are people that eate and deuoure men." Shakespeare's familiarity with this common term is shown by Othello's reference to "the Cannibals that each other eat, The Anthropophagi" (I.iii.143–144).

The activities of the spirits described by Lavater bear a certain

THE ASCENT OF MAN

resemblance to the treatment visited by Ariel and his fellows upon Caliban and the other plotters. As in Shakespeare, their location is indefinite, occurring at various points in the New World and "the greate Ocean sea." Most significant is Lavater's placing the spirits particularly in the lands of the Anthropophagi, or cannibals. Since the name Caliban is an apparent metathesis of *canibal*, we find in Lavater's account of spirits who plague the cannibals a parallel with Shakespeare's contrast between Ariel and Caliban.

We know that Shakespeare had read Montaigne's essay *Of the Caniballes*, in which the author describes certain savages from the New World and tells what he has learned concerning their native society (below, p. 199). He is favourably impressed with this view of the "natural man" and his praise is reflected in Gonzalo's glowing description of the utopian state (II.i.147–168). Montaigne refers to the cannibals only incidentally as eaters of human flesh and seems more concerned with studying mankind in a primitive stage of social development. He says they were brought from "Antartike France." Eden places the savage worshipers of Setebos at "the 49 degree and a halfe vnder the pole Antartyke" and a few lines earlier mentions a meeting with "certeyne Canibals" farther up the coast in Brazil.[13] The use of "Antartyke" and "Canibals" by both authors may have caused Shakespeare to connect the two accounts of primitive savages and to adopt Setebos as a deity of the cannibals, and hence of Caliban.

It is clear, however, that Shakespeare does not share Montaigne's enthusiasm for primitive man. Indeed, the personality of Caliban might be considered a refutation of the "noble savage" theory. He is a slave because he cannot live successfully with human beings on any other terms.[14] He is educable to a certain extent but seems completely lacking in a moral sense. He has repaid Prospero's kindness by attempting to violate Miranda's chastity, and he cannot be made to see anything wrong in his action. He has imagination and sufficient intelligence to learn human language, but neither punishment nor kindness can give him a sense of right and wrong. He is not particularly to blame for his character, "which any print of goodness will not take," since it resulted from his birth; and in fact his complete amorality makes him seem amusing rather than culpable. His love of music and his worship of Stephano as a god are probably based upon contemporary accounts of the Indians.[15] Prospero's condemnatory words, like Othello's phrase "the base Indian," align Shakespeare

176

with those who viewed the savages as a lower order of beings rather than with idealists of primitive man.[16]

Yet Caliban is something more than the primitive savage of the voyagers' narratives. His character is developed in accordance with a definite philosophical conception, the key to which is Prospero's phrase "the beast Caliban" (IV.i.140). This phrase is not spoken in anger but is intended to convey a precise meaning.

In my article "Misanthropy in Shakespeare" I have shown that Shakespeare used extensively the concept of bestiality as applied to human conduct and that he drew this concept directly from Aristotle's *Nicomachean Ethics*.[17] According to Aristotle, there are three evil states of the human mind: incontinence, malice, and bestiality. The incontinent man's evil appetites overcome his will to do good; the malicious man's will is itself perverted to evil purposes, though his reason perceives the difference between right and wrong; the bestial man has no sense of right and wrong and therefore sees no difference between good and evil. His state is less guilty but more hopeless than those of incontinence and malice, since he cannot be improved.

While men can degenerate into bestiality through continued wrongdoing, Aristotle declares, a natural state of bestiality is relatively rare in the human race, existing occasionally among remote and savage tribes. Illustrating natural bestiality, he writes,

> I mean bestial characters like the creature in woman's form [lamia?] that is said to rip up pregnant females and devour their offspring, or *certain savage tribes on the coasts of the Black Sea, who are alleged to delight in raw meat or in human flesh, and others among whom each in turn provides a child for the common banquet*.[18]

It is probable that Shakespeare remembered this particular passage in the following lines from *King Lear:*

> The barbarous Scythian
> Or he that makes his generation messes
> To gorge his appetite, shall to my bosom
> Be as well neighbour'd, pitied, and reliev'd,
> As thou my sometime daughter. (I.i.118–122)

The significant resemblance is the reference to tribes who eat their own children, a reference sufficiently uncommon to suggest a borrowing from the *Ethics*. His "barbarous Scythian" is also equivalent to Aristotle's "savage tribes on the coasts of the Black Sea," since the Scythians inhabited the northern and western shores of that sea. Herodotus gives many instances of their barbarities;[19] Montaigne follows Pliny and the medieval mapmakers in referring to them as cannibals.[20] The combining of the Black Sea savages (Scythians) and the childeaters in the same order by both authors suggests that Aristotle may be the source of Shakespeare's reference.

At any rate, it is difficult to see how Shakespeare could have avoided comparing Aristotle's Black Sea tribes with the savages of the New World. Aristotle convicts his tribes of bestiality on the ground that they ate their meat raw and had a taste for human flesh. Both Hakluyt and John Stow condemn the Indians for eating raw meat,[21] and numerous authors testify to their cannibalism.[22] Such adjectives as "brutish," "bestial," and "base" are applied to them, and they become the type of the debased savage in certain areas of popular opinion.[23] Stow also comments on the unintelligibility of their language,[24] a point of resemblance to Caliban and to the incubus-begotten savages of Jornandes.

In these parallels we can find a clue to the philosophic explanation of Caliban. The references to cannibals brought Aristotle and Montaigne together in Shakespeare's mind. Aristotle sees in the cannibal an example of bestial man in his natural state. Montaigne also uses the cannibal as an example of the "natural man" and praises highly the climate and customs of his country. Shakespeare uses that praise in Gonzalo's utopian speech, stating what such a country might be ideally, but he does not repeat Montaigne's praise of the cannibal as he actually exists. Rather, his Caliban, or *canibal*, is the embodiment of Aristotle's bestial man. The dramatist has sought to realize in the flesh the philosopher's concept of a primitive savage who has not attained the level of humanity.[25]

If Caliban is to be regarded as a type of the bestial man, it is desirable that we determine in what his bestiality consists. He is not an eater of human flesh, possibly from lack of opportunity; but neither Aristotle nor Montaigne gives major emphasis to the eating of human flesh. They use cannibalism simply as an illustration of primitive or bestial conduct. Bestiality, in Aristotle, results from the absence of certain mental faculties that distinguish men from beasts. As men have immortal souls and beasts do not, it has been the task of

178

philosophy to make the distinction with as much precision as possible.

As I have already stated (above, pp. 71–72), the nature of the soul is threefold. Every living thing has a soul. Plants have the vegetal soul, with powers of nourishment, growth, and reproduction. Beasts have the vegetal soul included in the sensible soul, which possesses simple powers of perception. Man has both the vegetal and sensible souls included in the rational soul, which gives him the power of thought. To determine the exact division of functions between the sensible soul and the rational soul is not easy. Thomas Aquinas attempts it in his commentary on Aristotle's treatise *On the Soul*. According to Aquinas, the sensible soul possesses intelligence, but only the rational soul possesses intellect. Intelligence has the power to apprehend, while intellect has the added power to judge. Intellect may be called "sapience" or "judgment."[26] Intelligence is susceptible to error through following false knowledge or opinion. It is also prone to follow the "phantasies" or first impressions of things, lacking the reflective power of reason that allows man to "judge" between the true and false, the right and wrong, in his own imaginings. When man's intellect is obscured in any one of three ways, he also follows his phantasies, in the same manner as a beast (above, p. 90). Intellect may be "veiled" by any strong passion, such as wrath, lust, or fear; by illness, such as frenzy or madness; and by sleep, as in dreams. In these instances a man cannot exercise rational control over his imaginings. He is then like a beast, for a beast is one in whom such a deficiency is permanent.

It should be noticed that Caliban has to a high degree the qualities of intelligence allowed by Aquinas to the beasts. He enjoys the sweet music of the isle, dreams of riches falling from heaven, and otherwise shows a fertile imagination. His foolish worship of Stephano as a god shows his lack of judgment (V.i.295–297), while his attempts upon Miranda's virtue and Prospero's life show his lack of a moral sense. Antonio and Sebastian are also would-be murderers, but at the end they are able to recognize the evil of their schemes, as Caliban cannot do, having no sense of right and wrong. It is this lack, rather than physical deformity or dullness of wit, that stamps him as a type of the bestial man.

Prospero believes that Caliban cannot develop the qualities of judgment that would stamp him as a man:

A devil, a born devil, on whose nature
Nurture can never stick; on whom my pains,
Humanely taken, all, all lost, quite lost. (IV.i.188-190)

Again he reproaches him:

Abhorred slave,
Which any print of goodness wilt not take,
Being capable of all ill. (I.ii.351-353)

Yet Caliban's recognition of his folly at the end of the play might indicate some latent capacity for the perception of error that would mark the beginning of judgment and the development of a moral sense. But, lacking that development, he remains a type of the bestial man.

Caliban is Shakespeare's most original character, but even he has literary forebears. His parentage is taken from contemporary demonology. His appearance and environment are suggested by writers on distant lands. His character results from Aristotle's conception of the bestial man. Yet here the whole is greater than the sum of its parts, which seem hardly more than hints for the remarkable creation that Shakespeare has based upon them.

2. The Figurative Beast

As Coriolanus takes leave of his mother after his banishment from Rome has been pronounced by the tribunes, he remarks, "The beast with many heads butts me away" (IV.i.1-2), in reference to the populace of Rome. This remark is a culmination of his many contemptuous references to the common people, which have prompted the tribunes to name him "an enemy to the people" (III.iii.118). Coriolanus's belief in the aristocratic ideal of leadership is in marked contrast to the democratic ideal of government "by the people," which received its best statement in Abraham Lincoln's Gettysburg Address. The people may govern through representatives who may be chosen in various ways; but when a large populace tries to manage directly the day-by-day affairs of government, the more impetuous and demagogic voices are likely to carry the day.[27]

180

Coriolanus's violent language masks a real concern for effective government in Rome. When decisions by the appointed leaders may be vetoed by jealous tribunes in the name of "the people," any effective action may become impossible in the face of a foreign threat or other emergency (III.iii.127–133).

Coriolanus's concern that Rome should have a workable plan of government appears in his speech after the tribunes propose to annul his appointment as consul:

> O good but most unwise patricians! why,
> You grave but reckless senators, have you thus
> Given *Hydra* here to choose an officer,
> That with his peremptory "shall," being but
> The horn and noise o' th'*monster's,* wants not spirit
> To say he'll turn your current in a ditch,
> And make your channel his? . . . By Jove himself!
> It makes the consuls base; and my soul aches
> To know, when two authorities are up,
> Neither supreme, how soon confusion
> May enter 'twixt the gap of both and take
> The one by th'other. (III.i.91–112)

The monster *Hydra,* with many heads, is here his term for the people. His complaint is that neither their representatives, the tribunes, nor the consuls, the nominal heads of the state, have clearly designated spheres of authority; consequently, confusion is inevitable. Coriolanus, though arrogant in manner, is not seeking personal power; he asked only to defend his city and then to live quietly within it. He stood for the consulship only at the insistence of friends who wished to honour him, but to have that honour granted and then withdrawn at the urging of demagogic tribunes is more of an insult than he can accept. Also, the event shows a basic fault in the form of government itself; in an emergency the "checks and balances" may prevent any action at all.

The phrase "a beast with many heads" stems from Horace's characterization of the Roman people, "Bellua multorum es capitum" (*Epistulae,* I.i.76). In an excellent article,[28] C. A. Patrides traces the use of the phrase in showing Renaissance disillusionment with "the people" or "the multitude." He cites examples from

Barnaby Rich (1606), Pierre Charron (1601, tr. 1606), Lancelot Andrewes (1629), Arthur Warwick (1632), and Sir Thomas Browne. Only the first two of these could have been actual sources for Shakespeare.[29] Andrewes cites Psalm 68:30, "inter Belluas populorum," as an early example of the phrase.

Patrides omits to mention Coriolanus's reference to the people as a "Hydra . . . monster" and also another Shakespearean use of the phrase in which the "beast" has become a "monster." In the introduction to *2 Henry IV* Rumour explains;

> Rumour is a pipe,
> Blown by surmises, jealousies, conjectures,
> And of so easy and so plain a stop
> That *the blunt monster with uncounted heads,*
> The still-discordant wav'ring *multitude,*
> Can play upon it. (lines 15–20)

In Patrides's quotation from Pierre Charron's *Of Wisdome,* he has omitted the lines that identify the people as a "monster." I quote the relevant lines with pagination from the 1670 edition:

> *The people . . . are a strange beast with many heads* (p.186). . . . They are *a monster* whose parts are all tongues; they speak all things, but know nothing; they look upon all, but see nothing; they laugh at all and weep at all; *fit to mutiny and rebel, not to fight.* Their property is rather to assay to shake off their yoke, then to defend their liberty (p.188). . . . To conclude, *the people are a savage beast.* . . . The Vulgar *multitude* is the mother of ignorance, injustice, inconstancy, idolatry, vanity, which never yet could be pleased. (p.189)[30]

The central portion of this quotation from Charron may be reflected in Coriolanus's opinion of the populace as poor soldiers to trust in an emergency:

> Being press'd to th' war,
> Even when the navel of the state was touch'd,
> They would not thread the gates. . . . Being i' th' war,
> *Their mutinies and revolts, wherein they show'd*
> *Most valour,* spoke not for them. (III.i.122–127)

This is remarkably close to Charron's "fit to mutiny and rebel, not to fight."

Florio's Montaigne thrice uses this image. In the essay "Divers Events from One Selfe Same Counsell," he writes,

> Being yet a childe, I saw a gentleman, who had the command of a great Citie, and by a commotion of a seditiously furious people greatly put to his plunges, who to suppress the rising fire of this tumult, resolved to sally out from a strongly assured place, where he was safe, and yeeld himselfe to that *many-headed monster mutinous rowt;* thrived so ill by it, that he was miserably slaine amongst them. . . . There is nothing lesse to bee expected or hoped for at the hands of this *monstrous faced multitude,* thus agitated by furie, than humanitie and gentlenesse.[31]

In "An Apologie of Raymond Sebond" Montaigne writes,

> This *many-headed,* divers-armed, and furiously-raging *monster,* is man; wretched, weake and miserable man: whom if you consider well, what is he, but a crawling, and ever-moving Ants-neast?[32]

In his essay "Of Diverting and Diversions" Montaigne refers to "this incensed *Hydra-headed-monster multitude,*" who in one instance were confused and then pacified by the quick wit and patient explanations of their proposed victim.[33]

In considering these passages as possible sources for Shakespeare, we meet the problem of dating. *2 Henry IV* was registered for publication on 23 August 1600 and was probably written in 1598. Since Charron's *De la Sagesse* appeared in 1601 and the translation by Samson Lennard about 1606, it could not have been a source for *2 Henry IV* but could have been a source for *Coriolanus* (ca. 1608). Neither could Shakespeare have used Florio's Montaigne (1603) for the earlier play unless he had seen it in manuscript, a circumstance that seems quite probable since both men were members of the earl of Southampton's circle of friends.[34]

If Shakespeare had read the French edition of Montaigne (1588), he would have found "many-headed monster mutinous rowt" translated from "cette tourbe mutine" and "this monstrous faced

THE ASCENT OF MAN

multitude" from "ce monstre." In the next example, "This many-headed, divers-armed, and furiously-raging monster" is in the original "ce furieux monstre, à tant de bras et à tant de testes [têtes]." In the last quotation "this incensed Hydra-headed-monster multitude" translates the French "cette tourbe esmeue." Thus in all but one instance "many-headed" was Florio's addition to Montaigne's text; Florio was greatly attracted by this image.

The fluctuating passions of the multitude are carefully portrayed by Shakespeare in the actions of the Roman populace after the murder of Julius Caesar. Brutus feels that he must appease "the multitude, beside themselves with fear" (III.i.180). In his subsequent speech and in that of Antony, the plebeians are swayed back and forth, finally reaching fever pitch and destroying without regard to guilt or innocence. Patrides notes similar references to the multitude, who are blown about as lightly as a feather in their emotions (*2 Henry VI*, IV.viii.56; *3 Henry VI*, III.i.84–89). We may add another instance in *Hamlet*, when the messenger brings news of Laertes's approach:

> The ocean, overpeering of his list,
> Eats not the flats with more impetuous haste
> Than young Laertes, in a riotous head,
> O'erbears your officers. The *rabble* call him lord,
> And, as the world were now but to begin,
> Antiquity forgot, custom not known,
> (The ratifiers and props of every word,)
> They cry, "Choose we! Laertes shall be king!"
> Caps, hands, and tongues applaud it to the clouds,
> "Laertes shall be king, Laertes king!" (IV.v.99–108)

The queen comments,

> How cheerfully on the false trail they cry!
> O, this is counter, you false Danish *dogs!* (IV.v.109–110)

Her characterization of the "rabble" as "dogs"[35] serves the same purpose as the "many-headed beast" in *Coriolanus*. King Claudius condemns "the distracted multitude, Who like not in their judgment, but their eyes" (IV.iii.4–5). Perhaps we should add to these examples Apemantus's remark in *Timon of Athens* that "the common-wealth of Athens is become a forest of beasts" (IV.iii.352).

The "many-headed beast" as applied to the common people is an example of historical or political allegory. In moral allegory it represents the multiple lusts and desires of the sensual appetite, or concupiscible faculty of the soul, which should be controlled by the dominance of reason. For the Renaissance the seven-headed beast of Revelation 17 politically represented the seven hills of Rome, but morally it represented the seven deadly sins.[36] The many-headed Hydra slain by Hercules and the three-headed Cerberus chained and dragged forth by him have a similar significance. Francesco Piccolomini interprets Hercules's killing of monsters as the rational faculty and/or the irascible faculty subduing the appetites and vices of the concupiscible faculty.[37] Natalis Comes, in his *Mythologiae*, identifies Hercules as probity, fortitude and other powers of the soul and body that expel all vices from the soul. Hercules killing the Hydra represents temperance overcoming vices; the Hydra's many heads show that from one crime many evil consequences may proceed.[38] Cerberus represents avarice; Hercules is the great-souled or magnanimous man who exposes avarice and drags it into the light.[39]

Plato in *Republic* IX (588–589) has reference to a man, a lion, and a many-headed monster as figures for the human soul. In his "Argument" to this book, Ficino identifies these as the rational, irascible, and concupiscible faculties of the soul. The many-headed monster must be disciplined and guided by his companions until all three can live in harmony together.[40]

Vincenzo Cartari, in his chapter on Pluto in *Imagini de i Dei de gli Antichi*, identifies Cerberus as the sensual appetite itself rather than the vices proceeding from it. Hercules, who bound Cerberus and brought him out of Hades, represents the prudent man who controls his appetite so as to avoid hellish vices and to follow the light of virtue.[41] The concupiscible faculty is necessary to physical life and must not be destroyed, but it must be controlled.

Shakespeare has reserved the term "many-headed" for his descriptions of the multitude, but he stresses the "beastliness" of uncontrolled appetite. In *Othello* Cassio reproaches himself for drunkenness: "I have lost the immortal part of myself, and what remains is *bestial*" (II.iii.264). Richard of Gloucester, later Richard

III, instructs Buckingham as to his campaign of slander against Edward IV:

> Moreover, urge his hateful luxury
> And *bestial appetite* in change of lust,
> Which stretch'd unto their servants, daughters, wives,
> Even where his raging eye or savage heart,
> *Without control,* lusted to make a prey. (*Richard III,* III.vi.80–84)

In *Troilus and Cressida* Ulysses uses the figurative beast in his long speech on degree. When degree is neglected or violated, all things fall into confusion and principles of justice disappear:

> Then everything includes itself in power,
> Power into will, will into appetite;
> And *appetite, an universal wolf,*
> So doubly seconded with will and power,
> Shall make perforce *an universal prey,*
> And last eat up himself. Great Agamemnon,
> This chaos, when degree is suffocate,
> Follows the choking. (I.iii.119–126)

I have earlier discussed the mental processes involved in this passage (above, p. 107); here I am concerned with the allegory of the beast. There is a threefold allegory: personal, political, and cosmic. In a person the concupiscible appetite, when unrestrained by will and reason, will indulge in such excesses as lead to his destruction. In a state the disregard of an established order of rank by self-willed individuals can lead only to anarchy and loss of political identity. In the cosmos if the planets could wander at will without control by the sun, the world would return to chaos. Appetite, if unrestrained, will lead to destruction on any level. It may be compared to a violent and voracious wolf; cosmically, a wolf with power to destroy the universe.

One suspects here an echo of Ragnarök, or doomsday, as it is pictured in Norse mythology. The account is given in the Prose Edda.[42] First two wolves devour the sun and the moon, destroying the source of light. Then the greatest wolf, Fenris (or Fenrir), breaks his chain and goes forth to battle the gods, accompanied by the

Midgard Serpent. The opposing forces destroy each other, and
Asgard, the home of the gods, is likewise destroyed. Fenris as an
agent of destruction is parallel with Typhon in Greek mythology
and also with "the dragon, that old serpent, which is the Devil and
Satan" and is chained in the bottomless pit for a thousand years until
he is unchained and comes forth again (Rev. 20:1–3).[43] But the Norse
image is that of a wolf; and Shakespeare's image is that of "an
universal wolf" that makes "an universal prey." Fenris and his
companion wolves seem to be a possible source for this image.[44]

3. The Paragon of Animals

The comparison between beasts and human beings appears several
times in *Hamlet*. In lamenting his mother's quick remarriage so soon
after her husband's death, Hamlet exclaims,

> O God! a beast that wants *discourse of reason*
> Would have mourn'd longer. (I.ii.150–151)

Here the "discourse of reason," or power to reason logically from
point to point (above, p. 95), is given as the distinguishing feature
between human beings and beasts. Just before his departure for
England, Hamlet uses the same term in reproaching himself for his
delay in avenging his father's death:

> *What is a man*
> *If his chief good and market of his time*
> *Be but to sleep and feed? A beast*, no more.
> Sure he that made us with such large *discourse*,
> Looking before and after, gave us not
> That capability and godlike *reason*
> To fust in us unus'd. (IV.iv.33–39)

He adds that either "bestial oblivion" (forgetfulness) or too much
caution as to the "event" (outcome) of his actions may be the cause
of his delay.

Here Hamlet recognizes the "discourse of reason" as the differen-
tial between a man and a beast, but he likewise recognizes the

likeness between them. A man who has no thought beyond the basic necessities of sleep and food is only a beast, for he functions as a beast does. The "capability" that makes him more than a beast is his power of reason, which makes him more like God; but a capability must be used if it is to be effective. The rational faculty enables man to reason from the past in order to foresee the future, but he must make an effort to do this. If he devotes himself solely to needs of the present moment, he does not progress beyond the status of a beast. Physically he is like a beast; it is the added mental capability that makes him a man. Hamlet does not here name the rational faculty as evidence of man's immortality; but in his soliloquy "To be or not to be" he declares the probability of such immortality in "the undiscovered country" (III.i.79).

The similarity of men and beasts, with some doubt as to man's immortality, is eloquently asserted by Solomon in Ecclesiastes 3:18–21:

> I said in my heart concerning the estate of the sons of men, that God might manifest them, and that they might see that they themselves are beasts.
>
> For that which befalleth the sons of men befalleth beasts; even one thing befalleth them: as the one dieth, so dieth the other; yea they have all one breath; so that a man hath no preëminence above a beast: for all is vanity [vain belief].
>
> All go unto one place: all are of the dust, and all turn to dust again.
>
> Who knoweth the spirit of man that goeth upward, and the spirit of the beast that goeth downward to the earth?

In the final chapter of Ecclesiastes, Solomon answers his own question. At the death of a man, "then shall the dust return to the earth as it was; and the spirit shall return unto God who gave it" (12:7).

The rational soul—or the rational faculty of the soul (above, p. 106)—is the "spirit" that shall return to God; the body shall join the bodies of beasts in the dust. The rational soul did not originate with the body in the first place but was added to the embryo some weeks after conception.[45] The embryo repeated the several stages of creation, existing first in the manner of a plant and later in the manner of a beast before becoming a man. La Primaudaye remarks, the soule of man seemeth in nothing or very little to differ from that of plants, as long as it is in the mothers wombe, nor from the soule of beasts during the time of his infancie.[46]

The difference consists in the child's "capability" of developing to a more advanced stage of mental proficiency.

Hamlet's rhetorical question "What is a man ... ?" may stem from the repeated use of "What is man?" in the Bible. In Job 7:17-18 the phrase appears,

> *What is man,* that thou shouldest magnify him? and that thou shouldest set thy heart upon him? And that thou shouldest visit him every morning, and try him every moment?

In the Prayer-Book version of Psalm 144:3-4 the phrase again appears.

> Lord, *what is man,* that thou hast such respect unto him? or the son of man that thou so regardest him?
> Man is like *a thing of nought;* his time passeth away like a shadow.

The words "a thing of nought" are echoed in Hamlet's phrase "a thing . . . of nothing" (above, p. 160; below, p. 234) and show his familiarity with this passage.

The most significant use of "What is man?" is found in Psalm 8 and is here quoted in the Prayer-Book version:

> When I consider thy heavens, even the work of thy fingers; the moon and the stars which thou hast ordained;
> *What is man,* that thou art mindful of him? and the son of man that thou visitest him?
> Thou madest him lower than the angels, to crown him with glory and worship.
> Thou makest him to have dominion of the works of thy hands; and thou hast put all things in subjection under his feet:
> All sheep and oxen; yea and the beasts of the field;
> The fowls of the air, and the fishes of the sea, and whatsoever walketh through the paths of the seas. (vv. 3-8)

189

THE ASCENT OF MAN

The first verse of this quotation recalls Psalm 19:1:

> The heavens declare the glory of God; and the *firmament*
> showeth his handy-work.

And again the theme appears in Psalm 102:25–27:

> Thou, Lord, in the beginning hast laid the foundations of the
> earth, and the heavens are the work of thy hands.
> They shall perish, but thou shalt endure: they shall wax old as
> doth a *garment;*
> And as a *vesture* shalt thou change them.

Shakespeare would probably have made these associations from a
work so familiar as the Psalter, and he may have associated with
them a similar observation from La Primaudaye:

> This hie ornament, this *firmament* so cleare, and face of heauen
> so sumptuous to behold, is a thing full of greatnesse. Therein we
> may behold the Master builder thereof, cloathed with the whole
> *frame* as with a *garment.*[47]

Psalm 8, with these associated passages, seems to be echoed in
Hamlet's explanation of his melancholy mood to Rosencrantz and
Guildenstern. Like Antonio in *The Merchant of Venice* (above,
p. 131), he says that he cannot understand his uncharacteristic mood
of sadness:

> Indeed, it goes so heavily with my disposition that this goodly
> *frame*, the earth, seems to me a sterile promontory; this most
> excellent canopy, the air, look you, this brave o'erhanging
> *firmament*, this majestical roof fretted with golden fire—why, it
> appeareth no other thing to me than a foul and pestilent con-
> gregation of vapours. *What a piece of work is a man!* how noble in
> reason! how infinite in faculties! in form and moving how
> express and admirable! in action how like an angel! in apprehen-
> sion how like a god! the beauty of the world, the paragon of
> animals! And yet to me what is this quintessence of dust? Man
> delights not me. . . . (II.ii.308–322—Kittredge text)

Like Psalm 8, this speech states first the wonder of the universe with its starry heavens and second the wonder of man. Hamlet begins with praise of "this goodly frame, the earth," which appears "sterile" to him in his melancholy mood. Since the obverse of sterility is fruitfulness, he may well be recalling Batman's praise of the earth as the "first springing Parent of all things" and the "receyuer of all fruitefulnesse" (above, p. 18). Then comes his praise of the upper air and the "firmament" of the starry sky. The second part of his speech begins with an exclamation, "What a piece of work is a man!" This has the same intent as the psalmist's rhetorical question, "What is man?" and is followed by a comparison of man to the angels and a statement of his superiority to all other animals.[48] Shakespeare adds a comparison to "a god."[49] The "action" and "apprehension" of the speech are the two functions of the rational soul as already described (above, pp. 93, 104), for it is these that elevate man above all other animals, making him the "paragon" of the class to which he belongs.[50]

Hamlet's words on man may also echo La Primaudaye's explanation of the microcosm:

> Likewise it is a common vse in schooles to teach, that man is a little world, and that within him the body is composed of the elements, the reasonable soule is celestiall, the vegetable power common to men and plants, the sense common to men and bruit beastes, the reason participated to Angels: and finally the image of God is therein seene and considered.[51]

Here are stated man's preëminence among animals, his likeness to angels, and his likeness to God. Hamlet's comparison of man to "a god" need not disturb us; for in Genesis 3:5 the serpent predicts that Adam and Eve may become "as gods" by eating the forbidden fruit, and in 3:22 God says that man has become "as one of us." This apparent reference to multiple deities takes away any suggestion of pagan polytheism that Hamlet's phrase may seem to have.

Hamlet's deprecatory reference to man as "this quintessence of dust" is likewise biblical. In the first creation "the Lord God formed man of the *dust* of the ground, and breathed into his nostrils the breath of life; and man became a living soul" (Gen. 2:7). The "quintessence" is the finest product of the dust but is nevertheless dust. As God said to Adam after the Fall:

191

In the sweat of thy face shalt thou eat bread, till thou return unto the ground; for out of it thou wast taken; for *dust* thou art, and unto *dust* shalt thou return. (Gen. 3:19)

And the psalmist says of God:

For he knoweth whereof we are made; he remembereth that we are but *dust*. (Psalms 103:14)

Shakespeare may also have recalled Horace's celebrated description of man as "pulvis et umbra" (dust and shadow).[52] And, finally, Hamlet's abrupt change from a statement of man's nobility to a statement of his origin may have drawn a hint from La Primaudaye:

For what wil it profit a man to take so great paines as to measure the whole world, and to compasse on euery side all the elementarie region, to know the things that are contained in them, and their nature, and yet in the meane time hee can not measure or know himselfe being but *a little handfull of earth?*[53]

These illustrative passages, all from works well known to Shakespeare, may serve to explain his concept of man as "the paragon of animals." Man has an origin from the "dust" in common with beasts and is like a beast in his earliest stages of life, but he has a capability of advancing beyond the bestial level through the exercise of reason. He may learn what is already known and may also extend the bounds of existent knowledge and understanding. In this creative function he most fully shares in the nature of God. It was Thomas Aquinas who declared that man's ultimate felicity lies in his power to "consider" *(intelligere)*, to exercise his power of thought.[54] And in *Paradise Lost* Milton's Belial puts it even more aptly in protesting against Moloch's desire for annihilation:

For who would lose,
Though full of pain, this intellectual being,
Those thoughts that wander through eternity? (II.146–148)

4. Nature and Art

Man's development of the arts is evidence of his advance beyond the capabilities of the beasts. The perennial debate upon the relative merits of nature and art proceeds ultimately from Plato's *Republic* (Book X) and from Aristotle's *Nicomachean Ethics* (VI.iv). For literary criticism the most significant work is Longinus's *On the Sublime*. Polydore Vergil quotes Seneca's *De Beneficiis* (IV) as saying that nature is God's divine reason inserted into the whole world and all its parts. He distinguishes nature from art by the need for human intervention. For example, an object falls downward by nature but is thrown upward by art.[55] Eating is not an art, but cookery is. The fine arts produce objects of beauty.

All commentators agree that the plastic artist imitates nature, but they disagree as to whether or not he can improve upon nature. Should the artist copy nature as closely as he can or should he change what he sees to a more ideal form in the attempt to give a clearer and deeper meaning?[56] This is the purpose of most modern artists, whether they be impressionists, surrealists, or abstractionists. All viewers recognize their purpose, but many doubt their success.

Two of Shakespeare's favourite authors take opposite positions on this question. In *The French Academie* La Primaudaye writes that nature is superior to art, that one soon tires of a scenic painting but never of a beautiful landscape. God's work is better than that of man:

> Those delights which we receiue of naturall thinges haue more force and are purer, and continue longer then artificiall pleasures. . . . For we being naturall, naturall things are more agreeable vnto vs then artificiall. . . . Therefore Arte laboureth alwayes to follow nature, and to expresse her workes as neere as it can. . . . For the least worke of his [God's] in nature is more excellent in his kinde, then the perfectest worke that humane arte is able to shew.[57]

Contrariwise, Palingenius writes in *The Zodiake of Life:*

> For without Art is nature wont to giue no perfect thing.[58]

Echoes of this debate appear in Shakespeare. In describing the horse of Adonis in *Venus and Adonis*, he writes,

> Look, *when a painter would surpass the life*
> In limning out a well-proportion'd steed,
> His *art* with *nature's* workmanship at strife,

As if the dead the living should exceed;
So did this horse excel a common one
In shape, in courage, colour, pace, and bone. (lines 289–294)

In seeking to paint an ideal horse rather than the one before his eyes, the painter tries to improve on nature and sets his art at strife with nature; the dead picture of a horse will look better than the living horse. But Adonis's living horse is equal to the painter's ideal horse.

In *Lucrece*, after Tarquin's departure, Lucrece spends some time in looking at a large picture showing the destruction of Troy:

A thousand lamentable objects there,
In scorn of *nature, art* gave lifeless life. (lines 1373–1374)

In the course of nature all things change and decay, but art overcomes this weakness of nature by preserving a record of things as they existed at a given moment in time. The "lifeless life" of art gives to the works of nature a greater degree of permanence than they would otherwise have.

Ficino refers to "the living and natural art" of nature, who is herself the great artificer of all things.[59] The "living art" appears in *Love's Labour's Lost* when the king plans to turn his court into a miniature university:

Our court shall be a little Academe,
Still and contemplative in *living art.* (I.i.13–14)

Their image as philosophic students will be "art" because it is planned by the mind of man, not instituted by nature; but it will be "living" because the figures in it are alive, as in a tableau, not the lifeless forms in a painting.

The "natural art" appears when Timon compliments the poet, "Thou art even *natural in thine art*" (V.i.88). Hamlet insists that the art of acting should "hold the mirror up to *nature*" (III.ii.24). In *Pericles* Marina is praised for her skill in sewing; with her needle she makes "*nature's* own shape of bud, birch, branch, or berry, That even her *art* sisters the *natural* roses" (V.Gower.6–7). Like La Primaudaye's artist, she succeeds by imitating nature as closely as possible.

In *A Midsummer Night's Dream* Lysander uses nature and art
figuratively when he first avows his love to Helena:

Transparent Helena! *Nature shows art,*
That through thy bosom makes me see thy heart.
(II.ii.104–105)

Because of Helena's simple and open personality, he can "see" with
his mind the emotions and sentiments of her heart. But it is nature
that enables his imagination to do this, and nature shows art in
providing an operation beyond the usual bounds of nature.

Ficino says something of the kind in his "Argument" to Plato's
Republic (Book X). God places in nature the exemplary ideas
according to which men and things are formed. Plato believes
strongly that the necessary forms of the arts are present in the pattern
of ideas. (This seems to mean that imagined forms like the centaurs
or the golden mountain, which have no real existence [above, p. 91]
but can be painted, are present in the pattern of divine ideas.) Ficino
comments,

> Nor should it seem remarkable that man has the forms of the arts
> by divine means, since the imaginations of the arts are also not
> present in beasts. And if forms of this kind are made in the soul,
> therefore we must say that they are made in nature, since they
> are naturally implanted.[60]

The essential act of artistic creation is the envisioning of forms in the
artist's mind before they materialize in stone or on canvas. It is these
forms that are implanted in the mind by nature, and in this sense art *is*
nature. The execution of the artist's design varies according to his
talent and cannot be called nature.

Acciaiolus quotes Aristotle as saying that nature is superior to art:

> He says also that nature is superior to art, and this seems to be
> true since art is the imitator of nature, and that which imitates
> anything is less perfect than that which it imitates; hence art is
> called perfect when it is most closely assimilated to nature.[61]

Shakespeare's longest comparison between art and nature comes

in *The Winter's Tale* in the dialogue between Perdita and Polixenes at
the sheep shearing. Perdita offers her guests flowers: rosemary and
rue, which will remain fragrant through the winter. Of autumn
flowers she has none:

> *Per.* The fairest flowers o'th' season
> Are our carnations and streak'd gillyflowers,
> Which some call *Nature's bastards*. Of that kind
> Our rustic garden's barren; and I care not
> To get slips of them.
> *Pol.*   Wherefore, gentle maiden,
> Do you neglect them?
> *Per.*   For I have heard it said
> There is an *art* which in their piedness shares
> With *great creating Nature*.
> *Pol.*   Say there be;
> Yet Nature is made better by no mean
> But Nature makes that mean; so, over that art
> Which you say adds to Nature, is an art
> That Nature makes. You see, sweet maid, we marry
> A gentler *scion* to the *wildest stock*,
> And make conceive a bark of baser kind
> By bud of nobler race. This is an art
> Which does mend Nature, change it rather, but
> The art itself is Nature.
> *Per.*   So it is.
> *Pol.* Then make your garden rich in gillyflowers,
> And do not call them *bastards*.
> *Per.*   I'll not put
> The dibble in earth to set one slip of them;
> No more than were I painted I would wish
> This youth to say 'twere well, and only therefore
> Desire to breed by me. (IV.iv.81–103)

Today Perdita would doubtless be a doughty champion of
organic gardening. She detests anything artificial, including in this
category hybridized flowers. Polixenes defends this part of flower
culture and adds the grafting and budding of fruit trees as another
example. These are not artificial in the sense that a statue or a

painting is. The "art" of changing flowers and trees utilizes the natural powers of the plants and guides them rather than opposes them. Hence the "art" is itself a "natural" operation. The crossbreeding of plants often takes place in nature without human intervention. When the human "art" is exercised, it is really a part of nature.

Perdita accepts the argument but retains her prejudice against gillyflowers. They are bred to have showy exteriors. It is as though Florizel should love her only for her painted face—whether painted on her skin or on canvas is not clear. It would be love artificially excited, not a natural affection for one's whole personality. She does not wish her lover to love only outward appearance, as Pygmalion fell in love with his statue.[62]

Polixenes's use of grafting and budding fruit trees as an art that is really nature seems indebted to Lucretius's account of various human *arts,* such as skill in weaving:

> But *nature* herself, *creatress* of things, was first a pattern for sowing and was the beginning of *grafting,* since berries and acorns fallen from the trees in due time put forth swarms of shoots beneath; from *nature,* too, they learned *to insert scions into branches,* and to plant young saplings in the ground over the fields.[63]

Lucretius's phrase "natura creatrix," which he also uses elsewhere,[64] may have suggested "great creating Nature" in connection with the process of grafting fruit trees.

In the beginning of his Second Georgic, on the cultivation of trees, Virgil describes and advocates the process of grafting (lines 32–34). He urges the farmer to "soften *wild fruits* by cultivation" (line 36). He then explains how natural sprouts from the roots can be used.

> Those shoots which spring up spontaneously into the shores of light are indeed unfruitful, but they rise strong and vigorous, for *nature* is strong in the soil. Also, if one *inserts scions* into these or transplants them into prepared trenches, they will put off their savage character and, by frequent cultivation, will follow willingly whatever *arts* you may call them to. (lines 47–52)

These lines state Polixenes's view of the "art of nature" by which a "gentler scion" is married to the "wildest stock" in order to improve the quantity and quality of the fruit produced.

Ficino uses a similar figure when he distinguishes between the art of a painter or sculptor, who deals with lifeless materials, and that of a farmer or a physician, who deals with living plants or bodies. In the second case the art is really nature, for nature often produces grain or heals a sick body without any outside aid. The practitioner of agriculture or medicine should be called "excitator naturae et minister" (a stimulator and a minister of nature); for the art involved is really that of nature.[65]

George Puttenham borrows Ficino's two instances—but without pronouncing that the "art" is really "nature"—in the final chapter of his *Arte of English Poesie* (1589):

In some cases we say arte is an ayde and coadiutor to nature, and a furtherer of her actions to good effect, or peraduenture a meane to supply her wants, by renforcing the causes wherein shee is impotent and defectiue [for example, a physician aids the natural processes of the body to restore health, and a gardener fertilizes, waters, and weeds his plants.] In another respect arte is not only an aide and coadiutor to nature in all her actions, but an alterer of them, and in some sort a surmounter of her skill, so as by meanes of it her owne effects shall appeare more beautifull or straunge and miraculous, as in both cases before remembred. The Phisition by the cordials hee will geue his patient, shall be able not onely to restore the decayed spirites of man, and render him health, but also to prolong the terme of his life many yeares ouer and aboue the stint of his first and naturall constitution. And the Gardiner by his arte will not onely make an herbe, or flowr, or fruite, come forth in his season without impediment, but also will embellish the same in vertue, shape, odour, and taste, that nature of her selfe woulde neuer haue done: as to make single *gillifloure,* or marigold, or daisie, double: and the white rose, redde, yellow, or carnation, a bitter mellon sweete, a sweete apple, soure, a plumme or cherrie without a stone, a peare without core or kernell, a goord or coucumber like to a horne, or any other figure he will: any of which things nature could not doe without mans help and arte.[66]

Sometimes, writes Puttenham, art is neither an aider nor surmounter but a bare imitator of nature.[67] His specific reference to the hybridizing of gilliflowers marks this passage as a likely source for the scene in *The Winter's Tale*.[68]

Ficino's and Puttenham's use of the farmer whose art is really nature is analogous to the hybridizer and grafter of flowers and plants. Shakespeare also uses their other instance of the physician guiding nature to cure bodily disease. In *All's Well*, the king states that his physicians have decided "that labouring *art* can never ransom *nature* From her inaidable estate" (II.i.121-122), that he cannot be cured. But Helena thinks "my *art* is not past power nor you past cure" (line 161), yet the cure will be heaven's action working through her art as its instrument. She uses Ficino's word *minister* to describe her own part in the cure:

> He that of greatest works is finisher
> Oft does them by the weakest *minister*. (lines 139-140)

The cure is successful.

In Montaigne's essay, "Of the Caniballes," there occurs a passage that is generally acknowledged as a principal source of Gonzalo's utopian vision of a "natural" condition of society (*Tempest*, II.i.143-168).[69] A few lines before this passage in Montaigne, he describes the "natural" primitive society and the "artificial" civilized society by an analogy to fruit trees, on which subject he disagrees with Lucretius and Virgil. He writes,

> They [the cannibals] are even savage, as we call those *fruits wilde*, which *nature* of herselfe, and of her ordinarie progresse hath produced: whereas indeed they are those which our selves have altered by our artificiall devices, and diverted from their common order, we should rather terme savage. In those are the true and most profitable vertues, and naturall properties most lively and vigorous, which in these we have *bastardized*, applying them to the pleasure of our corrupted taste. And if notwithstanding, in divers fruits of those countries that were never tilled, we shall finde, that in respect of ours they are most excellent, and as delicate unto our taste; there is no reason, *art*

should gaine the point of honour of our *great* and puissant mother *Nature*. We have so much by our inventions surcharged the beauties and riches of her workes, that we have altogether overchoaked her: yet, where ever her puritie shineth, she makes our vaine and frivolous enterprises wonderfully ashamed.[70]

Here the emphasis upon grafting fruit trees as a "bastardizing" of nature's fruits provides a striking resemblance to the similar discussion in *The Winter's Tale*.[71] *"Our great. . . mother Nature"* provides a verbal parallel to *"great* creating *Nature,"* with Lucretius's "natura creatrix."

Another form of art is the interpretation of nature. In *Antony and Cleopatra* Charmian and Iras wish the soothsayer to read their palms and tell their fortunes. When asked if he is the man that "knows things," he replies,

> In *nature's* infinite *book of secrecy*
> A little I can read. (I.ii.9–10)

Paracelsus, in the introduction to his book *Azoth*, sets himself the task of investigating the *arcana* or "secrets" of natural things. Man himself is a "book" in which these secrets can be studied, since he is a microcosm or model of the great world.[72] La Primaudaye uses the image repeatedly. In the "Forespeach" to part II of *The French Academie* (1594), he writes that the Bible presents "this whole visible world as a *great booke of Nature*. . . . So I thinke that euen now we haue an other good occasion to reade in this *great booke of nature* (page 333); the "booke of nature" is repeated on page 337. In the "Forespeach" to part III (1603), he writes that "the world is a shadow of the brightnesse of God, and like a *great booke of Nature* and naturall Theologie" (page 635). He adds that in part II he had studied the microcosm, or little world of man; in part III he proposes to study the macrocosm, or great world (page 636). The soothsayer's phrase is probably traceable to such images as these.

As shown by the illustrations in this section, Shakespeare had an active interest in discussions of art and nature, their relative merits, their relation to each other, and their significance in the upward struggle of the human race.

MUSIC OF MEN'S LIVES

5. *The Music of Men's Lives*

Music is another of the arts that both aids and signalizes man's advance from a primitive state into the creative life of thought. It is at once apparent to any reader of Shakespeare that he makes extensive use of music in his plays. His original songs in the comedies, his use of old folksongs in *Hamlet* and *Othello,* his frequent references to musical instruments, the calls for instrumental and vocal music by his characters—all these attest to his interest in music.[73]

Equally effective are his figurative uses of music. When Hamlet urges Guildenstern to play the recorder, then compares playing the recorder to "playing upon" Hamlet himself, he gives a typical example of this figurative usage (III.ii.360–388). Another such usage occurs in *Richard II* as Mowbray prepares to go into banishment to France:

> The language I have learn'd these forty years,
> My native English, now I must forgo;
> And now my tongue's use is to me no more
> Than an unstringed viol or a harp,
> Or like a cunning instrument cas'd up,
> Or, being open, put into his hands
> That knows no touch to tune the harmony. (I.iii.159–165)

The last two lines are suggestive of Hamlet's words to Guildenstern.

In *Henry VIII* Sandys contrasts his rural "plain-song" with the artificial French melodies, by which he means to contrast his own "honest" manners with the alleged trickery of French gallants at court (I.iii.41–47). When Pericles detects through the riddle the secret incest of King Antiochus with his beautiful daughter, he says to the daughter:

> You are a fair viol, and your sense the strings;
> Who, finger'd to make man his lawful music,
> Would draw heaven down and all the gods to hearken;
> But being play'd upon before your time,
> Hell only danceth at so harsh a chime. (I.i.81–85)

These analogies reach a climax in Richard II's soliloquy in prison at Pomfret Castle, as he meditates upon his former follies:

> Music do I hear?
> Ha, ha! keep time! How sour sweet music is,
> When time is broke and no proportion kept!
> So is it in *the music of men's lives.*
> And here have I the daintiness of ear
> To check time broke in a disord'red string;
> But for the *concord* of my state and time
> Had not an ear to hear my true time broke. (V.v.41–48)

Concord is an ambivalent word, meaning a musical harmony and also peaceful agreement within a state. Richard's inattention has caused the welfare of himself and his kingdom to go awry. His comparison of man's life to a musical harmony is ultimately derived from Plato's *Republic* (Books IV [443] and IX [591]).

Lovers are particularly susceptible to music, which often fits their mood of agitation or of reflective melancholy. The voice of the beloved sounds musical to the lover. In lamenting Hamlet's apparent madness, Ophelia says,

> And I, of ladies most deject and wretched,
> That suck'd the honey of *his music vows,*
> Now see that noble and most sovereign reason,
> Like *sweet bells jangled, out of tune* and harsh. (III.i.163–166)

Henry V, after proposing marriage to Princess Katharine, says, "Come, your answer in *broken music*; for *thy voice is music* and thy English broken" (V.ii.263). And Othello, who ordinarily dislikes music (III.i.17), yet says of Desdemona, "O she will sing the savageness out of a bear" (IV.i.200).

The special relationship of music to love is expressed by Orsino in the first line of *Twelfth Night*: "If music be the *food of love,* play on." In *Antony and Cleopatra* Cleopatra calls, "Give me some music; *music,* moody *food* Of us that trade in *love* (II.v.1–2).

Lucretius uses *pabula amoris* (foods of love) in a general reference to all those things that excite the passion of love, but with no mention of music.[74] The substance of the phrase, though not the wording, may stem from Plato's *Republic* (III [403]), "The end of music is the love of beauty," translated by Ficino as "Oportet enim musicam in amatoria pulchri finiri."[75] This could be construed as "For it is proper that music be ended [find its objective] in the passionate love of a beautiful one," since *amatoria* applies specifically to sexual love. But I suspect that there is some intermediate source for the "food of love" that has not yet been detected.[76]

A conception that appealed powerfully to Shakespeare was the music of the spheres, the sounds the courses of the planets supposedly make by their friction against each other. Plato in the Vision of Er[77] added to this a siren singing in each star; in Christian mythography the sirens became angels. The Lord had described to Job the creation of the earth "when the morning stars sang together, and all the sons of God shouted for joy" (Job 38:7). The sons of God were angels, since humanity was not yet created.

Aristotle did not believe that there was any music of the spheres.[78] Palingenius, in *The Zodiake of Life*, supports Aristotle's view, since sound is made by a percussion of the air and there is no air among the stars, which are in a region of fire.[79] The Platonic view was popularized by Cicero's *Somnium Scipionis* (chapter V) and Macrobius's *Commentarium* (II.i.–iv). These seem to have provided material for Lorenzo's speech on music in *The Merchant of Venice:*

> Lor. Sit, Jessica. Look how the floor of heaven
> Is thick inlaid with patines of bright gold.
> There's not the smallest orb which thou behold'st
> But in his motion like an angel sings,
> Still quiring to the young-ey'd cherubins.
> Such harmony is in immortal souls;
> But whilst this muddy vesture of decay
> Doth grossly close it in, we cannot hear it. . . .
> Jes. I am never merry when I hear sweet music.
> Lor. The reason is, your spirits are attentive;
> For do but note a wild and wanton herd,
> Or race of youthful and unhandled colts,
> Fetching mad bounds, bellowing and neighing loud,
> Which is the hot condition of their blood,
> If they but hear perchance a trumpet sound,
> Or any air of music touch their ears,
> You shall perceive them make a mutual stand,
> Their savage eyes turn'd to a modest gaze
> By the sweet power of music; therefore the poet

203

Did feign that Orpheus drew trees, stones, and floods;
Since nought so stockish, hard, and full of rage,
But music for the time doth change his nature.
The man that hath no music in himself,
Nor is not mov'd with concord of sweet sounds,
Is fit for treasons, stratagems, and spoils.
The motions of his spirit are dull as night
And his affections dark as Erebus.
Let no such man be trusted. (V.i.58-88)

In Cicero's *Somnium Scipionis* Scipio the Younger, having ascended in a dream to the circle of fixed stars, asks his ancestor, Scipio Africanus, what is the great and sweet music that fills his ears. Africanus replies that it comes from the motion of the spheres but is too great to be heard by mortal men, just as the Catadupa [cataract] of the Nile so deafens the ears of men living nearby that they no longer hear it. Human ears cannot take it in, just as human eyes cannot gaze directly on the sun (chapter v).

This illustration of the cataract of the Nile is repeated by Macrobius,[80] by St. Ambrose,[81] by Palingenius,[82] and by Sir Philip Sidney in his *Apologie for Poetrie*.[83] These uses illustrate the continued popularity of Cicero's fanciful analogy.

Macrobius first explains why the revolving spheres must necessarily produce musical sounds as they turn against each other. The world-soul itself proceeds from a harmony of musical numbers. Plato's fable of the sirens means that in the motion of the spheres song is produced by heavenly spirits (*numinibus*). Most peoples, cultured or primitive, sing at funerals, believing that souls after leaving their bodies return to the source of sweet music, the sky:

For in this life every soul is captivated by musical sounds ... for into the body it brings the memory of music which it knew in the sky and is so taken with soothing melodies that no bosom may be so hard or rough as not to be held by affection for such harmony. Hence I judge the fables of Orpheus and Amphion— by one of whose songs the witless animals, by the other's songs the stones, were moved to draw near—to have taken their origin; because they first strongly drew the barbarous races, either without the culture of reason or like stones softened by no emotion, to a sense of pleasure from singing. . . . By musical law, therefore, all that lives is captivated because the celestial soul, which animates the universe, has taken its origin from music.[84]

Macrobius further explains that the human soul, receding from its origin in the sky, is surrounded by greater density in the sphere of earth, which impairs its perceptions and prevents it from hearing the sphere harmonies.[85]

For the generalized density of the earth's sphere, Shakespeare has substituted the fleshly body or "muddy vesture of decay";[86] when released from the body, the soul can once again hear the divine sphere harmonies, as was the case with Scipio in his dream.

Macrobius's use of Orpheus and Amphion in conjunction, one moving beasts and the other moving stones by the power of music, was probably drawn from Horace's *Ars Poetica* (lines 391–402), where they are given the same figurative meaning. Ovid tells their stories separately and attributes to Orpheus the power by his music to draw wild animals, trees, and stones to follow him.[87] Aquinas interprets the legend of Orpheus in his commentary on Aristotle's *De Anima*:

> It should be known that this Orpheus was one among the first philosophers who were, as it were, poet-theologians, speaking in verse of philosophy and of God. And there were as many as three of these: Samius [Pythagoras of Samos], Orpheus, and one other. And this Orpheus first led men into dwelling together and was a most beautiful harmonizer, in that he brought bestial and solitary men into a civilized society. And because of this it is said of him that he was the best musician, so much so that he made or might make stones to dance; that is, he was so beautiful a harmonizer that he softened stony men.[88]

This is Shakespeare's figurative usage, naming Orpheus alone and not Orpheus-Amphion in conjunction. He repeats the Orpheus theme in *Henry VIII* in the song that comforts Queen Katherine:

> Orpheus with his lute made trees
> And the mountain tops that freeze
> Bow themselves when he did sing.

To his music plants and flowers
Ever sprung as sun and showers
There had made a lasting spring.

Everything that heard him play,
Even the billows of the sea,
Hung their heads, and then lay by.
In sweet music is such art,
Killing care and grief of heart
Fall asleep, or hearing, die. (III.i.3–14)

In Lorenzo's speech the account of the cattle and colts who become quiet at the sound of music seems to proceed from Shakespeare's own observation.[89] Also, Lorenzo's description of the man insensitive to music as "fit for treasons, stratagems, and spoils" seems to be an addition of Shakespeare's own. In Julius Caesar's characterization of Cassius as a dangerous plotter (above, p. 127) is the detail, "he hears no music."

Montaigne may have provided some material for Shakespeare's lines on music. In his essay "Of Custome" he borrows Cicero's illustration of the inhabitants who become deaf to the sound of the cataract of the Nile:

We need not goe seeke what our neighbours report of the Cataracts of *Nile,* and what Philosophers deeme of the celestiall musicke, which is, that the bodies of it's circles, being solid smooth, and in their rowling motion, touching and rubbing one against another, must of necessitie produce a wonderfull harmonie: by the changes and entercaprings of which, the revolutions, motions, cadences, and carrols of the asters [stars] and planets are caused and transported. But that universally the hearing senses of these low worlds creatures, dizzied and lulled asleepe, as those of the Aegyptians are, by the continuation of that sound, how loud and great soever it be, cannot sensibly perceive or distinguish the same.[90]

Again Montaigne writes in "An Apologie of Raymond Sebond":

There is no heart so demisse, but the ratling sound of a drum, or the clang of a Trumpet, will rowze and inflame; nor mind so harsh and sterne, but the sweetnesse and harmony of musicke, will move and tickle.[91]

George Puttenham, in *The Arte of English Poesie,* uses the material cited from Macrobius and Aquinas:

The profession and vse of Poesie is most ancient from the beginning, and not, as manie erroniously suppose, after, but before any ciuil society was among men. For it is written, that Poesie was th'originall cause and occasion of their first assemblies, when before the people remained in the woods and mountains, vagrant and dispersed like the wild beasts, lawlesse and naked, or verie ill clad, and of all good and necessarie prouision for harbour or sustenance vtterly vnfurnished: so as they litle diffred for their maner of life, from the very brute beasts of the field. Whereupon it is fayned that *Amphion* and *Orpheus,* two Poets of the first ages, one of them, to wit *Amphion,* builded vp cities, and reared walles with the stones that came in heapes to the sound of his harpe, figuring thereby the mollifying of hard and stonie hearts by his sweet and eloquent perswasion. And *Orpheus* assembled the wilde beasts to come in heards to harken to his musicke, and by that meanes made them tame, implying thereby, how by his discreete and wholsome lesons vttered in harmonie and with melodious instruments, he brought the rude and sauage people to a more ciuill and orderly life.[92]

How many of these works were actual sources of Shakespeare's lines is difficult to say. Quite probably he had read most or all of them; and Lorenzo's speech may be a composite from several sources in Shakespeare's reading.

Shakespeare has several casual references to the music of the spheres. Pericles, realizing that his daughter Marina is still alive, is so transported with joy that he hears imaginary music: "the music of the spheres . . . most heavenly music" (V.i.231–234). In *A Midsummer Night's Dream* Oberon mentions a time when "certain stars shot madly from their spheres To hear the sea-maid's music" (II.i.153–154). This may be a complimentary reference to queen

207

Elizabeth;[93] the stars recognize her music as more beautiful than their own sphere harmonies. In *Twelfth Night* Olivia states that she would rather hear Cesario's (Viola's) voice proposing marriage "than music of the spheres" (III.i.121). In *Henry VIII* Queen Katherine, dying, meditates "on that celestial harmony I go to" (IV.ii.80). "Heavenly harmony" is twice used in compliment to a girl's singing voice (*Taming of the Shrew*, III.i.5; *Titus Andronicus*, II.iv.48).

In *As You Like It* the duke says of Jaques, who has attempted to sing a song,

> If he, compact of jars, grow musical,
> We shall have shortly discord in the spheres. (II.vii.5-6)

Jaques is basically a disharmonious man, while sphere music is a pattern of the harmonious man; if Jaques becomes musical, then the spheres must be the opposite, full of discord and "jars" instead of harmony.

Shakespeare repeatedly stresses the therapeutic usefulness of music to calm the mind, induce sleep, and restore the wits of those who verge on insanity. Christopher Sly, Henry IV, Mariana, Brutus, and Lear all receive solace from music. Figuratively, a well-ordered constitution of the body is a harmony, as La Primaudaye describes the four humours when they are in balance.[94] Both Censorinus and Polydore Vergil attribute to Herophilus the statement that the pulse of a person's veins beats with a musical rhythm.[95] When Hamlet's mother thinks that he suffers the ecstasy of madness, he replies,

> My pulse, as yours, doth temperately keep time
> And makes as healthful music. It is not madness
> That I have uttered. (III.iv.140-142)

The Venerable Bede also refers to the "musical" pulse of the veins in a significant context:

> For the world itself is said to be constituted of a certain harmony of sounds, and the sky itself to be revolved by a modulation of harmony. . . . Music refreshes disturbed souls, since it removes

headache and depression, dispels unclean spirits and depraved and languorous humours. Hence it is found useful to the welfare of body and soul. . . . Music itself also comforts reptiles, aquatic creatures, and flying creatures by its sweetness. But whatever we say—and the way we are moved by *pulses of the veins*—is proved to be harmony and is allied to utility.[96]

Here are repeated ideas already mentioned, together with the effect of music on the animal kingdom.

Finally, in *The French Academie* La Primaudaye uses musical harmony to express the accord of different ranks within a city, of the elements and qualities in "this vniuersal frame" of the physical world, of the several parts of the human body, and of the people and officials of a commonwealth.[97]

Shakespeare uses music as a figure for political harmony. In *Henry V* the duke of Exeter says,

> For government, though high and low and lower,
> Put into parts, doth keep in one consent,
> Congreeing in a full and natural close,
> Like music. (I.ii.180–183)

The archbishop of Canterbury takes up the theme with a lengthy account of the well-ordered society in a hive of honey bees. In *2 Henry VI*, at the quarrel of Gloucester and cardinal Beaufort, king Henry says,

> How irksome is this music to my heart!
> When such strings jar, what hope of harmony? (II.i.55–56)

When the chief men of the state cannot harmonize their views, the state itself is in danger from their differences.

At the end of *Cymbeline*, when peace is concluded to the satisfaction of both sides, the soothsayer says,

> The fingers of the powers above do tune
> The harmony of this peace. (V.v.466–467)

The harmony of heaven is at last reflected in the harmony of peace on earth for men.

6. Heirs of Eternity

The art of letters is yet another evidence of man's advance beyond the level of the beasts. In the opening scene of *Love's Labour's Lost*, the king of Navarre swears his three associates to a mutual pact to devote their whole time to study for three years, admitting no distracting influences. His motive is given in the first lines:

> Let fame, that all hunt after in their lives,
> Live regist'red upon our brazen tombs
> And then grace us in the disgrace of death;
> When, spite of cormorant, devouring Time,
> Th'endeavour of this present breath may buy
> That honour which shall bate his scythe's keen edge
> And make us *heirs of all eternity*. (I.i.1–7)

The purpose of this intensive study is to acquire knowledge (line 56), but the nature of the study is not specified, except that it is a study of books. Presumably their eternal fame will be achieved by writing their own books as a result of their studies or by imparting their acquired wisdom in some other way.

The defeat of death or time by extending one's fame and name beyond death is a familiar theme. In *Troilus and Cressida* Troilus objects to surrendering Helen to the Greeks:

> She is a theme of honour and renown,
> A spur to valiant and magnanimous deeds
> Whose present courage may beat down our foes,
> And *fame in time to come* canonize us. (II.ii.199–202)

In the sonnets Shakespeare proposes to immortalize his friend by his verse:

> But thy eternal summer shall not fade
> Nor lose possession of that fair thou ow'st;
> Nor shall Death brag thou wand'rest in his shade,
> When in eternal lines to time thou grow'st;

So long as men can breathe or eyes can see,
So long lives this, and this gives life to thee. (18)

Yet do thy worst, old Time. Despite thy wrong,
My love shall in my verse live ever young. (19)

The theme is repeated in sonnets 54, 55, 60, 63, 65, 81, 100, 101, and 107.

Troilus hopes for fame through military glory. Shakespeare's friend will be remembered for youthful beauty. In sonnet 146 the poet seems to echo the king's speech from *Love's Labour's Lost*. Addressing his own soul, he urges it to have less care for fine raiment and ornamentation of the body, which will fade so soon, and to cultivate the mind:

Buy terms divine in selling hours of dross:
Within be fed, without be rich no more.
So shalt thou feed on Death that feeds on men,
And Death once dead, there's no more dying then.

Immortality through the writing of verse is not an unusual theme; we find it stated at the end of Ovid's *Metamorphoses* and in Horace's *Carmina* (III.xxx). But immortality through *study* is less common. We find it illustrated, however, in Emblem 132 of Andreas Alciatus's *Emblemata*. The emblem is "Ex literarum studiis immortalitatem acquiri" (Immortality may be won by the study of letters). The picture shows Triton blowing his conch shell as a trumpet; he is encircled by a serpent that holds its tail in its mouth. The poem reads as follows:

Neptuni tubicen (cuius pars ultima cetum
  Aequoreum facies indicat esse Deum)
Serpentis medio Triton comprenditur orbe,
  Qui caudam incerto mordicus ore tenet.
Fama viros animo insignes, praeclaráque gesta
  Prosequitur, toto mandat & orbe legi.
(Neptune's trumpeter Triton—whose hinder part shows as a
sea-fish, whose face shows him to be a god—is enclosed in the
mid-circle of a serpent who with his teeth holds his tail in an

uncertain mouth. Fame attends upon men eminent in mind, and upon famous deeds, and commands that they be celebrated in the whole circle of the world.)[98]

Claudius Minos's commentary repeats from Macrobius's *Saturnalia* (I.viii) the explanation that images of Tritons with their horns were placed atop the temple of Saturn to show that from his age to the present history has been recorded and is as if vocal, whereas before then the great deeds of great men are mute, dark, and unknown:

Triton marinus Deus, Neptunique filius, & tubicen schemate serpentis circulo continetur, quod refertur quidem ad *perpetuam & numquam intermorituram doctorum virorum memoriam.* Tuba enim famae & commendationis nota est, ut quae ab omnibus exaudiatur. Serpens in se revolutus, *aeternitatem* designat, ut docet Orus Niliatus in ipso Hieroglyph. principio. (Triton, a sea-god, son and trumpeter of Neptune, is contained in the drawn circle of a serpent, which indeed refers to *the perpetual and never-dying memory of learned men.* For the trumpet is a sign of fame and praise, as that which may be heard by all peoples. The serpent revolved upon itself designates *eternity,* as Orus Niliatus teaches in the beginning of his *Hieroglyphica.*)[99]

The great popularity of Alciatus's *Emblemata* (Minos's notes were added in 1573 and were used thereafter) makes it likely that Shakespeare was familiar with this emblem. In the king's speech, "devouring Time" is the *Tempus edax rerum* of Ovid,[100] and time as an old man with his scythe is also found elsewhere.[101] But the elevation of students and scholars to *eternal* fame probably proceeded from Alciatus.

In the Variorum edition of Alciatus's *Emblemata* (1621), the editors repeat Minos's notes[102] but add a cautionary word. The true cause of fame and glory is not study but the virtue that may be developed by study; ignominy is the reward of vice. "Sola virtus in Aeternitatis templo trophaea figit" (Only Virtue fixes her trophies in the temple of Eternity).[103]

Macrobius had already made a comment similar to that of Minos on "dark ages" of the past for which no written records survive.

Who would not judge the world to have begun quite recently, he asks, since our records go back only about two thousand years (he was writing about A.D. 400).[104] Since Minos quotes the *Saturnalia*, he may also have recalled this passage from the *Commentarium in Somnium Scipionis*:

> For if from the beginning of time, or before the beginning, as philosophers think, the world existed, why through the innumerable series of centuries was there not developed such a civilization as we now have? *Nor the use of letters, by which alone an eternity of memory is sustained?*[105]

He concluded that the world antedated historical time and that earlier civilizations did develop but were periodically destroyed by fire or flood; therefore present written records cannot extend back very far.

Some significance attaches to Macrobius's statement that "an eternity of memory" can be sustained only by the use of letters, the same sentiment later expressed by Alciatus and Minos. It is by the development of letters and the other arts that man can extend his memory on earth beyond the term of his mortal life and have an earthly as well as a heavenly immortality. It is the man of understanding whose fame will endure, unlike "the beasts that perish" (Psalm 49:20). As Horace comments on the *Iliad*, the epic of the Trojan War:

> Vixere fortes ante Agamenmona
> Multi: sed omnes illacrimabiles
> Urgentur, ignotiqui longa
> Nocte, carent quia vate sacro.
>
> (Many brave men lived before Agamemnon: but all of them, unlamented and unknown, are overwhelmed by a long night, because they lack a sacred bard [to recount their deeds].)[106]

And I may add the words of La Primaudaye:

> For wee see how our predecessours teach vs after their death by their bookes and writings and how by this meanes their words are not onely visible vnto us, but also as it were *immortal*.[107]

213

* * *

In considering the relationship of beasts to men, a modern reader inevitably thinks in terms of the theory of evolution. There is no evidence that Shakespeare thought in this way, though one critic has sought to identify Caliban as the "missing link" in Darwinian evolution.[108] For the Elizabethans men and beasts were akin only because God created them from similar patterns; men's "capability and godlike reason" were proof that they were not descended from bestial forms of life. But Shakespeare and his contemporaries did believe in a form of cultural evolution by which men had raised themselves from a savage to a civilized society through the exercise of their rational powers. It was this achievement that constituted the special glory of man.

VIII

The Conduct of Life

THE DIDACTIC ELEMENT in Shakespeare's works is not so much studied now as it was early in the century, when Richard G. Moulton wrote *The Moral System of Shakespeare* (1903). To some extent an element of moral instruction is present in all of Shakespeare's plays, particularly the tragedies. When Albany hears of Cornwall's death after the blinding of Gloucester, he exclaims,

> This shows you are above,
> You justicers, that these our nether crimes
> So speedily can venge! (*King Lear*, IV.ii.78–80)

He is passing a moral judgment: sinners must expect punishment from God. In *Hamlet* King Claudius makes the same point: the rich and powerful evildoers—"offence's gilded hand"—may evade punishment by earthly law, "but 'tis not so above" (III.iv.57–60).

Comments of this kind are quite numerous in the plays and all serve the purpose of moral instruction. In one instance the title of a play, *Measure for Measure*, is taken from the Sermon on the Mount (Matt. 7:2) and suggests a moral *exemplum*. Occasionally a long speech is a direct moral admonition: Katherine on the duty of wives to their husbands (*Taming of the Shrew*, V.ii.136–179), Portia to Shylock and Isabella to Angelo on the obligation to be merciful (*Merchant of Venice*, IV.i.184–205; *Measure for Measure*, II.ii.57–79), the duke-friar's speech on the ills of life to reconcile Claudio to approaching death (*Measure for Measure*, III.i.5–41), and

Polonius's advice to Laertes as the latter departs for France (*Hamlet*, I.iii.58–80). Sometimes a single phrase is used to recall a familiar biblical passage that imparts a moral lesson. Sometimes an ethical issue is debated at length, for example the argument between Hector and Troilus on the proposed return of Helen to her husband (*Troilus and Cressida*, II.ii).[1] Sometimes moral teaching is implicit in the action of a scene and not merely in the words of the characters. Shakespeare usually contrives to have his didactic teaching serve a dramatic purpose in the plot or the characterization and thus seem appropriate in its context.

1. Proverbial Wisdom

The coining of short, pithy phrases to express moral truth or practical wisdom seems to have been a favourite activity of the Elizabethans.[2] When Hamlet stops in the midst of agonizing suffering to write down a striking phrase that occurs to him, "that one may smile, and smile, and be a villain" (I.v.108),[3] he illustrates a fashion of Shakespeare's time. In *The Dark Lady of the Sonnets* Bernard Shaw humorously pictures Shakespeare himself as keeping a notebook of striking phrases. The fashion survives in such later works as Benjamin Franklin's *Poor Richard's Almanac* (1732), Martin Tupper's *Proverbial Philosophy* (1838–1867), and the "paragraphs" of modern newspapers.

Erasmus's *Adagiorum Chiliades*, in which he traces hundreds of proverbs to their sources, classifies proverbs according to the vices or virtues illustrated: Assiduitas, Garrulitas, Invidia, and so forth. The book seems to be designed for clergymen or others who may wish to ornament a moral discourse with a striking phrase. A selection of these proverbs was translated into English by Richard Taverner (1539). Perhaps better known to English schoolboys was the *Sententiae* of Publius Syrus, a collection of maxims made before the Christian era.[4] Nor should we forget Solomon's Book of Proverbs from the Bible. Shakespeare seems to have used all of these, besides the English collection by John Heywood (1562). When he borrows a proverb, he is likely to transform and amplify it or to restate it in other terms. A few examples will illustrate his method.

Polonius's first maxim to Laertes is

Give thy thoughts no tongue,
Nor any unproportion'd thought his act.

The second line seems to be Shakespeare's amplification and continuation of the proverbial thought expressed in the first line. The Oxford *Dictionary of English Proverbs* (1936) lists two similar examples, both used by John Heywood in a slightly different form:

A still tongue makes a wise head (p. 28).
Let not your tongue run at rover [random] (p. 231).

A few lines later Polonius says,

Give every man thine ear, but few thy voice;
Take each man's censure, but reserve thy judgment.

The Oxford *Proverbs* gives

It is better to play with the ears than the tongue (J. Davies, 1611)
(p. 231).
A word spoken is past recalling (Chaucer, Barclay) (p. 32).

These two have only a general resemblance to Polonius's words, but the second of them is echoed by Hamlet in an exchange with the king just before the performance of *The Murder of Gonzago*:

King: How fares our cousin Hamlet?
Ham. Excellent, i' faith—of the chameleon's dish. I eat the air, promise-cramm'd. You cannot feed capons so.
King. I have nothing with this answer, Hamlet; these words are not mine.
Ham. No, nor mine now. (III.ii.97–103)

Hamlet means that, according to the proverb, a word once spoken is no longer controlled by the one who speaks it (cf. Tilley's *Dictionary*, W776).
    Polonius further advises Laertes:

The friends thou hast, and their adoption *tried*,
Grapple them to thy soul with hooks of steel;

217

But do not dull thy palm with entertainment
,Of each new-hatch'd, unfledg'd comrade.

The Oxford *Proverbs* cites Lyly's *Euphues and His England:* "Friends are *tryed* before they are to be trusted" (p. 555). Publius Syrus writes, "Cave amicum credas, nisi quem provaberis" (Beware of one whom you may believe a friend, until you shall have tried him). Again from Syrus: "Si novos parabis amicos, veterum ne oblivisceris" (If you will make new friends, forget not the old friends).

In these speeches of Polonius, one cannot definitely name any single proverb as his source, yet they clearly reflect a background of proverb lore. Shakespeare does quote many proverbs verbatim; the Oxford *Proverbs* and Tilley's *Dictionary* conveniently list these after the other examples cited in each case. His transformations of proverbs are somewhat harder to detect.

Polonius's final admonition to Laertes is as follows:

To thine own self be true,
And it must follow, as the night the day,
Thou canst not then be false to any man.

The first line may have some affinities with *Nosce teipsum* (Know thyself), one of the most celebrated of all proverbs.[5] The Oxford *Proverbs* cites a most interesting quotation from Bacon's *Advancement of Learning* (1605), which has parallels with two separate speeches of Polonius:

There are few men so *true to themselves* and so settled, but that . . . they open themselves; specially if they be put to it with a counterdissimulation, according to the proverb of Spain, *Di mentira, y sacaras verdad; tell a lie and find a truth.* (page 412)

This second use of "truth to oneself" suggests that the phrase is proverbial (unless Bacon is copying Shakespeare). The Spanish proverb cited is expanded by Polonius in his scene with Reynaldo (II.i). In Paris Reynaldo is to tell small lies about Laertes in the hope of eliciting from his hearers true reports of Laertes's conduct: "Your bait of falsehood takes this carp of truth" (line 63). Shakespeare has developed a proverb into a masterpiece of characterization.

In *Measure for Measure,* when Isabella asks that Angelo "show some pity," he replies,

> I show it most of all when I show justice,
> For then I pity those I do not know,
> Whom a dismiss'd offence would after gall;
> And do him right that, answering one foul wrong,
> Lives not to act another. (II.ii.99–104)

This speech is apparently based on two "sentences" from Publius Syrus:

> Bonis nocet, quisquis pepercerit malis (Whoever has spared evil men injures good men).
> Injuriam ipse facias, ubi non vindices (You yourself may do an injury when you leave one unavenged).

This second statement may be echoed by Hamlet after his recital to Horatio of Claudius's offenses:

> Is't not perfect conscience,
> To quit him with this arm? And is't not to be damn'd
> To let this canker of our nature come
> In further evil? (V.ii.67–70)

In *Troilus and Cressida* Shakespeare has utilized another maxim of Publius Syrus:

> Laus nova nisi oritur, etiam vetus amittitur (Unless new praise is born, even the old praise is lost).

Here "praise" is used in the sense of prestige or reputation. When Achilles, who has withdrawn from the battle, is ignored by the Greek chiefs, who now flatter Ajax, he asks Ulysses what is the reason. Ulysses replies at great length, including these lines:

> The present eye praises the present object.
> Then marvel not, thou great and complete man,
> That all the Greeks begin to worship Ajax;
> Since things in motion sooner catch the eye

219

Than what not stirs. The cry went once on thee,
And still it might, and yet it may again,
If thou wouldst not entomb thyself alive
And case thy reputation in thy tent. (III.iii.180–187)

Here the Latin proverb is more like a text for Ulysses' "sermon"
than the verbal source of his lines.

In the succeeding speeches, when Achilles asks how his love for
Priam's daughter, Polyxena, had become known, Ulysses replies,

The providence that's in a watchful state
Knows almost every grain of Plutus' gold,
Finds bottom in th'uncomprehensive deeps,
Keeps place with thought and almost, like the gods,
Does thoughts unveil in their dumb cradles.
There is a mystery . . . in the soul of state;
Which hath an operation more divine
Than breath or pen can give expressure to. (III.iii.196–204)

This speech seems to have its origin in Richard Taverner's explanation of a proverb from Erasmus:

Multae regem aures, atque oculi. Kings haue many eares and
manye eyes, as who shulde saye, nothynge can be spoken,
nothynge doone so secretly againste kynges and rulers, but by
one meanes or other at lengthe it wyll come to theyr knowledge. (Oxford *Proverbs*, p. 252)

Ulysses is more than a match for Polonius in spinning out a proverb
to great length.

These few instances, which are hardly more than a sampling,
illustrate the manner in which Shakespeare adapted proverbs and
commonplaces for use in his plays.

2. Good Name

In *Othello* Iago speaks the following passage:

Good name in man and woman, dear my lord,
Is the immediate jewel of their souls.

220

Who steals my purse steals trash; 'tis something, nothing;
'Twas mine, 'tis his, and has been slave to thousands;
But he that filches from me my *good name*
Robs me of that which not enriches him,
And makes me poor indeed. (III.iii.155–161)

An early parallel to this speech is Proverbs 22:1, "A *good name* is
rather to be chosen than great riches." Publius Syrus writes, "Bona
opinio hominum tutior pecunia est" (the good opinion of men is
more worthwhile than money). The idea of robbery of one's good
name was introduced by La Primaudaye:

For seeing good fame and credite is more precious than any
treasure, a man hath no lesse iniurie offered him when his *good
name* is taken away, than when he is spoiled of his substance. . . .
[The envious man], *fearing their vertue whom he hateth from his
heart,* hee will seeme to welcome, to honour, and to admire
them, and yet vnder hand and behind their backes he will cast
abroad and sow his slanders.[6]

This passage contains not only the reference to "good name" but
also an excellent statement of Iago's attitude toward Cassio. It
involves more than mere jealousy that Cassio had obtained the
lieutenancy Iago coveted. Cassio must die because "if Cassio do
remain, He hath a daily beauty in his life That makes me ugly"
(V.i.18–20). Both Iago's hypocritical actions and his inner motiva-
tions are indicated in La Primaudaye's words (above, p. 136).

Where Iago's concern for his "good name" is hypocritical or at
least exaggerated, Othello's concern is geniune. Expecting to die, he
does not wish to be remembered as worse than he actually is. He is
"an honourable murderer, if you will, For nought I did in hate, but
all in honour" (V.ii.294–295). He further urges that his name not be
needlessly blackened:

When you shall these unlucky deeds relate,
Speak of me as I am; nothing extenuate,
Nor set down aught in malice. Then must you speak
Of one who lov'd not wisely but too well;
Of one not easily jealous, but, being wrought,
Perplex'd in the extreme. (V.ii.341–346)

221

Othello's fault was one of too easy suspicion and imperfect perception. His attitude toward wifely infidelity was that current in his
day. Thomas Heywood's play, *A Woman Killed with Kindness,* is an
ethical study of the question. John Frankford is tempted to kill his
unfaithful wife and her lover but pauses and thanks God for saving
him from the crime of murder. But his wife's brother, Sir Francis
Acton, who has himself attempted to seduce Susan Mountford, says
that his sister should have been killed for infidelity to her husband.[7]
His attitude reflects the "unwritten law" still current in some parts of
the world.

Hamlet, dying, is likewise concerned for his good name:

> O good Horatio, what a wounded *name,*
> Things standing thus unknown, shall live behind me.
>
> (V.ii.355–356)

He has just asked Horatio to "report me and my cause aright To the
unsatisfied" (lines 350–351). But Horatio, greatly moved, takes the
poisoned cup to follow his friend in death. Hamlet summons the
strength to wrench the cup from his hand and to repeat his request.
He is primarily interested in saving Horatio's life. Horatio can help
him more by living than by dying, he urges, for no other person alive
has even a clue to the reasons for what has happened. Horatio must
live "to tell my story" even if dying seems momentarily more
desirable. Thus what has seemed to some readers a selfish self-
concern in Hamlet is actually an instance of supreme unselfishness.

3. The Father as a God

In *A Midsummer Night's Dream* Theseus urges Hermia to obey her
father's wishes and to marry Demetrius:

> To you your *father* should be *as a god,*
> *One that compos'd your beauties,* yea, and one
> To whom you are but as a form in wax
> *By him imprinted,* and within his power
> To leave the figure or disfigure it. (I.i.47–51)

Aquinas states in his commentary on the *Nicomachean Ethics* that one's parents should be honoured as gods, for they have caused our very existence through generation.[8] In La Primaudaye's chapter "Of the dutie of Children towards their Parents," he asserts that children should obey their parents in all things:

> The *Father* is the true image of the great and soueraigne *God*, the vniuersal father of all things, as *Proclus* the Academike saide, Yea, *the childe holdeth his life of the father* next after God, & whatsoeuer else he hath in this world.[9]

Whether the fathers' godlike prerogatives include the right to select their children's mates is a favorite question with Shakespeare. Portia is determined to follow her father's prescribed method of selecting a husband; but Hermia, Silvia, Juliet, Jessica, Anne Page, Desdemona, Imogen, and Florizel refuse to accord their fathers the right of selection. Shakespeare's sympathies seem to be with the children who follow the dictates of their own hearts rather than the wishes of their fathers when selecting a partner in marriage.

4. Sermons in Stones

In *As You Like It* the banished duke in the Forest of Arden opens Act II with his speech on "the uses of adversity." This theme has been discussed already in my *Shakespeare's Derived Imagery* (chapter 13), but two passages in the speech require further explanation. In one, the duke says,

> And this our life, exempt from public haunt,
> Finds *tongues in trees, books in the running brooks,*
> *Sermons in stones,* and good in everything. (II.i.15–17)

In these lines the duke, with determined optimism, is finding compensations for the lack of his library. He must now draw his lessons from nature instead of from books, and the change may actually be beneficial to him.

Plato has a somewhat similar passage in *Phaedrus* (275). Socrates professes weariness with the artificial and complicated arguments in

223

THE CONDUCT OF LIFE

books of rhetoric and thinks that spoken wisdom may be simpler and better. The ancients heard prophetic words from an oak tree in the temple of Jove at Dodona and, unlike modern people, were content to hear wisdom from stones and trees, if only they spoke the truth. The resemblance to the duke's lines is greatly increased in Ficino's Latin translation:

> *Phaedrus.* Facile tu, o Socrates, Aegyptios, et alios cuiusvis gentis *sermones* facis.
> *Socrates.* At, o amice, qui in Iovis Dodonaei templo versantur, *ex quercu sermones* primos fatidicos erupisse asserunt. Priscis itaque illis, utpote qui non ita ut vos recentiores, sapientes erant, satis erat ob eorum inscitiam *petras et quercus audire*, modo vera promerent.
> (*Phaedrus.* O Socrates, you easily make up *sermons* about the Egyptians or any other peoples that you please.
> *Socrates.* But O friend, those who are situated in the temple of Jove at Dodona assert that the earliest prophetic *sermons* burst forth *from an oak-tree.* And so, to those ancient ones who were wise men—though not in the manner of you moderns—it was sufficient to their lack of knowledge *to hear stones and trees,* provided only that they set forth the truth.)[10]

Here Ficino's use of *sermones* to translate Plato's *logoi* (words) has determined the character of Shakespeare's lines. The "sermons" that had burst forth as speech from an oak tree and the implied meaning that "sermons" were heard from stones as well as trees account sufficiently for "tongues in trees" and "sermons in stones."

Socrates continues his argument that for effective teaching spoken language is superior to a written book. He draws an analogy to a farmer who will sow his seeds carefully in earth and await their maturity rather than seek a quick blossoming by sowing them in "gardens of Adonis" (forcing-pots). So it is with the wise man who wishes to "sow" his thoughts or "sermons" in the minds of others:

> Non igitur *in aqua nigra* studiose ipsa calamo cum *sermonibus* seminabit, cum succurrere illis periclantibus nequeat, nequeat et ex ipsis veritatem sufficienter ostendere. (Accordingly, he will not carefully, by his pen, sow with *sermons in dark water,* since it

224

cannot aid in those hazards [of being misconstrued] and cannot sufficiently demonstrate the truth from [the sermons] themselves.)[11]

Socrates means that in drawing words from a book one cannot ask the author for clarification of doubtful points, while this is possible if the author is present and speaking. Ficino's "dark water" means ink, and "sowing with sermons in dark water" is the process of writing a book. The *sermones* connect this passage with the earlier one and provide a probable suggestion for "books in the running brooks."

In Ficino the three images are not quite parallel, since the *sermones* in stones and trees are a substitute for books, while the *sermones* in "dark water" are metaphorically the books themselves. Shakespeare has made them parallel, with the "running brooks" a substitute for books, to be enjoyed in the absence of printed books. All three images then illustrate the preferability of learning from nature instead of learning from books.

The prophetic stones and trees appear in Macbeth's apprehensions after seeing the ghost of Banquo:

> It will have blood, they say; blood will have blood.
> *Stones have been known to move and trees to speak*;
> Augures and understood relations have
> By maggot-pies and choughs and rooks brought forth
> The secret'st man of blood. (III.iv.122–126)

The oracles were often appealed to in deciding questions of guilt or innocence—as in Sophocles' *Oedipus Rex* and in Shakespeare's *The Winter's Tale*. Macbeth recalls the same image as the duke in *As You Like It* but recalls it in a different connection.

Erasmus, in his *Adagiorum Chiliades* (or *Adagia*), gives the proverb, "Ex quercubus ac saxis nati" (to be born from oak trees and stones). He derives this from Homer's *Odyssey* (XIX.163), where Penelope asks the beggar's lineage, "for thou was not born from the traditional oak-tree or stone." Erasmus translates this line as "Nam neque fatidica quercu natus es, neque saxo"; he employs *fatidica,* the same adjective that Ficino had used. He thinks that Homer may be referring to the traditional creation of the human race from stones thrown by Deucalion and Pyrrha,[12] and to the fact that primitive peoples sometimes lived in hollow trees. The proverb suggests obscure birth, rural uncouthness, and perhaps insensitiveness.[13]

This proverb provides background for two speeches in *Julius Caesar*. Reproaching the populace for forgetting Pompey so soon, Marullus calls them

> You *blocks*, you *stones*, you worse than senseless things,
> O you hard hearts, you cruel men of Rome. (I.i.40–41)

Antony, exciting their sympathy for Caesar, says,

> You are not *wood*, you are not *stones*, but men. (III.ii.147)

As men, they have human emotions and cannot maintain the insensitiveness of wood and stones.

Thus two passages that employ the same words and images may be derived from different sources and are used for different purposes.

5. The Penalty of Adam[14]

The second phrase from the duke's speech in *As You Like It* that needs explication occurs near the beginning in reference to the cold weather:

> Here feel we not the *penalty of Adam*,
> The seasons' difference, as the icy fang
> And churlish chiding of the winter's wind. . . . (II.i.5–7)

Theobald emended *not* to *but* in the first line, since the subsequent lines indicate that the duke did suffer from the cold and *not* seems to be a self-contradiction. The objection is sometimes met by punctuating the sentence as a rhetorical question. Or, alternatively, *feel* may not refer to physical sensation but to mental concern: "We do not *mind* the cold, though we feel it physically." Whichever reading is adopted, we still must explain Shakespeare's transformation of Genesis 3:19, where Adam's penalty is given as the need to work hard for his living: "In the sweat of thy face shalt thou eat bread." This penalty has been changed to "the seasons' difference," with

particular reference to the discomfort of cold weather. By what logic
has this change been made?

Not much of significance has been added to the extensive discussion the *Variorum* gives of this passage. Furness lists several references to the tradition that in Eden it was always spring. One or two
commentators recalled that in Ovid's *Metamorphoses* Jupiter introduced a change of seasons at the end of the golden age and suggested
a possible connection. But in the absence of any written authority or
source for this connection, it has remained somewhat tenuous.
Thomas Keightley sought for such a source but wrote, "It does not
appear that any author anterior to Milton made the change of seasons
a part of Adam's penalty."[15] And there the matter rests.

Yet there was such a source as Keightley sought, in a work that
was unquestionably known and used by Shakespeare. Arthur Golding's translation of Ovid's *Metamorphoses* (1567) has been shown to
be a source of Shakespeare's writing.[16] In his prefatory *Epistle,*
addressed to the earl of Leicester, Golding aligned himself with
those mythographers who saw classical mythology as an allegorical
setting forth of the biblical narrative. He believed, for example, that
the creation of man by Prometheus as described by Ovid was a
"fabling" representation of the creation of Adam by God (lines
421–454). He even identified Prometheus specifically as "theternall
woord of God" (line 453), that is, as the Logos or second person of
the Trinity. He then proceeded to identify Adam's life in paradise
with life in the golden age and Adam's expulsion from paradise with
man's loss of the golden age.[17] The punishments of bread-earning
toil and seasonal changes in temperature are combined as parts of
Adam's penalty:

> Moreover by the golden age what other thing is ment,
> Than Adams tyme in Paradyse, who beeing innocent
> Did lead a blist and happy lyfe untill that thurrough sin
> He fell from God? From which tyme foorth all sorrow did
>   begin.
> The earth accursèd for his sake, did never after more
> Yeeld foode without great toyle. *Both heate and cold did vexe him*
>   *sore.*
> Disease of body, care of mynd, with hunger, thirst and neede,
> Feare, hope, joy, greefe, and trouble, fell on him and on his
>   seede.
> And this is termd the silver age. (lines 469–477)

There is a certain logic to combining the change of seasons with the labour of tilling the ground because, according to Ovid, one was the cause of the other. In the perpetual spring of the golden age, fruits and grain ripened the year round without any effort by man. With the change of seasons, it became necessary to till the soil and to store food for use in the barren winter months (below, p. 230). Golding's translation of Ovid's lines makes clear this cause and effect.

> But when that into *Lymbo* once *Saturnus* being thrust,
> The rule and charge of all the worlde was under *Jove* unjust.
> And that the silver age came in more somewhat base than golde,
> More precious yet than freckled brasse, immediatly the olde
> And auncient Spring did *Jove* abridge and make thereof anon,
> Foure seasons: Winter, Sommer, Spring, and Autumne of and
> on.
> Then first of all began the ayre with fervent heate to swelt.
> Then Isycles hung roping downe: then for the colde was felt
> Men gan to shroud themselves in house: their houses were the
> thickes,
> And bushie queaches, hollow caves, or hardels made of stickes.
> Then first of all were furrowes drawne, and corne was cast in
> ground.
> The simple Oxe with sorie sighes, to heavie yoke was bound.[18]

The last two lines indicate the advent of soil tillage and its attendant labour.

In the light of Golding's words, Shakespeare's phrase becomes clear. Ovid and Moses were telling the same story; the golden age and paradise were the same. When their perpetual springtime gave way to a change of seasons as a consequence of Adam's sin, he suffered from the extremes of heat and cold and from the necessity of hard agricultural labour. Hence "the seasons' difference" was the immediate cause of his discomforts and might properly be indentified as "the penalty of Adam."

6. *The General Curse*

When a gentleman of Cordelia's court encounters King Lear in his madness, he remarks,

> Thou hast one daughter
> Who redeems nature from *the general curse*
> Which twain have brought her to. (IV.vi.209-211)

This speech involves a biblical parallel. The "twain" (Adam and Eve) brought upon all of nature the curse from which the "one" (Christ) shall redeem nature. The curse upon nature was pronounced by God in his words to Adam after the Fall:

> Cursed is the ground for thy sake; in sorrow shalt thou eat of it all the days of thy life. Thorns also and thistles shall it bring forth to thee; and thou shalt eat the herb of the field. In the sweat of thy face shalt thou eat bread, till thou return unto the ground; for out of it thou wast taken; for dust thou art, and unto dust thou shalt return. (Gen. 3:17-19)

Thus the penalty of Adam, which I have already discussed, involved a curse upon the ground itself and upon the plants that grow out of it. The first part of the penalty was the necessity of manual labour, but the second part was subjection to death, a cessation of earthly existence. It is this penalty from which Christ would redeem man by his own death and resurrection. St. Paul stresses this:

> For as in Adam all die, even so in Christ shall all be made alive.
> (1 Cor. 15:22)

> As by one man sin entered into the world, and death by sin; and so death passed upon all men. . . . Death reigned . . . even over them that had not sinned after the similitude of Adam's transgression, who is the figure of him that was to come.
> (Romans 5:12, 14)

The one to come is Christ, the "second Adam," of whom the first Adam is a figurative presentation as well as being an actual person.[19]

The extension of the curse to include animals as well as earth, plants, and men is found in a very interesting Greek work, *The Revelation of Moses,* included in the New Testament Apocrypha.[20] This gives an account of Adam and Eve after their departure from

229

paradise until their deaths. Within it Eve gives her children an account of what happened to her in the garden.

When Adam becomes ill, Eve and her son Seth journey to paradise (the garden of Eden) to ask for some oil from the tree of life in order to heal Adam and to prolong his life. On their way Seth is attacked and wounded by a wild beast. Eve reproaches the beast for attacking man, the image of God. The beast replies,

> O Eve, not against us thy upbraiding nor thy weeping, but against thyself, since the beginning of the wild beasts was from thee. How was thy mouth opened to eat of the tree about which God had commanded thee not to eat of it? For this reason also our nature has been changed.[21]

Recall at this point that upon the coming of Christ the wild beasts will become gentle again; "they shall not hurt nor destroy in all my holy mountain" (Isa. 11:9).

Eve's request for oil to heal Adam is denied, but she is told that he will not suffer death forever. She calls together her children beside Adam's bed to tell them the account of the happenings in the garden during their stay there. She expands the version given in Genesis. Of God's reproof to Adam, she says,

> .God says to Adam, Since thou hast disobeyed my commandment, and obeyed thy wife, cursed is the ground in thy labours. For whenever thou labourest it, and it will not give its strength, thorns and thistles shall it raise for thee; and in the sweat of thy face shalt thou eat thy bread. And thou shalt be in distresses of many kinds. Thou shalt weary thyself, and rest not; thou shalt be afflicted by bitterness, and shalt not taste of sweetness; thou shalt be *afflicted by heat, and oppressed by cold;* and thou shalt toil much, and not grow rich; and thou shalt make haste, and not attain thine end; and the wild beasts, of which thou wast lord, shall rise up against thee in rebellion.[22]

Here again we find the extremes of heat and cold listed as part of Adam's penalty (above, p. 227), suggesting that the interpretation of Ovid in terms of Genesis may go back to the earliest years of the Christian era.

230

The Revelation of Moses ends with the deaths of Adam and Eve and their burial, with Abel, in the soil of paradise. The Lord promises them eventual resurrection.

What would have happened to men and women if Adam and Eve had not sinned? Augustine would have us believe that they would live in paradise for a very long time and would then be translated to a higher sphere without undergoing the pangs of death.[23] Abelard thought that since God had commanded man to "replenish the earth" (Gen. 1:28), his descendants would have gone out into different parts of the earth, but they would have found the ground "pleasant"—fertile, easily tillable, without thorns and thistles—since it would have received no curse from God.[24] Shakespeare's phrase "the general curse" serves the purpose of moral instruction by recalling the fall of man and his promised redemption through Christ.

7. A Wheel of Fire and Fortune

When King Lear awakes from the slumber that follows his fit of madness and finds his daughter Cordelia bending over him, he fancies that they are both dead:

> You do me wrong to take me out of the grave.
> Thou art a soul in bliss; but I am bound
> Upon *a wheel of fire*, that mine own tears
> Do scald like molten lead. (IV.vii.45–48)

She is in heaven; he is in hell. Lear seems to be recalling Dives' anguished cry to Lazarus after their deaths, when Dives is in hell and Lazarus is "in Abraham's bosom" (Luke 16:22–26).

The use of the fiery wheel as a hellish or purgatorial punishment is discussed elsewhere (above, p. 56–57). But there is yet another use of the wheel that makes the image especially applicable to King Lear. Macrobius explains that the body is the prison of the soul and that the conception of hell among the ancients is really symbolic of the punishments visited upon human beings in this life:

> They say that those hang, bound to the spokes of wheels, who,

231

THE CONDUCT OF LIFE

foreseeing nothing by counsel, moderating nothing by reason, regulating nothing by virtues, and submitting themselves and all their actions to [the caprices of] fortune, are always whirled about by chances and fortuitous circumstances.[25]

The impulsive acts, lack of foresight, and carelessness of consequences are evident in Lear's banishment of Cordelia and Kent and in his refusal to take any advice. He thus makes himself subject to the caprices of fortune and realizes this in his cry, "I am even The natural fool of fortune" (IV.vi.194–195). Macrobius had used the wheel of Ixion in Hades, a fiery wheel, as emblematic of the wheel of fortune; and elements of both appear in the image as applied to King Lear. The earl of Kent likewise recognizes the turns of fortune after he is put into the stocks: "Fortune, good-night! Smile once more; turn thy wheel!" (II.ii.180).

Fortune's wheel appears again in *Henry V* when Pistol begs Fluellen's aid to save Bardolph's life:

> Bardolph, a soldier, firm and sound of heart,
> And of buxom valour, hath, by cruel fate
> And giddy Fortune's furious fickle wheel,
> That goddess blind,
> That stands upon the rolling restless stone. (III.vi.26–30)

Fluellen interrupts, repeats the same details to give the moral that fortune "is turning, and inconstant, and mutability, and variation," but angers Pistol by refusing to aid Bardolph.

In Emblem 56 of Alciatus's *Emblemata* the fall of Phaethon from the fiery chariot of the sun is pictured; the motto is "In Temerarios" (On Bold Ones). The poem concludes,

> Sic plerique rotis fortunae ad sidera Reges
> Evecti, ambitio quos iuvenilis agit;
> Post magnam humani generis clademque suamque,
> Cunctorum poenas denique dant scelerum.
> (So often Kings, whom youthful ambition urges, are raised to the stars by the turns of Fortune's wheel; and, after their great injuries to the human race, they finally submit to the punishment of all their crimes.)

232

Minos's gloss on *rotis fortunae* states that "the wheel of Fortune, at which she sits, is assigned to her because of her fickleness and inconstancy."[26]

A second portrayal of Fortune, showing her foot upon the rolling stone, is given in Emblem 98, "Ars naturam adiuvans" (Art assisting nature). She is shown with Hermes (or Mercury), who sits upon a cubical stone, which is stable, whereas the round stone beneath Fortune's foot is unstable. The poem reads,

> Ut sphaerae Fortuna, cubo sic insidet Hermes:
> Artibus hic variis, casibus illa praeest.
> Adversus vim Fortunae est ars facta: sed artis
> Cum Fortuna mala est, saepe requirit opem.
> Disce bonas artes igitur studiosa iuventus,
> Quae certae secum commoda sortis habent.

(As Fortune [stands] upon a sphere, so Hermes sits upon a cube: he rules over various arts, she over various chances. Against the power of Fortune art was made; but, when Fortune is bad, one often requires the aid of art. Therefore, studious youth, learn good arts which have with themselves advantages of a certain lot [in the lottery of life].)

Minos explains that the student who has a firm foundation of studies and of the liberal arts cannot be shaken by any stroke of Fortune.[27] Fortune is blind. She has one foot upon a round stone to signify her instability; the other foot is in the sea, since the fluctuation of the waves represents the ups and downs of Fortune. She is contrasted with Hermes, patron of useful arts, who sits solidly upon the cube-shaped stone.[28]

There seem to be two images of Fortune involved, one of Fortune sitting at a spinning wheel, the other of Fortune standing on a spherical stone; it would be difficult to combine the two images into one. The images were conventional, and Alciatus's *Emblemata* is a convenient channel through which Shakespeare may have known them.

8. *Lear and the Psalmist*[29]

In an earlier study of biblical influences in *Hamlet*,[30] I have shown that when Shakespeare used biblical phrases their context often

233

lingered in his memory. An interesting example of this is a biblical
echo in *Hamlet*, the context of which serves as a source for a passage
in *King Lear*.

In *Hamlet* (IV.ii.30–32) Hamlet says, "The king is a thing . . . of
nothing" (above, p. 160), echoing Psalms 144:4 as given in the Great
Bible (1539):

> *Man is lyke a thynge of nought*, his time passeth awaye like a
> shadowe.
> Bowe thy heauens, O Lord, and come downe, touche the
> mountaynes, & they shall smoke.
> Sende forth the lyghtnyng, and scater them, shute out thyne
> arowes, and consume them.
> Sende downe thyne hande from aboue, deliuer me, & take me
> out of ye great waters, *from ye hande of straunge chyldren*,
> Whose mouth talketh of vanitie, & their ryght hande is a ryght
> hande of wickednes. . . .
> Saue me, and delyuer me *from the hande of straunge chyldren*,
> whose mouth talketh of vanit[i]e, and their ryght hande is a
> ryght hande of inquit[i]e. (vv. 4–8, 11)

With this passage compare Lear's rage on the heath:

> Blow, winds, and crack your cheeks! rage! blow!
> You cataracts and hurricanoes, spout
> Till you have drench'd our steeples, drown'd the cocks!
> You sulphurous and thought-executing fires,
> Vaunt couriers of cleaving thunderbolts,
> Singe my white head! And thou, all-shaking thunder,
> Strike flat the thick rotundity of the world!
> Crack nature's moulds, all germens spill at once,
> That makes ingrateful man! . . .
> Rumble thy bellyful! Spit, fire! spout, rain!
> Nor rain, wind, thunder, fire, are my daughters.
> I tax not you, you elements, with unkindness;
> I never gave you kingdom, *call'd you children*,
> You owe me no subscription. Then let fall
> Your horrible pleasure. (III.ii.1–19)

The psalmist's wish that the heavens may fall, the mountains be consumed, and the lightnings smite mankind, together with the reference to the "great waters," is a general parallel to the floods, lightnings, and destruction of the world that Lear invokes because of his wicked children. The most obvious influence, however, results from the psalmist's use of the phrase "straunge chyldren." To Shakespeare and other Elizabethans the word *strange* frequently meant "estranged, unfriendly, unnaturally hostile"; and this usage seems the most logical in interpreting the biblical phrase. Even though the meaning of the original may have been "strangers," a reading given in some sixteenth-century versions of the Bible, the phrase "straunge chyldren" would seem more applicable to estranged and unnatural offspring than to foreign persecutors.

Accepting this as Shakespeare's probable interpretation, we find that the parallel gains in significance thereby. Both the psalmist and Lear seem to regard the ingratitude of children as an unnatural aberration from universal laws and to think of a vast convulsion in nature as the fitting accompaniment of such an aberration (above, p. 33) The conception of men's actions as manifestations of a titanic struggle between good and evil in both the moral and the physical worlds gives to the play much of its tremendous power and dignifies Lear as something more than a foolishly irate old man. The germ of this conception is found in the words of the psalmist.[31] Perhaps his invoking the lightnings and arrows of the Lord may further have suggested Gloucester's somber prophecy:

> But I shall see
> The *winged vengeance* overtake such *children*. (III.vi.65–66)

9. The Duel Scene in King Lear[32]

In the *Explicator* for December, 1944, the editors question Shakespeare's introduction of the duel between Edmund and Edgar in the final scene of *King Lear*. They feel that it breaks the continuity of interest by taking Lear and Cordelia from the stage and contributes only a melodramatic effectiveness that is hardly in keeping with the intensity of emotion in the balance of the scene. Several considerations refute or modify this view.

235

First, while the fates of Lear and Cordelia are the points of greatest interest, they are not the only points of interest. Shakespeare has developed throughout the play the parallel situations of the two families, Gloucester's and Lear's. The fates of Gloucester, Edgar, Edmund, Goneril, and Regan are all of interest, and all are precipitated or revealed by the duel. The reported death of Gloucester and the successive deaths of Regan, Goneril, and Edmund are a series of events to which the deaths of Cordelia and Lear are the terrible climax. But to reserve this climax for the end of the play, Lear and Cordelia must be off the stage while the fates of the other characters are being decided.

Second, since the fortunes of a royal family and the future of a kingdom are involved, it is necessary to consider the effects upon public opinion. Albany is satisfied as to Edmund's guilt and publicly declares him a traitor, but the personal disloyalty of seducing Albany's wife is not necessarily treason to the kingdom.[33] Furthermore, though Albany has shrewdly dismissed Regan's troops, there is a real question as to his authority; for both Goneril and Regan support Edmund, and Goneril later declares that the power of the law resides in herself. The necessity of settling these confusing points is obviated by Albany's simple appeal to the divinely judged trial by combat. Shakespeare had used the device before, in the incomplete duel between Mowbray and Bolingbroke in *Richard II,* an account drawn in part from Froissart's *Chronicles.*[34]

Third, the issue of the combat dramatically supports the belief that heavenly justice will eventually triumph over wrong. Albany had expressed this belief in speaking of Cornwall's death (IV.ii.79); both Edgar and Edmund recognize it in the outcome of the duel. Like Laertes in *Hamlet,* Edmund, upon receiving his death wound, perceives the evil of his acts and tries to do "some good" before he dies. Because he has waited too late, the deaths of Cordelia and Lear provide a final crowning agony of suffering. But this does not alter the main contention. The duel is not solely or even primarily a melodramatic device. It will determine publicly the guilt or innocence of all three criminals: Edmund, Goneril, and Regan. Throughout the play their evil conspiracy has triumphed; now their cause is submitted to an acknowledged test of heavenly justice, and they are overthrown. Only if we accept the belief that divine providence controls the outcome of such a combat can we appreciate the full significance of the duel scene in *King Lear.*

* * *

One might cite numerous other scenes in Shakespeare in which the action suggests a moral or religious significance. In *The Winter's Tale,* when Leontes' jealous obsession with his wife's guilt makes him impiously denounce the divine oracle, the news of his son's death brings him to his senses. This is reminiscent of the death of the first-born as one of the plagues of Egypt (Exod. 12:29). The downfall of Wolsey in *Henry VIII,* the poisoning of Laertes by his own sword in his attempt to murder Hamlet, and the swift reversal of Shylock's fortunes in the courtroom scene of *The Merchant of Venice* all carry moral implications for the proper conduct of life. Shakespeare was a teacher as well as a poet.

Afterword

PERHAPS THE BEST KNOWN of all allusions to Shakespeare is the cheerful man's visit to the theater in Milton's *L'Allegro:*

> Then to the well-trod stage anon,
> If Jonson's learned sock be on,
> Or sweetest Shakespeare, Fancy's child,
> Warble his native woodnotes wild. (lines 131–134)

Milton seems to be recalling a performance of *As You Like It.*

This sentimentalized description of Shakespeare leaves an impression of untutored and unlearned genius, as though the author were another Robert Bloomfield or John Clare. The impression is heightened by the implied contrast with Jonson's learning. Yet I doubt that Milton intended such an implication. To him fancy and learning were not mutually exclusive, and he may have considered *L'Allegro* an example of his own "native woodnotes." His reference to Jonson's "sock," the low shoe worn by actors in classical comedy, may refer to Jonson's care in following the dramatic unities in his comedies, as contrasted with Shakespeare's disregard of the unities in most of his plays. The comment suggests a lack of discipline rather than a lack of knowledge in Shakespeare's writing, an unwillingness to fit his work into a prescribed mould.

It is true that Shakespeare wears his knowledge lightly, like a garland of bay leaves instead of a ceremonial crown. But he had a good deal of learning and used it extensively in his plays. It is always subordinate to portrayals of character and action; but it is there in the background, all but invisible, providing a solid underpinning of fact for his exuberant fancy. He had not only a creative mind but also a well-stocked mind, for the worker needed materials on which to work. In his writing one finds to a remarkable degree a successful synthesis of learning with life.

While it is not necessary to regard Shakespeare as "a progeny of learning," to quote Mrs. Malaprop, we should consider him a well-read man with a keen interest in books as well as in people. In London the intellectual currents of his day swirled about him, for these were not at all confined to the halls of Oxford and Cambridge. His profession probably allowed him ample time for reading, for he did not act in many plays so far as we can tell and he wrote an average of two plays per year. This was not a high rate of production for the Elizabethan period, when even a careful workman like Ben Jonson could boast in his prologue to *Volpone* that he wrote the entire play in five weeks. We do not know how much time Shakespeare spent in supervising productions, whether much, little, or none; and we certainly cannot assume that he was too busy to do any serious reading.

The evidence as to what Shakespeare read is still incomplete, and we cannot be sure that every parallel herein quoted was his actual source. But we can be sure that many of his ideas and images had literary progenitors. Through whatever avenues these may have finally reached him, they have left an indelible stamp upon his thought and upon the content of his works.

Appendix

Text of Translated Passages

ACCIAIOLUS, *Donatus*

p. 82. Nam primo homo vigilat, postea accidit somnus, qui vigiliae quaedam privatio est et operationis. Ligantur enim sensus, unde somnus ligamen sensuum externorum appellari solet: soluto deinde somno iterum fit vigilia in ebrio quoque ascendunt vapores, et perturbant spiritum vitalem et cerebrum, et instrumentum quo utitur ratio: soluto autem vapore illo rursus spiritus incipit meare purus, et instrumentum idoneum reddere ad operationes exercendas.

p. 113. . . . cum amicus verus sit quasi alter ipse.

p. 126. . . . quia ira oritur ex ebullitione sanguinis circa cor.

p. 127. At temerarii et celeres qui sunt acuti et melancholici, maxime agunt incontinenter secundum eam incontinentiam quam appellant temeritatem, quia acuti propter velocitatem cholerae cito agunt. Illi vero melancholici celeriter agunt, quia habent vehementes imaginationes propter humorem atrum, et ducuntur vehementi phantasia potius quam ratione, ideo neutri rationem expectant.

p. 147. Plato dixit eas [potentias animae] distingui non solum ratione, sed etiam subiecto. Itaque aliam esse in corde, aliam in cerebro, aliam in hepate collocavit, id est rationem in cerebro, irascibilem in corde, concupiscibilem in hepate posuit, ut in Tusculanis refert etiam Cicero.

p. 195. Dicit etiam quod natura est praestantior arte et hoc videtur esse verum cum ars sit imitatrix naturae, et id quod imitatur aliquid, est imperfectius eo quod imitatur: unde ars dicitur perfecta quando maxime assimilatur naturae.

ALANUS DE INSULIS

p. 169-70. *Vermis,* proprie. Dicitur Christus, unde David: *Ego sum vermis et non homo.* Vermis de terra nascitur sine semine, sine strepitu; graditur, conculcatur, vilipenditur. Sic Christus natus est de Virgine sine virili semine, inter homines humiliter vixit . . . a Judaeis contemptus et conculcatus, occisus fuit. Dicitur peccatum, unde in Job: *Putredini dixi: Pater meus es, mater mea et soror mea vermibus;* propter hoc quod *dixi: Pater meus es,* insinuavit quod omnis homo ab origine vitiata descendit; unde et addit: *Mater mea et soror mea vermibus,* quia scilicet et ab ipsa putredine, et cum ipsa in hunc mundum venimus: quantum ad materiam quippe corruptibilis carnis mater mea et soror mea vermes sunt, quia de putredine processimus, et cum putredine venimus quam portamus. . . . Dicitur carnalis delectatio, unde in Job de luxurioso: *Dulcedo illius vermis,* quia is qui in desiderio carnalis corruptionis exaestuat, ad fetorem putredinis anhelat.

AQUINAS, *Thomas*

p. 90. Unde quando intellectus non dominatur, agunt animalia secundum phantasiam. Alia quidem, quia omnino non habent intellectum, sicut bestiae, alia vero quia habent intellectum velatum, sicut homines. Quod contingit "tripliciter." Quandoque quidem ex aliqua passione irae, aut concupiscentiae, vel timoris aut aliquid huiusmodi. Quandoque autem accidit ex aliqua infirmitate, sicut patet in phreneticis vel furiosis. Quandoque autem in somno, sicut accidit in dormientibus. Ex istis enim causis contingit quod intellectus non praevalet phantasiae, unde homo sequitur apprehensionem phantasticam quasi veram.

p. 93. Substantia spiritualis tametsi non possit a corpore compraehendi, potest tamen esse suum corpori communicare, et proper hoc uniri corpori ut forma.

p. 93. Dicendum quod exstasim pati aliquis dicitur, cum extra se ponitur. Quod quidem contingit et secundum vim apprehensivam, et secundum vim appetitivam. Secundum quidem vim apprehensivam aliquis dicitur extra se poni, quando ponitur extra cognitionem sibi propriam; vel quia ad superiorem sublimatur, sicut homo, dum elevatur ad comprehendenda aliqua quae sunt supra sensum et rationem, dicitur extasim pati, inquantum ponitur extra connaturalem apprehensionem rationis et sensus; vel quia ad inferiora deprimitur, puta cum aliquis in furiam vel amentiam cadit, dicitur extasim passus. Secundum appetitivam vero partem dicitur aliquis extasim pati, quando appetitus alicuius in alterum fertur, exiens quodammodo extra seipsum.

p. 99. Amicis autem et fratribus debet homo fiduciam et communicationem rerum.

p. 125. Ira videtur aliqualiter audire rationem, inquantum scilicet iratus quodammodo ratiocinatur quod propter injuriam sibi factam deberet inferre vindictam. Sed obaudit, idest imperfecte audit rationem, quia non curat attendere judicium rationis circa quantitatem et modum vindictae. . . .

Et ita est de ira: quod audit quidem in aliquo rationem: sed propter naturalem caliditatem et velocitatem cholerae commoventis ad iram, antequam audiat totum praeceptum rationis, movet ad puniendum.

p. 133. Et dicit, quod melancholici secundum naturalem dispositionem semper indigent medicina contra tristitias, quia corpus eorum patitur corrosionem quamdam propter siccitatem complexionis. Et ideo habent vehementem appetitum delectationis per quam huiusmodi tristitia repellatur. . . . Et quia melancholici vehementer appetunt delectationes, inde est quod frequenter fiunt intemperati et pravi.

p. 205. Sciendum est quod Orpheus iste fuit unus de primis philosophis qui erant quasi poetae theologi, loquentes metrice de philosophia et de Deo, et fuerunt tantum tres, Samius, Orpheus, et quidam alius. Et iste Orpheus primo induxit homines ad habitandum simul et fuit pulcherrimus concionator, ita quod homines bestiales et solitarios reduceret ad civilitatem. Et propter hoc dicitur de eo, quod fuit optimus cytharaedus, in tantum quod fecit vel faceret lapides saltare, id est, ita fuit pulcher concionator, quod homines lapideos emollivit.

BEDE, *The Venerable*

pp. 19-20. Elementa autem, quibus mundus constat, quilibet sibi locum capit, secundum sui naturam, ignis sui levitate supremum, terra gravitate infimum, huic aqua circumfunditur, his duobus aer. Supra firmamentum autem secundum divinos sunt supercoelestes aquae, supra quas sunt spirituales coeli, in quibus angelicae virtutes continentur. Terra vero una ita se mediam locavit, ut aequaliter undique a firmamento distet, praeter exstantias montium et subsidentias vallium, transitque per meditullium eius intellectualis linea de arctico polo ad antarcticum, quae et aeris circumfusione ita ligatur, ut nusquam deflectatur.

pp. 208-9. Etenim ipse mundus quadam harmonia sonorum dicitur esse constitutus, et ipsum coelum sub harmoniae revolvi modulatione. . . . Turbatos animos musica recreat, quoniam dolorem capitis et tristitiam tollit, immundos spiritus humoresque pravos et languores depellit. Unde et utilis ad salutem corporis et animae invenitur. . . . Ipsa quoque reptilia, necnon et aquatilia, verum et volatilia, sua dulcedine musica consolatur; sed et quidquid loquimur, et venarum pulsibus commovemur, harmonia probatur esse, utilibus sociatum.

BRUNO

p. 94. . . . per quem ecstasim et mentis excessum . . . in quem nullis aliis quam spiritualibus pedibus ascendere possumus.

CICERO

p. 95. Est enim vis et natura quaedam, quae cum observatis longo tempore significationibus, tum aliquo instinctu inflatuque divino futura praenuntiat. . . .

Age ea, quae quamquam ex alio genere sunt, tamen divinationi sunt
similiora, videamus:

atque etiam ventos praemonstrat saepe futuros
inflatum mare, cum subito penitusque tumescit.

pp. 154-55. Pertinere autem ad rem [Stoici] arbitrantur, intelligi natura
fieri ut liberi a parentibus amentur; a quo initio profectam communem
humani generis societatem persequimur. Quod primum intelligi debet figura
membrisque corporum, quae ipsa declarant, procreandi a natura habitam
esse rationem. Neque vero haec inter se congruere possent ut natura et
procreari vellet et diligi procreatos non curaret. Atque etiam in bestiis vis
naturae perspici potest; quarum in fetu et in educatione laborem cum
cernimus, naturae ipsius vocem videmur audire. Quare ut perspicuum est
natura nos a dolore abhorrere, sic apparet a natura ipsa ut eos quos
genuerimus amemus impelli. Ex hoc nascitur ut etiam communis hominum
inter homines naturalis sit commendatio, ut oporteat hominem ab homine ob
id ipsum quod homo sit non alienum videri.

FICINO, *Marsilio*

p. 23. Atque etiam prope ipsum mundi centrum per terrenos hiatus
flumina, ignis & aeris & aquae undique fluunt.
pp. 36-37. [Amor] semina in germen pullulare compellit, & vires cuiusque
eius educit sinu, foetusque concipit, et quasi clavibus quibusdam conceptus
aperiendo producit in lucem: quamobrem omnes mundi partes, quia unius
artificis opera sunt, eiusdem machinae membra inter se in essendo et vivendo
similia, mutua quadam charitate sibi invicem vinciuntur, ut merito dici possit
amor nodus perpetuus et copula mundi, partiumque et eius immobile
sustentaculum, ac firmum totius machinae fundamentum.
p. 39. Quinetiam anni temporum constitutio utrisque his plena est. Nam
quotiens illa quae modo dicebam, calida et frigida, sicca et humida, con-
gruum inter se sortiuntur amorem, et harmoniam temperiemque oppor-
tunam suscipiunt, salubrem et fertilem annum hominibus, animantibus
omnibus, atque plantis afferunt, neque quicquam laedunt. Contra vero cum
petulans et contumeliosus amor in anni temporibus praevalet, iniuria multa
corrumpit. Pestes siquidem ex his oriri consueverunt, aliique morbi permulti
et variis brutis ac plantis innasci. Quoniam pruina, glacies, grando, segetum-
que rubigines, et putredines ex immoderato et excedente qualitatum amore
proveniunt.
pp. 39-40. Ex illo aeris grata temperies, aquae tranquillitas, terrarum
fertilitas, animalium sanitas: ex hoc contraria proficiscuntur.
p. 87. Isti enim tui oculi per meos oculos ad intima delapsi praecordia,
acerrimum meis medullis commovent incendium.
p. 108. . . . quia per potentiam confusio regnat, & chaos, distinctio fit per
actum.

LATIN TEXT

p. 110. . . . pulchritudinem esse gratiam quandam vivacem et spiritalem, dei radio illustrante angelo primum infusam: inde et animis hominum, corporumque figuris, et vocibus: quae per rationem, visum, auditum, animos nostros movet atque delectat, delectando rapit, rapiendo ardenti inflammat amore.

pp. 112-13. Omnia ex deo ita sunt, ut nusquam vel minima quaeque deserantur a deo. Ubique enim divina viget unitas: per quam res quaeque consistunt: ac perpetuo quodam intimoque circulo ad deum ipsum a quo & in quo sunt mirabiliter revolvuntur, alioquin in nihilum repente proruerent. Ab unitate divina omnia prodeunt: prodeuntiaque unitatem quandam ipsis impressam retinent divinae unitatis imaginem: qua revocantur in illam, & revocata perficiuntur. Haec ipsa animas rapit ad vota, quibus unio cum deo nobis penitus imploratur. . . . Ad voti vero profectionem quinque praecipua pertinent. Primum quidem est notio quaedam eius quod adorandum est, & qua ratione colendum. Secundum vero assimulatio quaedam vitae nostrae ad divinam vitam, puritate, castitate, sanctimonia, disciplina, ordine proficiscens, divinamque captans benevolentiam, & animas divinae largitioni subjiciens. Tertium est contactus aliquis: per quem essentiam divinam ferme iam attingimus: & in ipsam summitate quadam animae vergimus. Quartum ingressio quaedam in luminis divini vestibulum. Quintum denique unio, unitatem animae propriam divinae unitati insinuans penitus & connectens: unamque iam actionem eandem animae deique conflans: adeo ut nec ultra nostri iuris, sed dei simus, splendore obruti & circumfusi divino. Huius autem adorationis quae absque intermissione agenda est, supremus est finis, ut videlicet conversionem animae cum ipsa permansione coniungat: & quicquid a divina unitate processit, rursus idem firmiter restituat unitati: lumenque nostrum superno lumine circumfundat. Sola igitur adoratio recta animas beatae reddit patriae. Sola sanctimonia est plena virtus. Solus vir bonus, ut Plato scribit in legibus, deum decenter feliciterque precatur. Sola cum superis consuetudo beatos facit.

p. 166. Virtus quidem Solis universalis hunc hominem, qui est particularis effectus, non produci nisi per hominem alium tanquam particularem causam atque propriam.

p. 195. Neque mirum videri debet hominem artium formas habere divinitus, quum imaginationes artium bestiis quoque non desint. Ac si eiusmodi formae in anima fiant, idcirco dicentur fieri in natura, quia naturaliter inserantur.

LUCRETIUS

p. 19. Principio magnus caeli si vortitur orbis,
ex utraque polum parti premere aera nobis
dicendum est extraque tenere et claudere utrimque.
p. 197. At specimen sationis et insitionis origo
ipsa fuit rerum primum natura creatrix,
arboribus quoniam bacae glandesque caducae

tempestiva dabant pullorum examina supter;
unde etiam libitumst stirpis committere ramis
et nova defodere in terram virgulta per agros.

MACROBIUS

p. 17. Physici mundum magnum hominem, et hominem brevem mundum esse dixerunt.

p. 21. In omni orbe vel sphaera medietas centron vocatur, nihilque aliud est centron nisi punctum, quo sphaerae aut orbis medium certissima observatione distinguitur. Item ducta linea de quocumque loco circuli, qui designat ambitum, in quamcumque eiusdem circuli summitatem orbis partem aliquam dividat necesse est. Sed non omni modo medietas est orbis, quam separat ista divisio, illa enim tantum linea in partes aequales orbem medium dividit, quae a summo in summum ita ducitur, ut necesse sit eam transire per centron, et haec linea quae orbem sic aequaliter dividit, diametros nuncupatur. . . . Terra autem in medio caelestis circuli, per quem sol currit, ut centron locata est, ergo mensura terrenae umbrae medietatem diametri caelestis efficiet, et si ab altera quoque parte terrae par usque ad eundem circulum mensura tendatur, integra circuli, per quem sol currit, diametros invenitur.

p. 21. Mundanae autem sphaerae terra centrum est.

p. 24. Sine fratris radiis luna non luceat.

p. 25. *Dux* ergo est, quia omnes luminis maiestate praecedit, *princeps*, quia ita eminet, ut propterea, quod talis solus appareat, sol vocetur, *moderator reliquorum* dicitur, quia ipse cursus eorum recursusque certa spatii definitione moderatur. Nam certa spatii definitio est, ad quam cum una quaeque erratica stella recedens a sole pervenerit, tamquam ultra prohibeatur accedere, agi retro videtur, et rursus, cum certam partem recedendo contigerit, ad directi cursus consueta revocatur. Ita solis vis et potestas motus reliquorum luminum constituta dimensione moderatur.

p. 28. Nec dubium est, quin ipsa [luna] sit mortalium corporum et auctor et conditrix adeo, ut non nulla corpora sub luminis eius accessu patiantur augmenta, et hac decrescente minuantur.

p. 28. Quia si quis diu sub luna somno se dederit, aegre excitatur, et proximus fit insano, pondere pressus humoris, qui in omne eius corpus, diffusus atque dispersus est, proprietate lunari: quae ut corpus infundat, omnes eius aperit et laxat meatus.

pp. 32-33. Cum vero stellas *globosas et rotundas* dicat, non singularium tantum exprimit speciem, sed et earum, quae in signa formanda conveniunt. Omnes enim stellae inter se, etsi in magnitudine aliquam, nullam tamen habent in specie differentiam. Per haec autem duo nomina solida sphaera describitur, quae nec ex globo, si rotunditas desit, nec ex rotunditate, si globus desit, efficitur, cum alterum forma, alterum soliditate corporis deseratur. Sphaeras autem hic dicimus ipsarum stellarum corpora, quae omnia hac specie formata sunt.

pp. 204-205. Nam ideo in hac vita omnis anima musicis sonis capitur. . . . quia anima in corpus defert memoriam musicae, cuius in caelo fuit conscia, et ita delinimentis canticis occupatur, ut nullum sit tam inmite tam asperum pectus, quod non oblectamentorum talium teneatur affectu. Hinc aestimo et Orphei vel Amphionis fabulam, quorum alter animalia ratione carentia, alter saxa quoque trahere cantibus ferebantur, sumpsisse principium, quia primi forte gentes vel sine rationis cultu barbaras vel saxi instar nullo affectu molles ad sensum voluptatis canendo traxerunt. . . . Iure igitur musica capitur omne, quod vivit, quia caelestis anima, qua animatur universitas, originem sumpsit ex musica.

p. 213. Si enim ab initio, immo ante initium fuit mundus, ut philosophi volunt, cur per innumerabilem seriem saeculorum non fuerat cultus, quo nunc utimur, inventus? Non litterarum usus, quo solo memoriae fulcitur aeternitas?

pp. 231-32. Illos [aiunt] radiis rotarum pendere districtos, qui nihil consilio praevidentes, nihil ratione moderantes, nihil virtutibus explicantes, seque et actus omnes suos fortunae permittentes, casibus et fortuitis semper rotantur.

MINOS, *Claudius* (Claude Mignaut)

p. 233. Fortunae rota, cui insidet, tributa est, propter varietatem et inconstantiam.

OVID

pp. 21-22. Orbe locus medio est inter terrasque fretumque
caelestesque plagas, triplicis confinia mundi,
unde quod est usquam, quamvis regionibus absit,
inspicitur, penetratque cavas vox omnis ad aures.
Fama tenet summamque domum sibi legit in arce
innumerosque aditus ac mille foramina tectis
addidit et nullis inclusit limina portis:
nocte dieque patet. tota est ex aere sonanti,
tota fremit vocesque refert iteratque, quod audit.
nulla quies intus nullaque silentia parte.
nec tamen est clamor, sed parvae murmura vocis,
qualia de pelagi, siquis procul audiat, undis
esse solent, qualemve sonum, cum Iuppiter atras
increpuit nubes, extrema tonitrua reddunt.
atria turba tenet: veniunt, leve vulgus, euntque
mixtaque cum veris passim commenta vagantur
milia rumorum confusaque verba volutant.
e quibus hi vacuas inplent sermonibus aures,

247

hi narrata ferunt alio, mensuraque ficti
crescit, et auditis aliquid novus adicit auctor.
illic Credulitas, illic temerarius Error
vanaque Laetitia est consternatique Timores
Seditioque repens dubioque auctore Susurri.
ipsa, quid in caelo rerum pelagoque geratur
et tellure, videt totumque inquirit in orbem.

PARACELSUS

p. 165. Quia putrefactio res magnas parit, sicut huius pulchrum exemplum
in sacro Evangelio habemus ubi Christus dicit: Nisi granum tritici in agrum
proiiciatur, & putrefiat, non potest centuplum fructum ferre. Ex hoc sciendum est, multas res in putrefactione multiplicari, ita ut nobilem fructum
pariant. Putrefactio enim est mutatio & mors omnium rerum, & destructio
primae essentiae omnium rerum naturalium, unde nobis prodit regeneratio
& nova generatio millies melior.

SCALIGER, *Julius Caesar*

p. 164. Habet enim cum omnibus animalium generationibus hominis
generatio aliquid commune: propterea quod imperfectum continetur a
perfecto potestate quadam. Nam si e semine fit ovum, ex ovo animal. Ergo in
eo semine, ex quo fit statim animal, ovi vis continetur. Si ex putrefactis lignis,
aut aliis corporibus fit animal: eodem modo fit e cibo mutato in semen. Et
quae vis particularis in genere certo est, ut simile procreet per formam
similem: eadem est in communi ambitu naturae potestatis, ut e fimo generet
murem similem ei muri, cuius species in eiusdem naturae mente est. Habet
omnia praesentia Deus, ipseque est omnia: nec plus operae ponit in animando
semine, ut homo fiat, quam fimum, ut murem faciat. Nam quis dedit homini
formam per quam forma similis contineretur in eius seminis potestate?
Deveniendum omnis enim ad unum principium est: quod est Deus: cuius
voluntas fortuna appellatur, potestas natura est.

SENECA

p. 80. Maximis minimisque corporibus par est dolor volneris.
p. 109. . . . sic haec immensa multitudo unius animae circumdata illius
spiritu regitur, illius ratione flectitur pressura se ac fractura viribus suis, nisi
consilio sustineretur. . . . Ille [imperator] est enim vinculum, per quod res
publica cohaeret, ille spiritus vitalis, quem haec tot milia trahunt, nihil ipsa
per se futura nisi onus et praeda, si mens illa imperii subtrahatur.

VIRGIL

p. 197. Sponte sua quae se tollunt in luminis oras,
Infecunda quidem, sed laeta et fortia surgunt:
Quippe solo natura subest. Tamen haec quoque si quis
Inserat, aut scrobibus mandet mutata subactis,
Exuerint silvestrem animum: cultuque frequenti,
In quascunque voces artes, haud tarda sequentur.

Notes

Chapter I: Introduction

1. Sidney, *Apologie for Poetrie,* in G. Gregory Smith, ed., *Elizabethan Critical Essays,* 2 vols. (Oxford: The Clarendon Press, 1904), Vol. I, p. 160. In all quotations, italics are mine except when used for proper names, titles of books, or when otherwise specified.

2. *Merchant of Venice,* V.i.64. References are to the complete plays and poems of Shakespeare in the edition by W. A. Neilson & C. J. Hill (Cambridge, Mass.: Houghton Mifflin, 1942).

3. Muir, in *Shakespeare Newsletter,* 14 (1964), 35.

4. Wilson, in *Shakespeare Survey,* 10 (1957), 12–26.

5. See also "Shakespeare's Reading," in W. A. Neilson & A. H. Thorndike, *The Facts about Shakespeare* (New York: Macmillan, 1913, reprint 1961), ch. iii; Selma Guttman, *The Foreign Sources of Shakespeare's Works* (New York: Columbia University Press, 1947). In Latin passages I print the letters *u* and *v* according to modern usage.

6. G. H. Plimpton, *The Education of Shakespeare* (London: Oxford University Press, 1933), p. 83.

7. Ben Jonson, *Works,* ed. William Gifford (London: George Routledge & Sons, 1869), pp. 77, 81–82, 803–806.

8. *Taming of the Shrew,* I.i.32; *Troilus and Cressida,* II.ii.166. For discussion, see my *Character of Hamlet & Other Essays* (Chapel Hill: University of North Carolina Press, 1941, reprint New York: Arno Press, 1970), p. 116, n. 5.

9. There were earlier editions of Acciaiolus, with Argyropoulos's translation of the *Nicomachean Ethics,* in 1535, 1559, 1560.

10. See T. W. Baldwin, *Shakspere's 'Small Latine and Lesse Greeke,'* 2 vols. (Urbana: University of Illinois Press, 1944), index entries.

11. Craig, *The Enchanted Glass* (New York: Oxford University Press, 1936).

12. Harmon in *PMLA*, 57 (1942), 988-1008; Hodgen in *Huntington Library Quarterly*, 16 (1952), 23-42. My references to Montaigne are to Florio's translation in the Modern Library Edition (New York, 1933).
13. Robertson, *Montaigne and Shakespeare* (London: The University Press, 1897); Taylor, *Shakespeare's Debt to Montaigne* (Oxford: Oxford University Press, 1925); Türck, *Shakespeare und Montaigne* (Berlin: Junker &Dünnhaupt, 1930); Henderson in *Shakespeare Association Bulletin*, 15 (1940), 40-54; Deutschbein in *Shakespeare Jahrbuch*, 81 (1946), 70-107; Prosser in *Shakespeare Studies*, 1 (1965), 261-264; Kermode in *The Tempest*, Arden Edition, pp. xxxv, 145-147; Brown in note to *Merchant of Venice*, V.i.60, Arden Edition.

Chapter II: The Universal World

1. A very useful background study for this chapter is a German article by Gisela Prym-von Becherer, "Der Makrokosmos im Weltbild der Shake-spearezeit," *Shakespeare Jahrbuch*, 82 (1948), 52-87. Cf. also Cumberland Clark, *Shakespeare and Science* (Birmingham: Cornish Bros., 1929).
2. Macrobius, *Commentarium in Somnium Scipionis*, II.xii.11, in *Opera*, ed. F. Eyssenhardt (Leipzig: B. G. Teubner, 1893). This edition also contains the *Saturnalia* of Macrobius.
3. Cf. Hankins, *Shakespeare's Derived Imagery* (Lawrence: University of Kansas Press, 1953, reprint New York: Octagon Books, 1967), pp. 32-34.
4. *Commentarium in Somnium Scipionis*, II.xi.12; *Saturnalia*, I.xviii.15.
5. Marcellus Palingenius Stellatus, *The Zodiake of Life* (London: R. Newberie, 1576, reprint New York: Scholar's Facsimiles & Reprints, 1947), p. 232.
6. *Shakespeare's Derived Imagery*, pp. 150-158.
7. Stephen Batman, *Batman vppon Bartholome his booke De Proprietatibus Rerum* (London: Thomas East, 1582), XI (Supp.), v; p. 166. Hereafter referred to as Batman.
8. Plutarch, *Moralia*, trans. Philemon Holland (London: A. Hatfield, 1603), p. 1023.
9. Robert Allott, *Wits Theater of the Little World* (London: James Roberts, 1599), ff. 5-6. Italics not mine. Dante gives a similar account in *Convito*, III.v.
10. Lucretius, *De Rerum Natura*, V.510-512, trans. Munro.
11. In *Patrologia Latina*, ed. J. P. Migne, 222 vols, (Paris: Garnier Frères, 1844-1903), XC.882 C. Bede's *Opera Omnia* appeared in 1573.
12. *Commentarium in Somnium Scipionis*, I.xx.14-15, 22.
13. *Ibid.*, I.xix.11.
14. *Ibid.*, I.xxii.4.
15. Ovid, *Metamorphoses*, XII.39-63.
16. *Commentarium in Somnium Scipionis*, I.xxii.9-10.

SHAKESPEARE'S THOUGHT

17. In favor of "slander" consider the "slanderous tongue" of *Measure for Measure*, III.ii.199. Richard Knowles, in *Shakespeare Studies*, 2 (1966), 134, reproduces a woodcut of Fama in a robe painted with tongues, from Vincenzo Cartari's *Imagines Deorum* (Latin version, 1589), p. 264.

18. Marsilio Ficino, *De Immortalitate Animorum* (or *Theologia Platonica*), VI.vi; p. 378 in Ficino's *Opera Omnia* (Basel: 1561). A second edition (Basel: Henricus Petrina, 1576) has identical paging with the first edition. Paging is continuous throughout the entire book, which is sometimes bound as two or more volumes. Ficino's *Opera Omnia* must not be confused with Plato's *Opera Omnia* in Ficino's translation. Ficino's Italian writings are not included in his *Opera Omnia*. In this book references to Ficino are quoted from the *Opera Omnia* except for his *Commentarium in Convivium (Symposium)* and his *Compendium in Timaeum*, which are quoted from Plato, *Opera Omnia*, trans. Ficino (Basel: Froben, 1551).

19. Vincent de Beauvais, *Speculum Naturale*, VI.vii, in *Bibliotheca Mundi Vincenti Burgundi*, 4 vols. (Douai: Baltazaria Belleri, 1624), I.374. This set also includes *Speculum Historiale*, later quoted. An earlier edition appeared in 1591.

20. *Commentarium in Somnium Scipionis*, I.xv.10–12.

21. *Ibid.*, I.xxi.30.

22. *Ibid.*, I.xxii.13, II.v.20–36.

23. *Ibid.*, I.xv.16.

24. *The Zodiake of Life*, p. 214.

25. *Commentarium in Somnium Scipionis*, I.xvii.10.

26. Cf. also accounts of eclipses by Bede, *Elementorum Philosophiae*, in *Patrologia Latina*, XC.1156 C; and by Pierre de la Primaudaye, *The French Academie* (London: T. Adams, 1618), pp. 721–722. Cf. ch. III, n. 19, below.

27. *The Zodiake of Life*, p. 40.

28. *Commentarium in Somnium Scipionis*, I.xx.4–5.

29. *Saturnalia*, I.xxi. 17.

30. *The Zodiake of Life*, p. 40.

31. *Georgica*, I.233–239.

32. *Commentarium in Somnium Scipionis*, II.vii.9.

33. *Ibid.*, I.vi.61.

34. *Saturnalia*, I.xvii.42.

35. *Commentarium in Somnium Scipionis*, I.xii.14.

36. *Ibid.*, I.xi.7.

37. *Saturnalia*, VII.xvi.26.

38. Batman, V.iii. But herbs gathered by moonlight have superior medicinal qualities (*Merchant of Venice*, V.i.13; *Hamlet*, IV.vii.145–146). For discussion see Reynolds and Sawyer in *Shakespeare Quarterly*, 10 (1959). 515–517.

39. *Saturnalia*, VII.xvi.17.

40. *Ibid.*, VII.xvi.21.

41. For advocates of "sullied," see J. Dover Wilson in the New Cambridge Shakespeare edition of *Hamlet*, and Fredson T. Bowers in *Shakespeare Survey*, 9 (1965). 44–48. For advocates of "solid," see G. L.

Kittredge's notes to *Hamlet* (Boston: Ginn & Co., 1939); Samuel A. Weiss in *Shakespeare Quarterly,* 10 (1959), 219–227; Malcolm Ware and Richard Flatter in *ibid.,* 11 (1960), 490–493; Sidney Warhoft in *English Literary History,* 28 (1961), 21–30.

42. *Saturnalia,* VII.xvi.31.

43. See James O. Wood in *Notes and Queries,* 11 (1964), 262–264. Wood seeks to identify the "vap'rous drop" with witches' broth as described in John Leslie's *De Origine Moribus et Rebus Gestis Scotorum* (Rome, 1578). He traces "profound" to Latin *perfundere.*

44. Douce, *Illustrations of Shakespeare and of Ancient Manners* (London, 1839, reprint New York: Burt Franklin, 1968), p. 17.

45. *The Zodiake of Life,* p. 158.

46. *Commentarium in Somnium Scipionis,* I.xvii.12.

47. *Ibid.,* I.xiv.1–2.

48. See *Shakespeare's Derived Imagery,* p. 225. Macrobius, in *Commentarium in Somnium Scipionis,* I.xii.6, attributes to Plato's *Timaeus* the description of the universe as a "fabric" of the world-soul, but without using the word *globe.*

49. A. C. Swinburne's *Garden of Proserpine,* final lines.

50. *Commentarium in Somnium Scipionis,* I.xii.5, 17.

51. *Ibid.,* I.x.9, xi.3. Cf. *Shakespeare's Derived Imagery,* pp. 147–149.

52. *Commentarium in Somnium Scipionis,* I.xiv.22–23.

53. *Ibid.,* I.xxii.6; Palingenius, *The Zodiake of Life,* pp. 111–112.

54. Kepler, *Prodromus Dissertationum Cosmographicarum Seu Mysterium Cosmographicum* (1596). Discussion by W. de Sitter, *Kosmos* (Cambridge, Mass.: Harvard University Press, 1932), pp. 21–22.

55. In the same speech Lear's references to "steeples" and "[weather] cocks" suggest that he has the earth in mind.

56. Lucretius, *De Rerum Natura,* I.59, 501.

57. *Ibid.,* I. 851–852.

58. *Ibid.,* II.550.

59. Ovid, *Metamorphoses,* I.9.

60. Virgil, *Bucolica,* VI.31–34.

61. Augustine, *De Genesi ad Litteram,* in *Patrologia Latina,* XXXIV. For extensive discussion, see Hankins, *Source and Meaning in Spenser's Allegory: "The Garden of Adonis,"* pp. 234–286.

62. Curry, "Tumbling Nature's Germens," in *Shakespeare's Philosophical Patterns* (Baton Rouge: Louisiana State University Press, 1937).

63. *De Genesi ad Litteram,* V.xxiii, in *Patrologia Latina,* XXXIV.337. Augustine's *Opera Omnia* appeared in 1531, 1541, 1543, 1577, 1586.

64. Ficino, *Commentarium in Plotinum,* Ennead IV, Bk. VIII, ch. vi, in Ficino's *Opera Omnia,* p. 1755.

65. Ficino, *Commentarium in Convivium,* III.iii; p. 382.

66. Cf. T. W. Baldwin, "Nature's Moulds," *Shakespeare Quarterly,* 3 (1952), 237–241.

67. *A Treatise of Melancholy* (London; J. Windet, 1586), ch. ix, p. 33. Cited by William R. Elton in *Modern Language Notes,* 65 (1950) 196–197.

68. Cf. Mary Lascelles in *Shakespeare Survey*, 26 (1973). 69-79.

69. For further discussion of chaos, see *Source and Meaning in Spenser's Allegory*, p. 67.

70. Montaigne derides man's tendency to see his own troubles as part of a commotion in "the world's vast frame." One may think that a violent local storm involves a whole hemisphere, but it is not so (*Essays*, I.xxv: "On the Education of Children," p. 120). Roy Walker, in *Shakespeare Survey*, 8 (1955), 112, quotes W. H. Clemen on Shakespeare's use of cosmic disturbances to reflect human disasters. Harold Skulsky, in *Shakespeare Quarterly*, 17 (1966), 3-17, discusses the figurative use of chaos in *Troilus and Cressida*.

71. Ficino, *Commentarium in Convivium*, I.iii; p. 374.

72. Plato, *Symposium (Convivium)*, 188, trans. Ficino; p. 1184 C in Plato's *Opera Omnia* (Frankfurt: "apud Claudium Marnium & haeredes Ioannis Aubrii," 1602).

73. Ficino, *Commentarium in Convivium*, III.iii; p. 382.

74. Macrobius, *Commentarium in Somnium Scipionis*, I.vi.24-28.

75. Ovid, *Metamorphoses*, I.19. Cf. Milton's account of chaos:
"For Hot, Cold, Moist, and Dry, four champions fierce,
Strive here for mastery, and to battle bring
Their embryon atoms." (*Paradise Lost*, II.898-900)

76. *Metamorphoses*, I.25.

77. Honorius, *De Imagine Mundi*, II.lviii, in *Patrologia Latina*, CLXXII. 154 C. An edition appeared in 1583.

78. Macrobius, *Saturnalia*, I.viii.8.

79. Cicero, *Tusculan Disputations*, I.xvii.41, xxvi. 65; *De Natura Deorum*, III.xiv.36.

80. Lucretius, *De Rerum Natura*, V.276.

81. Ficino, *Commentarium in Convivium*, VI.iii; p. 395.

82. Honorius, *De Imagine Mundi*, I.xvi-xviii, in *Patrologia Latina*, CLXXII.47.

83. *Ibid.*, I.liii; p. 136.

84. Aquinas, *De Substantiis Separatis*, ch. i, in *Opuscula Omnia*, one-volume edition (Paris: apud Gvillelmvm Pele, 1634), pp. 166-167. Many editions before 1600.

85. Paracelsus, *Libri Meteororum*, chs. iv and viii; pp. 300, 312 in *Opera Omnia* (Latin version, 2 vols., Geneva: I. A. & S. de Tournes, 1658), Vol. II. Earlier Latin editions were those of Basel, 1575, and Frankfurt, 1603.

86. Paracelsus, *De Elemento Aeris*, ch. v, in *ibid.*, p. 327. Vincent de Beauvais quotes Peter Lombard to the same effect (*Speculum Naturale*, IV.cxiv).

87. Paracelsus, *De Nymphis, Sylphis, Pygmaeis, et Salamandris, et de Caeteris Spiritibus*, in *op. cit.*, pp. 388-398.

88. Vincent, *Speculum Naturale*, II.iii.

89. Paracelsus, *De Philosophia Occulta: "De Tempestatibus,"* in *op. cit.*, p. 492.

90. Ficino, *Commentarium in Plotinum*, Ennead III: "De Fato" (Com. x), ch. vi; p. 1676 in Ficino's *Opera Omnia*.

91. Ficino, *Compendium in Timaeum:* Appendix, ch. xxiv, in *Opera Omnia,* p. 1469. This appendix is not included in Ficino's translation of Plato's works (Basel, 1551), from which all other references to the *Compendium in Timaeum* are cited.

92. Spenser's *Faerie Queene,* I.x.65; Nathan Drake, *Shakespeare and His Times,* 2 vols. (London: Cadell & Davies, 1817), Introduction and Vol. II, p. 325.

93. Curry, "Sacerdotal Science in *The Tempest,*" in *Shakespeare's Philosophical Patterns;* Frank Kermode in *The Tempest,* Arden Edition, Appendix B. C. J. Sisson, in *Shakespeare Survey,* 11 (1958), 70–77, compares Prospero's magic with that described in English court trials. R. H. West, in "Ariel and the Outer Mystery," concludes that Ariel does not fit any particular pneumatological pattern (E. A. Bloom, ed., *Shakespeare, 1564-1964* [Providence: Brown University Press, 1964]). See also Nelson S. Bushnell in *PMLA,* 47 (1932), 684–698; Rose Abdelnour Zimbardo in *Shakespeare Quarterly,* 14 (1963), 49–56; Harry Levin in *Shakespeare Survey,* 22 (1969), 47–58.

94. Drake, *op. cit.,* Vol. II, pp. 299–355; J. O. Halliwell, *An Introduction to Shakespeare's 'Midsummer Night's Dream'* (London: W. Pickering, 1841); Thomas Keightley, *The Fairy Mythology* (London: H. G. Bohn, 1850); T. F. Thiselton-Dyer, *The Folklore of Shakespeare* (London: Griffith & Farran, 1883, reprint New York: Dover Publications, 1966); Minor W. Latham, *The Elizabethan Fairies* (New York: Columbia University Press, 1930); Cumberland Clark, *Shakespeare and the Supernatural* (London: Williams & Norgate, 1931), pp. 47–62.

95. Cf. *The Character of Hamlet:* "On Ghosts," pp. 156–157.

96. Cf. Harry Berger, Jr., in *Shakespeare Studies,* 5 (1969), 255–257. Robert H. Reed, Jr., in *Shakespeare Quarterly,* 11 (1960), 61–65, finds Ariel a partial imitation of Anthony Munday's sprite Shrimp in *John a Kent and John a Cumber.*

97. Cf. Kathleen M. Briggs, *The Anatomy of Puck* (London: Routledge & Kegan Paul, 1959); Dorelies Kersten in *Shakespeare Jahrbuch,* 98 (1962), 189–200. Robert Weiman, in *ibid.,* 104 (1968), 17–33, distinguishes between Puck "the Kobold" and Ariel "the airy spirit."

98. First printed in *PMLA,* 71 (1956), 482–495.

99. August Rüegg, *Die Jenseitsvorstellungen vor Dante und die übrigen literarischen Voraussetzungen der "Divina Commedia,"* 2 vols. (Cologne: Benziger, 1945), the most complete study; Rudolf Palgen, *Das Mittelalterliche Gesicht der Göttlichen Komödie* (Heidelberg: Karl Winters, 1935); Alessandro d'Ancona, *I Precursori di Dante* (Florence: G.C. Sansoni, 1874); C. S. Boswell, *An Irish Precursor of Dante* (Vision of Adamnan, London: D. Nutt, 1908); Theodore Silverstein, "Dante and Vergil the Mystic," *Harvard Studies in Philology and Literature,* 14 (1932), 51–59 (on the four rivers of hell).

100. Useful discussions are: Thomas Wright, *Saint Patrick's Purgatory* (London: John Russell Smith, 1844); J. A. MacCulloch, *Early Christian Visions of the Other World* (Edinburgh, 1912); St. John Seymour, *Irish Visions*

of the Other World (New York: Macmillan, 1930); Howard R. Patch, *The Other World* (Cambridge, Mass.: Harvard University Press, 1950); J. J. L. Duyvendak, "A Chinese 'Divina Commedia,'" *T'oung Pao* (Leyden), 41 (1952), 255–316 (many useful references).

101. Vincent de Beauvais, *Speculum Historiale*, XXVII.1xxxviii-civ. For Middle English metrical version, see *The Visions of Tundale*, ed. W. B. D. D. Turnbull (Edinburgh: Thomas G. Stevenson, 1843).

102. *Visio Alberici*, ch. iii. Reprinted in *Miscellanea Cassinese* (Montecassino, 1932), and in French by J. H. Marchand, *L'Autre Monde au Moyen Age* (Paris: E. de Bocard, 1940), pp. 117–183. For a detailed comparison with the *Divina Commedia*, see Catello de Vivo, *La Visione di Alberico* (Ariano: Appulo-Irpino, 1899); also Ruegg, I.406–434. Alberic (ch. iii) says that he saw great heaps of ice, the cold from which burned the sufferers like fire. Cf. *Paradise Lost*, II.590–595.

103. Wright, p. 168; James Mew, *Traditional Aspects of Hell* (London: Swan, Sonnenschein, & Co., 1903, reprint Ann Arbor, Michigan: Gryphon Books, 1971), p. 260.

104. Wright, p. 147; Patch, p. 112.

105. Bede, *Ecclesiastical History*, Bk. V, ch. xii. In the Old English *Genesis B*, sinners remain in one place, but the climate varies from extreme heat during the day to extreme cold at night. For additional instances in Old English, see M. D. Clubb, ed., *Christ and Satan* (New Haven: Yale University Press, 1925, reprint Hamden, Connecticut: Archon Books, 1972).

106. *The Revelation of the Monk of Evesham*, Arber's reprint (London: Edward Arber, 1869), ch. xvii.

107. In Milton's hell, both the fiery continent and the frozen continent are volcanic regions: "O'er many a frozen, many a fiery Alp" (II.620). They both seem indebted to Olaus Magnus's account of Iceland in his *Epitome de Gentibus Septentrionalibus*, a copy of which Milton owned. See my article "Milton and Olaus Magnus" in *Studies in Honor of T. W. Baldwin*, ed. D. C. Allen (Urbana: University of Illinois Press, 1958). See also Saxo Grammaticus, *Danica Historia* (Frankfurt: "ad Moenum," 1576), Preface, p. 3.

108. Mew, pp. 97, 177, 185, 209; James Hastings, ed., *Encyclopedia of Religion and Ethics*, 13 vols. (New York: Scribner, 1908–1927): "Descent to Hades," "Eschatology," "State of the Dead."

109. For Milton's debt to Gregory the Great, see my original article in *PMLA*, 71 (1956), 482–495. I have omitted a portion of it here.

110. Gregory, *Dialogues*, IV.xxxix, in *Patrologia Latina*, LXXVII.393–396. J. A. MacCulloch writes that Gregory's comment is the first explicit statement of the doctrine of purgatory (*Medieval Faith and Fable* [Boston: Marshall Jones, 1932], p. 187).

111. Rüegg (I.305) states that Dryhthelm's vision (699) is the first to contain a clear distinction between hell and purgatory.

112. *Visio Alberici*, ch. ix.

113. Plutarch, *Moralia:* "De Daemone Socratis," ch. xxii.

114. *Ante-Nicene Fathers*, 8 vols. (Buffalo: Christian Literature Co., 1886), VIII.579. For the medieval Latin version, see Theodore Silverstein,

Visio Sancti Pauli (London: Christophers, 1935). Cf. Dante's reference in *Inferno*, II.32.

115. Cf. Wright, p. 122.

116. Douglas's *Aeneid*, Introd. to Bk. VI. Cf. *Aeneid*, VI.426-429, 477-534.

117. Rüegg notes several points of indebtedness but does not develop the fire-wind-water parallel.

118. *Revelation of the Monk of Evesham*, chs. xxxvii, xxxviii. Cf. *Aeneid*, VI.430-431.

119. See Domenico Comparetti, *Vergil in the Middle Ages* (London: Swan, Sonnenschein, & Co., 1895, reprint Hamden, Connecticut: Archon Books, 1966.).

120. See n. 110, above; also articles on "Purgatory" and "Limbo" in the *Catholic Encyclopedia*, 15 vols. (New York: Robert Appleton, 1907).

121. Plutarch, *Moralia:* "De Tarditate Iustitiae Divinae," ch. xxii. Plutarch has a hot lake of boiling gold, a cold lake of lead, and a turbulent lake of iron, corresponding to Virgil's threefold purgation. Quoting Plutarch's essay, Natalis Comes refers to them simply as lakes of fire and ice (*Mythologiae* [Padua: P.P. Tozzi, 1616], III.xi: "De Tartaro"). Cf. Patch, p. 81.

122. *Mythologiae*, III.xi.

123. Here quoted from Virgil, *Opera*, ed. G. Fabricius (Basel, 1586), p. 164 C.

124. See *Shakespeare's Derived Imagery*, p. 136.

125. Wright, p. 84.

126. Aquinas, *Summa Theologica*, Pt. III (Supp.), App. ii.

127. Quoted in Vincent de Beauvais, *Speculum Naturale*, IV.114.

128. Cf. the medieval English ballad *The Daemon Lover* (Child, I.24a):

> "O whaten a mountain is yon," she said,
> "All so dreary wi' frost and snow?"—
> "O yon is the mountain of hell," he cried,
> "Where you and I will go."

129. Reproduced in C. M. Gayley, *Classic Myths* (Boston: Ginn & Co., 1911), p. 358. Cf. *Aeneid*, VI.616-617. For other fiery wheels, see Patch, pp. 84, 88, 92-93.

130. Vincent de Beauvais, *Speculum Historiale*, XXIX.9. Cf. Patch, p. 117. Judas himself describes this wheel in the *Voyage of Saint Brandan*, ch. xii (Marchand, p. 59).

131. See Wright, p. 72; Duyvendak, p. 50.

132. Among Shakespearean editors, G. L. Kittredge rejects the suggestion. It is tentatively accepted by O. J. Campbell and by Hardin Craig.

133. "Viewless" means invisible. *Invisibilis* may be used as a near equivalent of *inanis*. In Gen. 1:2, "without form and void" appears in the Vulgate as "inanis et vacua," but in the Latin translation of the Septuagint as "invisibilis et incomposita." The latter form is quoted by Ambrose, Augustine, and other church fathers.

134. This wind has a certain resemblance to Milton's violent cross wind that blows the hypocrites from the gate of heaven to "the backside of the world," into the Paradise of Fools on the outer shell of the cosmos (*Paradise Lost*, III.487-497).
135. See *Parlement of Foules*, lines 78-84, and Skeat's notes.
136. Macrobius, *Commentarium in Somnium Scipionis*, II.xvii.13-14. Cf. *The Character of Hamlet*, p. 221.
137. "The Ghost in *Hamlet:* A Catholic Linchpin," *Studies in Philology*, 48 (1951), 161-192. Cf. I. J. Semper's rejoinder, "The Ghost in *Hamlet:* Pagan or Christian," *Month*, 9 (1953), 222-234. See also J. Dover Wilson's introductory discussion to his edition of *Hamlet* in the New Cambridge Shakespeare (1936).

Chapter III: Numbers

1. For example, Christopher Butler and Alastair Fowler, "Time-Beguiling Sport: Number Symbolism in Shakespeare's *Venus and Adonis*," in E. A. Bloom, ed., *Shakespeare, 1564-1964*, pp. 124-133.
2. Macrobius, *Commentarium in Somnium Scipionis*, I.vi.
3. See Macrobius's *Opera*, editions of 1519, 1524, 1528.
4. Bound with Wright's *The Passions of the Minde in Generall* (London: V. Sims, 1604).
5. Censorinus, *De Die Natali*, XIV.xiii.
6. *Antony and Cleopatra*, IV.ix.12-23.
7. *Oxford English Dictionary:* "year."
8. La Primaudaye gives a similar discussion of the ages of man in *The French Academie*, I.lii; p. 233.
9. See *juventus* in Charlton T. Lewis and Charles Short's *Latin Dictionary* (Oxford: Clarendon Press, 1966). Dante extends the period of "youth" to 45 years (*Convito*, IV.xxiv).
10. *Commentarium in Somnium Scipionis*, I.vi.71.
11. Matteo Bandello, in his *Novelle*, gives Juliet's age as 18; Arthur Brooke, in his poetic *Tragicall Historye of Romeus and Iuliet* (London: R. Tottel, 1562), gives her age as 16.
12. *The Character of Hamlet*, p. 255. The full discussion, pp. 247-256, attempts to show a pattern of planned changes from Q1 to Q2.
13. Macrobius, *Commentarium in Somnium Scipionis*, II.ii.
14. Plato, *Opera Omnia*, trans. Ficino (Basel, 1551).
15. Aquinas, *Commentarium in De Anima Aristotelis*, I.iv; sec. 50. References are to book and *lectio*, and to sections which some editors number in sequence throughout each book. Aquinas's *Opera Omnia* appeared in Rome, 1570, and in Venice, 1594.
16. A useful study of numbers is Vincent F. Hopper, *Medieval Number Symbolism* (New York: Columbia University Press, 1938). An excellent

NOTES TO PAGES 58-77

article, "Number as Cosmic Language," by Russell A. Peck of the University of Rochester, was distributed to interested members of the Modern Language Association of America in December, 1974.

17. *Commentarium in Somnium Scipionis,* I.v–vi, II.ii.

18. *Ibid.,* II.ii. In II.ii.14 he derives this sequence from Plato's *Timaeus,* which combines 2-4-8 and 3-9-27 for the "perfection" of solidity.

19. *The French Academie,* III.xxxvii; p. 725 in ed. of London: T. Adams, 1618 (all four parts). Page references are to this edition. First printings of earlier parts were: I (1586), II (1594), III (1601). All four editions are in the library of Yale University.

20. La Primaudaye defines God as "the vnitie from which all number proceedeth" in *The French Academie,* III.i; p. 639.

21. Virgil, *Bucolica,* VIII.75.

22. *Commentarium in Somnium Scipionis,* I.vi.1.

23. Cf. "a square deal" and "to stand foursquare" in modern usage.

24. Donatus Acciaiolus, *Commentarium in Ethica ad Nicomachum* (Venice: "apud Franciscum, & Gasparem Bindonum fratres," 1565), I.x.91; pp. 53–54.

25. Aristotle, *De Anima,* II.iii; 414b.

26. Batman, III.vii. Italics not mine.

27. Aquinas, *Opuscula Omnia,* pp. 188–202.

28. James E. Phillips, in *Shakespeare Quarterly,* 15 (1964), 147–159, equates Prospero, Ariel, and Caliban with the rational soul, the sensible soul, and the vegetal soul, respectively. See p. 71.

29. Aquinas, *De Potentiis Animae,* ch. iv, in *Opuscula Omnia,* p. 541D[2] (page, position, column).

30. Other uses of the five wits occur in *Much Ado,* I.i.66; *Romeo and Juliet,* I.iv.47; *Twelfth Night,* IV.ii.92; *King Lear,* III.vi.60.

31. Batman, III.vi.

32. Allott, *Wits Theater of the Little World,* f. 37.

33. Aquinas, *De Sensu Respectu Singularium et Intellectu Respectu Universalium,* in *Opuscula Omnia,* pp. 623–624 (paging confused).

34. Aquinas, *De Intellectu et Intelligibili,* in *Opuscula Omnia,* p. 625C[1].

35. Ficino, *Compendium in Timaeum,* ch. xxvi; pp. 684–685.

36. Aquinas, *Commentarium in De Anima Aristotelis,* I.iv; sec. 51.

Chapter IV: The Psychology of Perception

1. Dante, *Paradiso,* IV.40-42.

2. *Paradise Lost,* III.50.

3. Helen Keller, *The Story of My Life* (New York: Doubleday, Page, & Co., 1903).

4. Aquinas, *De Potentiis Animae,* ch. iv, in *Opuscula Omnia,* p. 541C[2].

5. Aquinas, *Summa Contra Gentiles,* II.xlvii.

6. Aquinas, *Commentarium in De Anima Aristotelis*, III.ii; sec. 601, and Dante, *Purgatorio*, IV.1-12. Our modern view of "common sense" as a realistic and practical attitude of mind may be a derived meaning from its action as the first internal sense.

7. Montaigne, *Essays*, I.xxxviii; p. 196.

8. Dante, *The New Life*, translation of Charles Eliot Norton (Boston: Houghton Mifflin, 1892), p. 17.

9. Lemnius, *The Touchstone of Complexions*, trans. Thomas Newton, (London: Thomas Marsh, 1576), I.ii; ff. 11-12.

10. Batman, V.i.

11. Seneca, *De Tranquillitate Animi*, viii.2.

12. Montaigne, *Essays*, I.xl; pp. 208-209.

13. See Gordon W. O'Brien, "*Hamlet*, IV.v.156-157," *Shakespeare Quarterly*, 10 (1959), 249-251.

14. La Primaudaye, *The French Academie*, I.xl, p.427; II. Epistle to the Reader, n.p.; II.lxv, p. 526.

15. Acciaiolus, *Commentarium in Ethica ad Nicomachum*, VII.iii.31; p.337.

16. Lemnius, *The Touchstone of Complexions*, I.ii; ff. 12-15.

17. La Primaudaye, *The French Academie*, II.lxiii, p.522; II.lxxviii, p. 564.

18. *Ibid.*

19. Ficino, *Commentarium in Convivium*, VI.ix; p. 400; Pierre Charron, *Of Wisdome*, trans. Samson Lennard (London: E. Blount & W. Aspley, 1606), I.xiv.7.

20. *The French Academie*, II.xxxix; p. 455.

21. Ficino, *Commentarium in Convivium*, VII.iv; p. 410.

22. Aquinas, *Commentarium in De Anima Aristotelis*, II.xiv; sec. 417.

23. *Ibid.*, II. lviii; sec. 459.

24. Holland, *Moralia* (1603): "Platonique Questions," no. 6, p. 1023.

25. Cf. Cecil S. Emden, "Shakespeare and the Eye," *Shakespeare Survey*, 26 (1973), 129-137.

26. Acciaiolus points out that one can *feel* oneself to be seeing but cannot see oneself seeing except in a mirror (*Commentarium in Ethica ad Nicomachum*, IX.ix. 68; p.460).

27. Batman, V.vii.

28. Batman, V.xiii.

29. Batman, V.v.

30. Batman, V.i.

31. Batman, V.i.

32. Aquinas, *De Natura Luminis*, in *Opuscula Omnia*, p. 621D[1] (after p.624; mispaged).

33. *Commentarium in De Anima Aristotelis*, II.xiv; sec. 417.

34. *De Natura Luminis*, p. 621C[1].

35. Macrobius, *Saturnalia*, VII.xiv.5-7.

36. Ficino, *Commentarium in Convivium*, VII.iv; p. 411.

37. See my Yale dissertation (1929), *The Poems of George Turbervile*, pp. 44, 463. Available from University Microfilms International, Ann Arbor, Michigan.

38. *Romeo and Juliet* (Baltimore: Penguin Books, 1960), pp. 147-148.
39. Dante, in *Convito*, III. ix, credits the theory that eyes emit rays to "Plato and other philosophers" but says that Aristotle refuted the theory in *De Sensu et Sensili*.
40. *The French Academie*, II.xxvii; p. 420. See also Bede, *Elementorum Philosophiae*, in *Opera Omnia*, ed. Migne, 1850, Vol I, p. 1174 D, in *Patrologia Latina*, Vol. XC; Aquinas, *De Potentiis Animae*, ch.iv, in *Opuscula Omnia*, pp. 541E², 542E¹. The three ventricles are allegorized in Spenser's *Faerie Queene*, II.ix.
41. Aquinas, *De Potentiis Animae*, ch. iv, in *Opuscula Omnia*, p. 542D². Cf. *The French Academie*, II./xxvii; p. 561.
42. *Commentarium in De Anima Aristotelis*, III.vi; sec. 670.
43. *De Potentiis Animae*, ch. iv, p. 542B²; *The French Academie*, II.iv; p. 351.
44. *The French Academie*, II.xxv; p. 414.
45. Montaigne, *Essays*, II.xvii; p. 572.
46. Aquinas, *De Spiritualibus Creaturis*, Art. ii, in *Quaestiones Disputatae* (Paris: Franciscus de Honoratis, 1557), chapter heading.
47. Aquinas, *Summa Theologica*, II.xxviii.3. Cf. Dante, *Purgatorio*, XVII.13-18.
48. Cf. Plato, *Phaedrus* (244-245) and *Ion*.
49. Bruno, in *Patrologia Latina*, CLXV.720-721.
50. *Summa Theologica*, II.xxviii.1-2.
51. Cicero, *De Divinatione*, I.vi.12.
52. *Ibid.*, I.vii.13.
53. Aquinas, *De Intellectu et Intelligibili*, in *Opuscula Omnia*, p. 626E¹. "Discurrendo" is explained in *De Potentiis Animae*, ch. iv, in *Opuscula Omnia*, p. 542E¹.
54. Holland's Plutarch, *Moralia*, ed. 1603, ch. 38 in Table of Contents; *The French Academie*, II. the Forespeach, p. 334, II.xxvii, p. 418, *et passim*.
55. *The French Academie*, I.vi; p. 28. Cf. my *Character of Hamlet*, p. 211.
56. Aquinas, *Expositio Ethicorum Aristotelis*, VII.x; sec. 1467. References are to book, *lectio*, and to sections which some editions number in sequence throughout each book.
57. *Shakespeare Quarterly*, 14 (1963), 163-166. Smith questions my earlier statement that Hermione kissed Polixenes (*Shakespeare's Derived Imagery*, p. 156). Cf. *Winter's Tale*, I.ii.286, "kissing with inside lip," suggestive if not conclusive.
58. In *Shakespeare Quarterly*, 19 (1968), 19-24, Norman Nathan explains how Hermione's conduct in the scene provoked Leontes's jealousy. In *ibid.*, pp. 317-327, Jonathan Smith studies the words of Latin derivation in the play.
59. Albertus Magnus, *De Apprehensione*, IV.i, vii-viii; Ficino, *Commentarium in Convivium*, VII.xiv, p. 415; Aquinas, *De Potentiis Animae*, ch. iv; *Commentarium in De Anima Aristotelis*, II.xiv, *et passim*.
60. Aquinas, *De Universalibus*, ch. ii, in *Opuscula Omnia*, pp.630-631. Dante uses *intenzione* with this meaning in *Purgatorio*, XVIII.23.

61. Aquinas, *Expositio Ethicorum Aristotelis*, IX.ii; sec. 1783.
62. Aquinas, *De Natura Luminis*, in *Opuscula Omnia*, p. 621D¹. See also *De Unitate Intellectus*, in *ibid.*, pp. 192B², 193E¹.
63. Albertus Magnus, *De Apprehensione*, III.ix.
64. *Expositio Ethicorum Aristotelis*, X.xiv; secs. 2150, 2153.
65. *De Unitate Intellectus*, in *Opuscula Omnia*, p. 192C²; also p. 201D¹.
66. Aquinas, *Summa Contra Gentiles*, II. xlviii, citing Aristotle's First *Metaphysics*, II.ix.
67. Macrobius, *Commentarium in Somnium Scipionis*, I.vi.9.
68. Aquinas, *Commentarium in De Anima Aristotelis*, III.iii; sec. 604.
69. Aquinas, *Expositio Ethicorum Aristotelis*, IX.iv; sec. 1817.
70. Augustine *De Quantitate Animae*, I.vi, in *Patrologia Latina*, XXX-II.1011.
71. Cf. my *Character of Hamlet*, pp. 99–100.
72. Cf. "Religion in *Hamlet*" in *The Character of Hamlet*, pp. 207–214.
73. Aquinas, *Commentarium in De Anima Aristotelis*, I.viii; sec. 119; Acciaiolus, *Commentarium in Ethica ad Nicomachum*, I.i.2; p. 2. Cf. Dante, *Convito*, IV.xxii.
74. *The French Academie*, II.xxviii; p. 423. Italics not mine.
75. *Ibid.*, II.xxxvi; p. 447.
76. In *ibid.*, II.xxvi, he makes a statement like the first one quoted above but describes the Will as "an other *power* of the soule" (p. 418).
77. *Ibid.*, II.lxxviii; p. 566.
78. *Ibid.*, II.xxii; p. 406.
79. Aristotle, *De Anima*, III.v; 430a.
80. Montaigne, *Essays*, II.xi; pp. 371–372. Cf. above, ch. I, n. 13, for the reference.
81. Cf. Ernest W. Talbert, *The Problem of Order* (Chapel Hill: University of North Carolina Press, 1962).
82. Aquinas, *Commentarium in De Anima Aristotelis*, I.iv; sec.51.
83. Cf. Acciaiolus, *Commentarium in Ethica ad Nicomachum*, II.v.26; p. 82.
84. Ficino, *De Immortalitate Animorum*, XV.xi; p. 349 in Ficino's *Opera Omnia*.
85. On reason versus will, and order versus confusion, see David Kaula and F. Q. Daniels in *Shakespeare Quarterly*, 12 (1961), 271–291.
86. Cf. "to hit the white" in archery.
87. *The French Academie*, I.liv; p. 242.
88. Seneca, *De Clementia*, I.iii.5, iv.1.
89. Similar uses of the "state" of man are found in Plato's *Republic* IV (435, 441), and in Aristotle's *Nicomachean Ethics*, IX.viii; 1168b. Acciaiolus comments that in man is something which commands and something which obeys, as in a state (*Commentarium in Ethica ad Nicomachum*, IX.viii.50; p. 454). Cf. Pierre Charron, *Of Wisdome*, I.xviii.
90. *De Immortalitate Animorum*, XV.xii; p. 351 in Ficino's *Opera Omnia*. See also n. 91.
91. Ficino, *Commentarium in Convivium*, II.iii; p. 377.
92. *Ibid.*, V.iv; p. 389.

93. *Ibid.*, VII.xv; p. 415.
94. *Ibid.*, V.vi; p. 391.
95. Ficino, *Compendium in Timaeum*, ch. vi; pp. 673–674.
96. Plato, *Symposium* (192).
97. Acciaiolus, *Commentarium in Ethica ad Nicomachum*, IX.ix.63; p. 459.
98. *Ibid.*, IX.viii.47; p. 453.
99. Montaigne, *Essays*, I.xxvii; p. 151.
100. *The French Academie*, I.xiii; p.57.
101. Martin L. Vawter, in *Shakespeare Studies*, 7 (1974), 173–195, analyzes Cicero's attack on Stoic philosophy in *De Finibus* and *Tusculan Disputations;* Cicero cites Brutus as an example of Stoicism.
102. Cf. Laurence J. Mills, *One Soul in Bodies Twain* (Bloomington: University of Indiana Press, 1937); also my *Shakespeare's Derived Imagery*, pp. 156–157, 229–230.
103. Aquinas, *Summa Theologica*, II.xxviii.1.
104. *Ibid.*, II.xxviii.2.
105. *Commentarium in Convivium*, II.viii; p. 379.
106. *Ibid.*, p. 380.
107. *Ibid.*, VI.ix; p. 400.
108. *The French Academie*, II.1; p. 484.
109. *Ibid.*, II.xiii; p. 378.
110. Lemnius, *The Touchstone of Complexions*, I.ii, f. 9r; II.vi, f. 139v.
111. *The French Academie*, II. Epistle to the Reader; n.p.
112. *Ibid.*, II.lxxiv; p. 552.
113. Macrobius, *Commentarium in Somnium Scipionis*, II.xvi.23–24.

Chapter V: The Unsettled Humours

1. Ruth L. Anderson, *Elizabethan Psychology and Shakespeare's Plays* (Iowa City: University of Iowa Press, 1927); Campbell (n.5, below); John W. Draper, *The Humors and Shakespeare's Characters* (Durham, N.C.: Duke University Press, 1945); Lawrence Babb, *The Elizabethan Malady* (East Lansing: Michigan State University Press, 1951); William I. D. Scott, *Shakespeare's Melancholics* (London: Mills & Boon, 1962); Bridget Gellert Lyons, *Voices of Melancholy* (New York: Barnes & Noble, 1971).
2. Aquinas, *Expositio Ethicorum Aristotelis,* VII.vii; sec. 1421; Acciaiolus, *Commentarium in Ethica ad Nicomachum*, VII.vii.55, p. 353.
3. Bright, *A Treatise of Melancholy*, ch. xv, pp. 78–87.
4. Honorius, *De Imagine Mundi*, II.lix, in *Patrologia Latina*, CLXXII.154 D.
5. Lily B. Campbell, *Shakespeare's Tragic Heroes: Slaves of Passion* (Cambridge University Press, 1930, reprint New York: Barnes & Noble, 1959), p. 110.
6. Cf. Leo Kirschbaum in *Shakespeare Survey*, 13 (1960), 20–29.

SHAKESPEARE'S THOUGHT

7. *A Treatise of Melancholy*, ch. xvi, p. 96.
8. *Ibid.*, ch xvi, pp. 97–98.
9. *Shakespeare's Tragic Heroes*, p. 112.
10. *Ibid.*, p. 88.
11. Cassio becomes choleric when he is drunk, but this is not his normal temperament.
12. Robert Weiman, in *Shakespeare Jahrbuch*, 108 (1972), 24–34, attributes the jauntiness of Faulconbridge and Edmund to the traditional figure of Vice in medieval morality plays.
13. Cf. R. C. Bald, "'Thou, Nature, Art My Goddess': Edmund and Renaissance Free Thought," *J. Q. Adams Memorial Studies*, edd. MacManaway, Dawson, Willoughby (Washington: Folger Library, 1948), pp. 337–349.
14. Aquinas, *Expositio Ethicorum Aristotelis*, VII.vi; sec. 1386.
15. *Ibid.* VII.vi; sec. 1387.
16. Acciaiolus, *Commentarium in Ethica ad Nicomachum*, IV.v.93; p. 182.
17. *Ibid.*, IV.v.91–93; p. 182.
18. *Shakespeare's Tragic Heroes*, pp. 59, 75–78.
19. *Commentarium in Ethica ad Nicomachum*, VII.vii.55; pp. 352–353.
20. Ficino, *Commentarium in Convivium*, VII.iii; p. 410. The same analysis is given in Bright's *Treatise of Melancholy*, ch. xviii, pp. 107–108.
21. *Ibid.*, p. 108.
22. *The French Academie*, II.lviii; p. 506.
23. Juan Huartes, *The Examination of Men's Wits* (1594) (London: A. Islip, 1604), p.59.
24. Lemnius, *The Touchstone of Complexions*, II.vi; f. 143v.
25. *De Studiosorum De Sanitate tuenda*, ch. v, p. 497 in Ficino's *Opera Omnia*. This work is cited by Babb, *The Elizabethan Malady*, pp. 26, 60–61.
26. *A Treatise of Melancholy*, ch. xvii, p. 99.
27. *Ibid.*, ch. xvii, p. 106.
28. *Ibid.*, ch. xvi, pp. 87–88.
29. Aquinas, *Expositio Ethicorum Aristotelis*, VII.xiv; sec. 1532.
30. Ficino, *Commentarium in Convivium*, VII.iii; p. 410.
31. Cf. "Misanthropy in Shakespeare," in my *Character of Hamlet*, p. 123.
32. *Ibid.*, pp. 125–127; and "The Misanthrope," in *Shakespeare's Derived Imagery*, pp. 159–178.
33. Taillepied, *A Treatise of Ghosts*, trans. Montague Summers (London: The Fortune Press, 1933), p. 17. Eldred D. Jones, in *Shakespeare Quarterly*, 14 (1963),178–179, considers Aaron's melancholy to be a theatrical pretense. This seems doubtful, since other Shakespearean villains are subject to melancholy.
34. See Coleridge's *Lectures on Shakespeare*. Reviewed in Paul N. Siegel's *His Infinite Variety* (Philadelphia: J. B. Lippincott, 1964), pp. 306–307.
35. Among recent commentators, Bernard Spivack thinks Iago is patterned after the medieval Vice of the morality plays (cf. n. 12, above) in *Shakespeare and the Allegory of Evil* (New York: Columbia University Press, 1958), Stanley Edgar Hyman disagrees and offers a Freudian explanation:

that Iago was unconsciously attracted to Othello and hence was jealous of both Cassio and Desdemona (*Iago* [New York: Athenaeum, 1970]).

36. *A Treatise of Melancholy*, ch. xxxiv, pp. 187-188.
37. *The French Academie*, II. Epistle to the Reader, n.p.
38. *Shakespeare's Tragic Heroes*, p. 112.
39. *Ibid.*, p. 113.
40. *American Speech*, 7 (1931-1932), 452-453.
41. Lemnius, *The Touchstone of Complexions*, II.vi; f. 143v.
42. Cf. *The Character of Hamlet*, pp. 99-100.
43. *The Touchstone of Complexions*, II.vi; f. 147r.
44. See n. 20, above.
45. *The French Academie*, II.lxvii; p. 534.
46. Levin, "The Antic Disposition," *Shakespeare Jahrbuch*, 94 (1958), 177.
47. Lyons, *Voices of Melancholy*, p. 92.
48. On Lear's madness, see Kenneth Muir in *Shakespeare Survey*, 13 (1960), 30-40, and Josephine Waters Bennett in *Shakespeare Quarterly*, 13 (1962), 137-155.
49. Ficino, *Commentarium in Convivium*, VII.ix; p. 413.
50. John W. Draper discusses an additional type, the mercurial man, on the authority of C. Dariot's *Astrologicall Iudgement of the Starres* (London: T. Purfoote, 1583). This type appears to be a variation of the sanguine man and is not listed separately by most commentators. See Draper, *The Humors and Shakespeare's Characters*, pp. 87-93.

Chapter VI: The Human Condition

1. *The French Academie*, II.xxxvi; p. 448.
2. Bright, *A Treatise of Melancholy*, ch. x, p. 46.
3. Aquinas, *Summa Contra Gentiles*, II.lviii.
4. Acciaiolus, *Commentarium in Ethica ad Nicomachum*, I.xiii.109; p. 61.
5. Cicero's discussion of the three "seats" or vital organs occurs in *Tusculan Disputations*, I.ix. A later explanation by the Roman poet Claudian occurs in his *Fourth Consulship of Honorius*, lines 228-254.
6. *A Treatise of Melancholy*, ch. x, p. 46.
7. Montaigne, *Essays*, II.xii; p. 491.
8. Cf. *Source and Meaning in Spenser's Allegory*, pp. 25-30.
9. Acciaiolus, *Commentarium in Ethica ad Nicomachum*, III.iv.65; p. 126.
10. *Ibid.*, VII.viii.58; p.355.
11. Lucretius, *De Rerum Natura*, II.34-39.
12. Montaigne, *Essays*, I.xlii, "Of the Inequalitie that is Betweene Us," p. 226.
13. *Ibid.*, p. 227.
14. "For there is no man so barbarous or wicked in all the *world*, who is not

touched with honesty, and who retaineth not somewhat of the light of *nature"* (*The French Academie*, I.xvi; p. 71).
15. *Ibid.*, I.xlii; p. 185.
16. Cicero, *De Finibus*, III.xix.62–63.
17. Aquinas, *Expositio Ethicorum Aristotelis*, IX.ii; secs. 1781–1783.
18. Helge Kökeritz, in *Shakespeare's Pronunciation* (New Haven: Yale University Press, 1923), lists Hamlet's *kin-kind* as a "jingle" or homonymic pun, but he also notes the probability that this and some others may involve eye-rimes rather than similar internal vowel sounds (pp. 77 ff.).
19. Hamlet, though a Dane, cannot be recalling the Danish word for "child," which is *barnet*, akin to Scots *bairn*.
20. Macrobius, *Commentarium in Somnium Scipionis*, II.xii.9–10. Quoted by Aquinas in *De Unitate Intellectus*, in *Opuscula Omnia*, p. 197B[1].
21. Montaigne, *Essays*, II.xii; p. 445.
22. Cf. J. Swart, "'I Know Not Seems': A Study of Hamlet," *Review of English Literature* (Leeds, 1961), II.iv.60–76.
23. First printed in *PMLA*, where it was entitled "Hamlet's 'god kissing carrion': A Theory of the Generation of Life," 64 (1949), 507–516.
24. *Modern Language Notes*, 41 (1926), 234–238. See Ovid's *Metamorphoses* in the translation by Arthur Golding (London: W. Seres, 1567), I.495–524, and Pliny's *Historia Naturalis*, IX.84.
25. Lucretius, *De Rerum Natura*, III.713–740.
26. Aristotle, *De Generatione Animalium*, I.i (715b.30).
27. *Ibid.*, III.xi (762a.3).
28. *Ibid.*, II.iii (737a.1).
29. *Ibid.*, III.xi (762b.27).
30. Aristotle, *De Generatione et Corruptione*, II.x (336b.1). Cf. Aquinas's commentary on Bk. II, X.x.4 and XI.xi.5.
31. Hippocrates, *De Natura Pueri*, ch. xxxv.
32. Galen, Bk. I, ch. vi.
33. Pico, *Conclusiones:* "Secundum Avicennam," no. 5.
34. J. C. Scaliger, ed. & trans., *Aristotelis Historia de Animalibus* (Greek & Latin, Toulouse: D. & P. Bosc, 1619), Bk. VII: Introd., p. 789. Scaliger's edition, with Latin text only, appeared in Lyons: A. de Harsy, 1584.
35. *De Generatione Animalium*, II.iii (737a.18–24). Cf. n. 43.
36. Aristotle, *Historia Animalium*, VII.iii (583a.24).
37. "Ferment," Scaliger, *op. cit.*, VII.ii.22; "coagulate," Pico, *In Astrologiam*, VII.ii; "putrefy," Paracelsus, below.
38. *De Generatione Animalium*, I.xx (729a.12), II.iii (737a.15), II.iv (739b.23).
39. Paracelsus, *De Natura Rerum*, Bk. VII: "De transmutationibus rerum naturalium," *Opera*, 2 vols. (Geneva, 1658), Vol. II, p. 97.
40. *Ibid.*, Bk. I: "De generationibus rerum naturalium," p. 85.
41. Aristotle, *De Partibus Animalium*, II.iii (650a.34, 651a.15), IV.iv (678a.8 ff.). Cf. Aquinas, *De Principiis Naturae*, in *Opuscula Omnia*, p.410B[1].
42. *De Generatione Animalium*, I.xix (726b.1–15).
43. As organic matter, the genital fluids possess a certain "life," and in the

NOTES TO PAGES 154-172

male there lies dormant the "efficient cause" which, awakened by heat, starts the process of generation; but the seed becomes a living organism only after that process has begun. Cf. Aristotle's *De Generatione Animalium*, II.iv (739b.35).

44. William Harvey, *De Generatione Animalium* (1651), Exercise 68. Cf. Bruno Bloch, "Die geschichtlichen Grundlagen der Embryologie bis auf Harvey," *Abhandlungen der Kaiserlichen Leopoldinisch-Carolinischen Deutschen Akademie der Naturforscher*, 82 (Halle, 1904), 215-334.

45. Aquinas, *Commentarium in De Anima Aristotelis*, III.iv.619; *Commentarium in De Generatione et Corruptione Aristotelis*, Bk. I, V.xiii.4; *Summa Theologica*, I.cxviii.1.

46. Scotus, *Summa Theologica*, compiled by H. de Montefortino from the works of Scotus (Rome: Sallustiana, 1900-1903), Part I, Q. 104, A. 2.

47. Vincent de Beauvais, *Speculum Naturale*, XXIII.xlvi, XXXI.xxxviii.

48. Hermeias, *A Platonic Demonstration of the Immortality of the Soul*, trans. in Thomas M. Johnson, *Opuscula Platonica* (Osceola, Mo.: Press of Republican, 1908), p. 28.

49. Ficino, *De Immortalitate Animorum*, XV.xi, in *Opera Omnia*, p. 350.

50. *Hamlet* (Variorum), 2 vols., Vol. I, p. 146.

51. Macrobius, *Saturnalia*, I.xvii-xxi.

52. Boccaccio, *De Genealogia Deorum* (Italian version, Venice: Valentini, 1627), VII.xxii.

53. Frazer, *The Golden Bough*, 3rd ed., 12 vols. (London: Macmillan, 1907-1927), "Balder the Beautiful," ch.ii, X. 22-100.

54. Hartland, *Primitive Paternity*, 2 vols. (Folklore Society Publications, London, D. Nutt, 1909), I.25, 89-98.

55. Hartland, *The Legend of Perseus*, 2 vols. (London: D. Nutt, 1894), I.99.

56. *De Genealogia Deorum*, V.x. For another treatment of these questions, see "The Garden of Adonis" in *Source and Meaning in Spenser's Allegory*, pp. 234-286.

57. For the medieval tradition of the sun as the instrument of God's generative power, and also as a sexual symbol, see H. Flanders Dunbar, *Symbolism in Medieval Thought* (New Haven: Yale University Press, 1929). The notion was a commonplace of Hermetic philosophy; cf. the Latin *Asclepius*.

58. Calvin, *Institutes*, I.xvii.5.

59. Alanus, *Distinctiones Dictionum Theologicalium:* "Vermis," in *Patrologia Latina*, CCX.997. An edition was printed at Strasbourg in 1473.

60. Carlyle, *Heroes and Hero-Worship:* "The Hero as Poet."

Chapter VII: The Ascent of Man

1. First printed in *PMLA*, 62 (1947), 793-801.
2. *Tempest*, Arden Ed., old series, Introd., pp. xxxii-xxxix.

3. For discussion and additional documentation, see my essay "On Ghosts" in *The Character of Hamlet*.

4. R. R. Cawley, "Shakspere's Use of the Voyagers in *The Tempest*," *PMLA*, 41 (1926), 721–722. For resemblance of Sycorax and Caliban to Spenser's Hag and Churl (*Faerie Queene*, III.vii), see Alwin Thaler in *Shakespeare Association Bulletin*, 10 (1935), 203, and J. A. S. McPeek in *Philological Quarterly*, 35 (1946), 378–381. For a character contrast of Caliban with Miranda, see August Rüegg in *Shakespeare Jahrbuch*, 89 (1953), 128–131; of Caliban with Prospero, see Frank Kermode in New Arden Edition of *The Tempest*. For *The Tempest* as allegory, see A. D. Nuttall, *Two Concepts of Allegory* (New York: Barnes & Noble, 1967). Cf. above, pp. 45–46.

5. See Scot's *Discoverie of Witchcraft*, ed. Brinsley Nicholson (London: E. Stock, 1886), p. 512. See above, pp. 45–47.

6. A Latin edition of Jornandes appeared in 1515. The same information appears in Franciscus Irenicus, *Totius Germaniae Descriptio* (Frankfurt: "ad Moenum," 1570), Bk. I, ch. 37.

7. Cf. *Tempest*, III.iii.44–47.

8. *Purchas His Pilgrimes*, II.ix.1556. Cunliffe's note is an annotation to *Tempest*, II.ii.35, in Brooke, Cunliffe, and MacCracken's *Shakespeare's Principal Plays* (New York: Century, 1914).

9. Caliban's head is also reminiscent of the dog-headed men, mentioned by Pliny and familiar in maps and travel tales. See R. R. Cawley, *Unpathed Waters* (Princeton: Princeton University Press, 1940), pp. 107–108.

10. Richard Eden, *Historie of Travayle*, quoted from Edward Arber, *The First Three English Books on America* (Westminster: Constable, 1895), p. 252.

11. See Cawley's "Shakspere's Use of the Voyagers," already cited, which proves the indebtedness beyond a reasonable doubt. Cf. also D. G. James, *The Dream of Prospero* (London: Oxford University Press, 1967).

12. Lavater, edd. Wilson and Yardley (Oxford: Oxford University Press, 1929), pp. 70, 75.

13. Eden, *op. cit.*, p. 251. Eden's cannibals were in the same area as Montaigne's, who were brought to France by Villegagnon, as Montaigne tells us. Villegagnon, a French missionary, had settled at Rio de Janeiro, but his fort was later captured by the Portuguese (Purchas, IV.vii.1438). It is perhaps worthy of mention that Eden has the meeting with Setebos's worshipers take place on an island, and that on p. 250 is given a description of St. Elmo's fire, much like the fires in Shakespeare's storm.

14. Cf. Lawrence E. Bowling, "The Theme of Natural Order in *The Tempest*," *College English*, 12 (1950–51),203–209. Bowling thinks Prospero's initial error was a too indulgent attitude towards his brother Antonio and towards Caliban, when strictness was called for.

15. Cf. Cawley, *The Voyagers and Elizabethan Drama* (Boston: MLA Monograph Series, VIII, 1938), pp. 369, 388.

16. See *ibid.*, pp. 344 ff., for instances of the two opposite views.

17. In *The Character of Hamlet*. See particularly p. 116, n. 5, for evidence

that Shakespeare had read the *Ethics*. For a later significant article, see George C. Taylor, "Shakespeare's Use of the Idea of the Beast in Man," *Studies in Philology*, 42 (1945), 530–543.

18. Aristotle, *Nicomachean Ethics*, VII.v.2 (Loeb ed.).
19. Herodotus, *History*, ch. iv.
20. Montaigne, p. 166; Cawley, *Unpathed Waters*, p. 108.
21. Cawley, *The Voyagers and Elizabethan Drama*, pp. 349, 357.
22. *Ibid.*, pp. 363–364.
23. *Ibid.*, pp. 347–348.
24. *Ibid.*, p. 357.
25. Caliban's parentage supports this view. The Catholic Church listed human copulation with demons and human copulation with beasts as similar examples of unnatural lusts, or *bestialitas* (Montague Summers, *History of Witchcraft* [New York: A. A. Knopf, 1926], pp. 92, 106). As the offspring of an incubus, Caliban's birth resulted from an act of bestiality by his mother, which may have influenced her offspring.
26. Aquinas, *Commentarium in De Anima Aristotelis*, III.iv; secs. 629–631.
27. A useful general study is Brents Stirling's *The Populace in Shakespeare* (New York: Columbia University Press, 1949).
28. *Shakespeare Quarterly*, 16 (1965), 241–246.
29. Patrides cites Lancelot Andrewes's *XCVI Sermons* (4th ed., 1641, pp. 278–279). The first edition was in 1629. Of course, if the sermon were written early enough, Shakespeare might have heard it delivered.
30. Charron, *Of Wisdome*, I.lii.
31. Montaigne, *Essays*, I.xxiii; p. 94.
32. *Ibid.*, II.xii; p. 421.
33. *Ibid.*, III.iv; p. 748.
34. See Frances Yates, *John Florio: The Life of an Italian in Shakespeare's England* (Cambridge: Cambridge University Press, 1934).
35. For a topical meaning of this passage, see my *Character of Hamlet*, p. 113.
36. See my *Source and Meaning in Spenser's Allegory*, pp. 103–104.
37. *Ibid.*, pp. 26, 72.
38. Comes, *Mythologiae*, VII.1; pp. 372–373.
39. *Ibid.*, III.v; p. 105.
40. *Source and Meaning in Spenser's Allegory*, p. 125.
41. Cartari, ed. Padua, 1626, p. 236.
42. I cite the Prose Edda from Mallet's *Northern Antiquities* (London: Bohn Library, 1859), pp. 451–455.
43. For Typhon and other cosmic destroyers, such as "the boar from the forest" (Ps. 80:13), see *Source and Meaning in Spenser's Allegory*, pp. 76–78.
44. I am not sure where Shakespeare could have read this legend. A colloquium at Liège in April, 1972, demonstrated a continual exchange of influences between Scandinavian and French literatures throughout the Middle Ages (*Les Relations Littéraires Franco-Scandinaves au Moyen Age*, Paris, 1975, Liège Congres et Colloques, no. 73). Conceivably, an intermediate version in Latin or French could have been known to Shakespeare, or the cosmic wolves may have survived in oral tradition.

SHAKESPEARE'S THOUGHT

45. Seven weeks (Ficino), ten weeks (Vincent de Beauvais), when articulation of the brain cells was complete (Dante). See *Source and Meaning in Spenser's Allegory*, p. 270.
46. *The French Academie*, II.xxxii; p. 435, also II. xxxiii; p. 439.
47. *Ibid.*, Part II, the Forespeach, p. 334.
48. For echoes of Psalm 8 and Ecclesiastes 3 in *The Comedy of Errors*, see *The Character of Hamlet*, pp. 182–183.
49. In Sebastian Castalio's Latin version of Psalm 8:5 (in his *Biblia* [Basel: J. Oporinus, 1551]), we are told that man was like unto God (*Atqui eum propemodum Deum fecisti*).
50. On "how infinite in faculties" Kittredge cites Marlowe's *Tamburlaine*, Part I, II.vii.21–25:
  "Our souls, whose *faculties* can comprehend
  The wondrous architecture of the world,
  And measure every wand'ring planet's course,
  Still climbing after knowledge *infinite*,
  And always moving as the restless spheres."
51. *The French Academie*, III.xiv; p. 672.
52. Horace, *Carmina*, IV.vii.16.
53. *The French Academie*, Part II, the Forespeach, pp. 336–337.
54. Aquinas, *De Unitate Intellectus*, in *Opuscula Omnia*, p. 197A[2].
55. Polydore Vergil, *De Prodigiis*, Bk. III, p. 266, in *Dialogues* (Basel: "apud Mich. Ising[rinium]," 1553). Bound with *De Inventoribus Rerum* (Basel: "apud Isingrinium," 1550).
56. Cf. Edward William Taylor, *Nature and Art in Renaissance Literature* (New York: Columbia University Press, 1964).
57. *The French Academie*, II.xlviii; p. 478.
58. *The Zodiake of Life*, Bk. V, p. 78. Cf. Sidney, *An Apologie for Poetrie*, in G.'Gregory Smith, *Elizabethan Critical Essays*, I.155–157; Charron, *Of Wisdome*, I.xiv.
59. Ficino, *Commentarium in Plotinum*, Ennead III: "De Natura et Contemplatione," p. 1723 in Ficino's *Opera Omnia*.
60. In Plato's *Opera Omnia*, trans. Ficino (Basel: 1551), p. 653.
61. Acciaiolus, *Commentarium in Ethica ad Nicomachum*, II.vi.32; p. 87.
62. See Ovid, *Metamorphoses*, X.243–297.
63. Lucretius, *De Rerum Natura*, V.1361–1366.
64. *Ibid.*, I.629, II.1117.
65. Ficino, *De Immortalitate Animorum*, XI.v, p. 256 in *Opera Omnia*. Earlier, in *ibid.*, IV.i,p.123, Ficino speaks of the "art" which is really nature, but without using an agricultural example. See also Dante, *Convito*, IV.ix.
66. Puttenham, *Arte of English Poesie*, Arber's Reprint (Westminster: Constable, 1895), III.xxv; pp. 308–309.
67. *Ibid.*, p. 310.
68. Puttenham's words have been noted by Harold S. Wilson in the *Shakespeare Association Bulletin*, 18 (1943),114–120. Wilson also notes a passage on tree-grafting as art improving nature in Bernardo Daniello's *Poetica* (1536), p. 5.

270

69. Reprinted in the notes to various editions of *The Tempest* and in my *Shakespeare's Derived Imagery*, p. 277.

70. Montaigne, *Essays*, I.xxx; p. 163. This passage has been detected and quoted by Frank Kermode in his introduction to *The Tempest* (Arden Ed., p. xxxv). Kermode interprets *The Tempest* as an example of art (Prospero) controlling nature (Caliban).

71. Henry David Thoreau adopts Montaigne's position in his essay *Wild Apples*, insisting that natural fruit tastes better than fruit from grafted trees.

72. *Azoth*, p. 675 in Paracelsus's *Opera*, Vol. II.

73. A few useful titles are: Louis Elson, *Shakespeare in Music* (Boston: L. C. Page & Co., 1901); Richmond P. Noble, *Shakespeare's Use of Song* (London: Oxford University Press, 1923); John H. Long, *Shakespeare's Use of Music: The Final Comedies* (Gainesville: Florida University Press, 1962); F. W. Sternfeld, *Music in Shakespearean Tragedy* (New York: Dover Publications, 1963); Peter J. Seng, *The Vocal Songs in the Plays of Shakespeare* (Cambridge, Mass.: Harvard University Press, 1967). See also articles by Sternfeld in *Shakespeare Survey*, 15 (1962), 1-10, and 17 (1964), 214-222, and in Muir & Schoenbaum's *A New Companion to Shakespeare Studies* (Cambridge: Cambridge University Press, 1971), pp. 157-167.

74. Lucretius, *De Rerum Natura*, IV.1063.

75. In Plato's *Opera Omnia* (Greek & Latin), trans. Ficino (Frankfurt: "apud Claudium Marnium, & haeredes Ioannis Aubrii," 1602), p. 620 E.

76. Erasmus cites "Musicam docet amor" (love teaches music) from Plutarch and quotes Bion as saying that the Muses are always companions of love (*Adagia* [Frankfurt: Johannis Petrus Zubrodt, 1670], p. 50).

77. Plato, *Republic* X (617).

78. Aristotle, *De Caelo*, 290b.

79. *The Zodiake of Life*, pp. 129-130, 212-213.

80. Macrobius, *Commentarium in Somnium Scipionis*, II.iv.14.

81. Ambrose, *In Hexaemeron*, II.ii.7, in *Patrologia Latina*, XIV.147. There were six or more editions of Ambrose's *Opera Omnia* before 1580.

82. *The Zodiake of Life*, p. 213.

83. Sidney, in G. Gregory Smith, *Elizabethan Critical Essays*, I.206-207.

84. Macrobius, *Commentarium in Somnium Scipionis*, II.iii.7-12.

85. *Ibid.*, II.iv.7, 14-15.

86. For analogues to this image of the body, see *Shakespeare's Derived Imagery*, p. 222.

87. Ovid, *Metamorphoses*, XI.1-2. Cf. Dante, *Convito*, II.i.

88. Aquinas, *Commentarium in De Anima Aristotelis*, I.xii; sec. 190.

89. Cf. the "unback'd colts" moved by music in *Tempest*, IV.i.176.

90. Montaigne, *Essays*, I.xxii; pp. 74-75. Noted in the Arden Edition of *The Merchant of Venice*, with other citations of Quintilian's *Institutes*, I.x.12, and Plutarch's *De Re Musica*, ch. xliv.

91. Montaigne, *Essays*, II.xii; p. 536.

92. Puttenham, *The Arte of English Poesie*, I.iii, in Arber's Reprint, p. 22.

93. In Brooke, Cunliffe, & MacCracken, *Shakespeare's Principal Plays*, the notes to this passage summarize and support the theory of a reference to Elizabeth's visit to Kenilworth in 1575.

94. *The French Academie*, II.lxv; p. 528.

95. Censorinus, *De Die Natali*, XII.iv; Polydore Vergil, *De Inventoribus Rerum*, I.xv; p. 50.

96. Bede, *Musica Quadrata seu Mensurata*, in *Patrologia Latina*, XC.922 C-923 A.

97. *The French Academie*, I.lxvi; p. 301.

98. Andreas Alciatus, *Emblemata* (Lyons: "apud Haeredes Gulielmi Rouillij," 1614), p. 474.

99. *Ibid.*, pp. 474-478.

100. Ovid, *Metamorphoses*, XV.234.

101. Time as an old man carrying a scythe or a sickle stems from the image of Chronos (Kronus, Saturn), who was originally a god of the harvest and came to represent Time (Oskar Seyffert, *A Dictionary of Classical Antiquities* [London: Swan, Sonnenschein, & Co., 1891], pp. 167-168).

102. Emblem 133 in the variorum edition of *Emblemata* (Padua: P. P. Tozzi, 1621).

103. *Emblemata* (1621), p. 571.

104. Macrobius, *Commentarium in Somnium Scipionis*, II.x.7.

105. Macrobius, *ibid.*, II.x.8. La Primaudaye translates this passage in *The French Academie*, III.viii; p. 657. Since Part III of *The French Academie* first appeared in English in 1601, it can hardly have been a source for the opening lines of *Love's Labour's Lost*. The English translator of Part III was R. Dolman.

106. Horace, *Carmina*, IV.ix.25-28.

107. *The French Academie*, II.xv; p. 384.

108. Daniel Wilson, *Caliban the Missing Link* (London: Macmillan, 1873).

Chapter VIII: The Conduct of Life

1. For discussion, see *The Character of Hamlet*, pp. 68-72.

2. Cf. Morris P. Tilley, *Elizabethan Proverb Lore* (New York: Macmillan, 1926), and *A Dictionary of the Proverbs in England in the Sixteenth and Seventeenth Centuries* (Ann Arbor: University of Michigan Press, 1950).

3. Cf. Chaucer's "the smylere with the knyf under the cloke" in the *Knight's Tale* (*Canterbury Tales*, 1999).

4. Cf. T. W. Baldwin, *Shakspere's 'Small Latine and Lesse Greeke,'* Vol. I, pp. 119-120, on the use of *sententiae* in the schools. Cf. also Charles G. Smith, *Shakespeare's Proverb Lore: His Use of the Sententiae of Lennard Culman and Publilius Syrus* (Cambridge, Mass.: Harvard University Press, 1963). Separate editions of Syrus's work appeared in 1514, 1550, and 1578; in other instances his work was bound with Cato's *Disticha* or Phaedrus's *Fabulae*. I quote from M. Nisard's edition (Latin and French, Paris: Firmin-Didot, 1878), where Syrus is included with Horace and other Roman poets. Since his "sentences" are arranged alphabetically, page references are not necessary. My examples supplement those given by Smith.

5. Erasmus, *Adagia*, pp. 506, 513. Smith quotes numerous echoes of "Know thyself" in Shakespeare (p.76).

6. *The French Academie*, I.xliii; p. 189.

7. *A Woman Killed with Kindness*, xvii.22.

8. Aquinas, *Expositio Ethicorum Aristotelis*, IX.ii; sec. 1782.

9. *The French Academie*, I.l; p. 221.

10. Plato, *Opera*, trans. Ficino (Frankfurt, 1602), p. 1240 E.

11. *Ibid.*, p. 1241 D.

12. Cf. Ovid, *Metamorphoses*, I.400-413.

13. Erasmus, *Adagia*, p. 556.

14. First printed in *Shakespearean Essays*, edd. Alwin Thaler & Norman Sanders (Knoxville: University of Tennessee Press, 1964), pp. 41-43.

15. *As You Like It*, Variorum Edition, p. 64.

16. See p. 5 of W. H. D. Rouse's introduction to his edition of Golding's translation of Ovid's *Metamorphoses*, published as *Shakespeare's Ovid* (1904; facsimile reprint by the Centaur Press, London, 1961).

17. For Shakespeare's extensive use of the golden age throughout his works, see ch. 21 of *Shakespeare's Derived Imagery*.

18. Ovid, *Metamorphoses*, trans. Golding, I.129-140. Italics not mine.

19. St. Augustine states that many commentators believed the biblical account to be figurative up to the time when Adam and Eve leave the garden. He considers it to be both literal and figurative; paradise was an actual place (*De Genesi ad Litteram*, VIII.i, in *Patrologia Latina*, XXXIV.372).

20. In *Ante-Nicene Fathers*, VIII.565-570.

21. *Ibid.*, p. 566.

22. *Ibid.*, pp. 567-568.

23. Augustine, *De Genesi ad Litteram*, IX.iii; p. 395.

24. Abelard, *Expositio in Hexaemeron*, in *Patrologia Latina*, CLXX-VIII.762.

25. Macrobius, *Commentarium in Somnium Scipionis*, I.x.14.

26. Alciatus, *Emblemata* (Lyons, 1614), p. 228.

27. *Ibid.*, pp. 344-345.

28. *Ibid.*, pp. 346-347.

29. First printed in *Modern Language Notes*, 61 (February, 1946), 88-90 (Baltimore: The Johns Hopkins University Press).

30. In *The Character of Hamlet*, pp. 172-191.

31. For an excellent study of the religious aspects of *King Lear*, see William R. Elton, *King Lear and the Gods* (San Marino, California: The Huntington Library, 1966).

32. First printed in *The Explicator*, April, 1945 (III.vi.48).

33. Cf. G. T. Buckley, "Was Edmund Guilty of Capital Treason?" *Shakespeare Quarterly*, 23 (1972), 87-94.

34. Jean Froissart, *Chronicles of England, France, and Spain* (Everyman Edition, abridged, New York: E. P. Dutton, 1921), ch. xxvi, pp. 590-595. Shakespeare could have studied the etiquette of the judicial trial by combat, including the king's right to stop the combat, in *The Booke of Fayttes of Armes and of Chyalrye* (1489), translated and printed by William Caxton from the

French of Christine de Pisan, Bk. IV, chs, vii-xiv (Early English Text Society, O. S., no. 189, London: Oxford University Press, 1932). He could also have read Olivier de la Marche, *Livre des Duels* (Paris: Jean Richer, 1586).

Index

Faulconbridge (KJ), 123, 264
Faustus, Doctor, 133
Fenris, 186, 187
Ferdinand, king (LLL), 78, 194, 210-212; prince (Tem), 82, 94, 149, 170
Feste (TN), 132, 133, 150
fever, 151, 152
Ficino, Marsilio, 120, 155, 202, 224, 225, 244, 245, 271, 273; *Opera Omnia*, 14, 67, 252, 255; *Argumentum ad Republicam*, 185, 195; *Commentarium in Convivium (Symposium)*, 14, 36, 38, 39, 42, 83, 87, 99, 100, 110-113, 115, 117, 128, 129, 133, 134, 142-144, 252-254, 260, 261-265; *Commentarium in Plotinum*, 36, 37, 44, 194, 253, 254, 270; *Compendium in Timaeum*, 14, 44, 67, 68, 70, 73-75, 112, 113, 252, 255, 263; *De Immortalitate Animorum (Theologia Platonica)*, 23, 108, 166, 198, 252, 262, 267, 270; *De Studiosorum De Sanitate tuenda*, 129, 264
fingers, 80, 139, 189, 209
firmament, the, 19, 190, 191
Flamineo, 59
Flaminius (Tim), 57
Flatter, Richard, 253
Florio, John, 15, 78, 107, 152, 183, 184, 251, 269
Florizel, prince (WT), 34, 35, 38, 129, 197, 223
flowers, 196-199, 206
Fluellen (H V), 232
folklore, 45, 167, 201 *see* myth
food (fig.), 202, 203
Ford (MWW), 121, 126; Mistress Ford, 69, 125, 149
forests, woods, 117, 128, 185, 207, 223, 269
form, forms, 69, 70, 72, 75, 93, 99, 110, 113, 146, 164, 165, 171, 193, 195, 222
Fortinbras (Ham), 121

fortune, Fortune, 102, 135, 139, 164, 231-233
fountains (fig.), 69, 108, 117, 118, 167
Fowler, Alastair, 258
France, French people, 124, 129, 176, 201, 216, 268, 275; language, 15, 183, 184, 256, 269
France, king of (AWEW), 158, 199; princess of (LLL), 78
Francis (1 H IV), 121
Frankford, John, 222
Franklin, Benjamin, 216
Frazer, James G., 166, 267
Frederick, duke (AYLI), 126
French Academie, The see Primaudaye
friends, friendship, 42, 46, 79, 98-100, 113-116, 129, 131-133, 155, 181, 183, 210, 217, 218
Froissart, Jean, 236, 273
fumes, fumal, 81, 82, 87
Furness, H. H., 227

Galen, 164, 266
gall, the, 138, 139
gardens, 196, 198; of Adonis, 224; of Eden, 230, 273
garment (fig.), 110, 190 *see* vesture
garner, a (fig.), 117, 118
Gayley, C. M., 257
generation (of life), 27, 36, 41, 44, 83, 161-171, 177, 223, 267; spontaneous, 162-165, 168-170
Genesis B (OE), 256
genital fluids, 35, 164-165, 266
genius (guardian spirit), 106
gentleman, a (KL), 228
geometry, geometrical, 67-70, 72, 73
Germany, language, 158
germens, 33-38, 234
Gertrude, queen (Ham), 20, 33, 77, 83, 94, 95-97, 103, 104, 139-142, 155, 156, 160, 184, 187, 208
ghosts, 43, 45-47, 55, 57, 58, 83, 86, 94, 103, 142, 175, 225, 255,

(1H IV), 27, 64, 123, 140; (H V), 151, 152, 154, 202; Henry VI (2 H VI), 130, 209; Henry VIII (H VIII), 139
Hercules, 185
Heresbach, Conrad, 140
Hermeias, 166, 267
Hermes, 233
Hermetic philosophy, 267
Hermia (MND), 23, 24, 79, 114, 222, 223
Hermione (WT), 56, 65, 97-100, 237, 261
Hero (MAAN), 134, 136
Herodotus, 162, 173, 178, 269
Herophilus, 208
Heywood, John, 216, 217
Heywood, Thomas, 273
Hill, Charles J., 250
Hippocrates, 163, 164, 266
Hodgen, Margaret T., 15, 251
Holland, Philemon, 14, 19, 84, 95, 251, 260, 261
Homer's *Iliad*, 18, 53, 213; *Odyssey*, 173, 225
Honorius of Autun, 41-43, 120, 121, 135, 254, 263
honour, honesty, 69, 71, 136, 154, 181, 200, 210, 221, 266
Hopper, Vincent F., 258
Horace, 152, 181, 192, 205, 211, 213, 270, 272
Horatio (Ham), 46, 79, 97, 139, 219, 222
horses, 41, 193, 194, 203, 206, 271
Hotspur (Henry Percy) (1 H IV), 38, 125
Huartes, Juan, 264
Hubert (KJ), 122
humanity, human race, mankind, 154, 155, 161, 172, 176-178, 187, 200, 203, 225, 232, 235
humours, the four, 81, 83, 86, 119-146, 208, 209; "humours of revenge," 125
Huns, the, 173

hybrids, 196-199
Hydra, the, 181-185
Hyman, Stanley E., 264

Iago (Oth), 66, 87, 97, 123, 124, 136, 137, 220, 221, 264, 265
Iceland, 9, 256
ideas, 76, 77, 86, 87, 110, 166, 195, 239; divine, 195; ideal, 178, 180, 193, 194
imagination *see* senses, internal
immortality, 32, 106, 146, 162, 163, 178, 185, 188, 210, 213
Imogen (Cym), 85, 89, 100, 223
incest, 96, 201
incontinence, 97, 127, 177
incubus, incubi, 43, 173, 174, 178, 269
Indian, American, 172, 173, 176, 178
infection (fig.), 78, 87, 98, 100, 101, 113
influence (astron.), 29
ingratitude, 235
ink, 137, 225
insanity, 28, 128, 208 *see* madness
insight, instinct, 95, 155
instruments, mental, 105, 106, 147, 199
intellect, the, 15, 20, 73, 87, 90, 92, 95, 100, 101, 106, 107, 172, 179, 192, 239; intellectual sense, 73-75
intelligence, 73-75, 90, 143, 176, 179
intention (image), 87, 98-100, 104, 261
Io, 166
Iras (AC), 200
Ireland, 134
Irenicus, Franciscus, 268
Isabella (MFM), 80, 111, 215, 219
islands, 155, 175, 179, 268
Ixion, 56, 232

James I, king, 59; *Demonologie*, 122, 139

284

James, D. G., 268
Jaquenetta (LLL), 134
Jaques (AYLI), 65, 134, 135, 208
jealousy, 97, 101, 121, 124, 136, 181, 182, 221, 237, 265
Jessica (MV), 203, 223
jests, jokes, 24, 48, 132, 133, 137, 166
Jews, the, 169
Joan of Arc (1 H VI), 111
Joanno dos Sanctos, friar, 174
John, Don (MAAN), 135, 136; king (KJ), 122, 149
Johnson, Dr. Samuel, 13, 161
Johnson, Thomas M., 267
Jones, Eldred D., 264
Jonson, Ben, 13, 14, 119, 143, 238, 239, 250
Jornandes (Jordanes), 174, 178, 268
Judas Iscariot, 56, 137, 257
judgment *see* senses, internal; Judgment Day, 56 *see* doomsday
Juliet (RJ), 48, 65, 66, 69, 83, 88, 89, 116, 125, 134, 223
Julius Caesar, 59; (JC), 38, 96, 105, 127, 184, 206, 226
Jupiter, Jove, 22, 166, 181, 224, 227, 228 *see* Zeus
justice, 107, 186, 219, 236

Kalendar of Shepherds, The, 50
Katharine, princess (H V), 202; Katherine, queen (H VIII), 205, 208; Katherine (TS), 126, 144, 215
Kaula, David, 262
Keightley, Thomas, 227, 255
Keller, Helen, 77, 259
Kenilworth, 271
Kent, earl of (KL), 38, 62, 63, 161, 232
Kepler, Johann, 33, 253
Kermode, Frank, 16, 251, 255, 268, 271
Kersten, Dorelies, 255
kin, kindred, kinship, 153-158
kings, 151, 152, 154, 156-160, 184,

232; (fig.), 25, 159, 160
kingdom, a (fig.), 80, 106, 108
Kirschbaum, Leo, 263
Kittredge, G. L., 190, 252, 253, 257, 270
Knowell, Edward, 143
Knowles, Richard, 252
Kocher, P. H., 12
Kökeritz, Helge, 266

Laertes (Ham), 26, 52, 125, 138, 139, 142, 156, 184, 216-218, 236, 237
La Feu (AWEW), 158
lakes, 50, 54, 57; of ice, 49, 50, 257; of fire, 49, 257
lamia, the, 177
land-fish, a, 174
language, 46, 173, 174, 176, 178, 181, 201, 224; (fig.), 110, 114 *see* speech
Lascelles, Mary, 254
Latham, Minor, 45, 255
Laurence, friar (RJ), 38, 51
Lavater, Ludwig, 16, 175, 176, 268
Lazarus (bibl.), 231; vision of, 50
Lear, king (KL), 33, 34, 38, 57, 62, 63, 70, 71, 80, 96, 121, 124, 125, 135, 143, 155, 208, 228, 231-236, 253
learning, 11, 12, 141, 212, 225, 238
Leicester, earl of, 227
Lemmi, C. W., 162, 266
Lemnius, Levinus, 16, 80, 82, 118, 119, 141, 142, 260, 263-265
Lennard, Samson, 183, 260
Leonato (MAAN), 136
Leontes (WT), 27, 56, 98-101, 104, 126, 237, 261
Lepidus (AC), 162
Leslie, John, 253
Lethe, the river, 49, 50, 53
letters, literature, 172, 210, 211, 213
Levin, Harry, 143, 255, 265
Lewis, Charlton T., 258
Liège, university of, 269
life force, the, 162, 163; "lifeless life" (art), 194, 198

285

Mercutio (RJ), 85, 92, 123, 134
meridian, the, 24
merman, a, 174
Mew, James, 56, 256
Michigan, 140
microcosm, the, 17, 33, 191, 200
microscope, the, 162
Migne, J. P., 251
Milky Way, the, 32
Millay, Edna St. Vincent, 70
Mills, Laurence J., 263
Milton, John, 14, 227; *L'Allegro,*
130, 238; *Paradise Lost,* 9, 17, 18,
49-51, 77, 192, 254, 256, 258,
259; *Il Penseroso,* 130
mind, the, 11, 16, 23, 62, 74, 76-80,
91-96, 98, 99, 106, 108, 110, 114,
118, 119, 121, 124, 129, 137, 141,
142, 146, 150-152, 160, 177-179,
194, 195, 207, 208, 211, 212, 224,
227, 239, 260; divine, 68, 110
Minos, Claudius (Claude Mignaut),
14, 212, 213, 233, 247
Minotaur, the, 91
Miranda (Tem), 48, 65, 66, 149,
176, 179, 268
mirrors, 85-87, 117, 260; (fig.), 110,
115, 194
misanthropy, 135, 264
"missing link," the, 214, 272
mistletoe, the, 103
Moloch, 192
Monk of Evesham, vision of the, 50,
52, 53, 256, 257
monsters, 162, 172-175, 181-185;
(fig.), 97
Montaigne, 15, 78, 81, 92, 107, 114,
148, 152, 160, 176, 178, 183, 184,
199, 200, 206, 207, 251, 254,
260-263, 265, 266, 268, 269, 271
Montano (Oth), 97, 111
Montefortino, H. de, 267
moon, the, 20, 21, 23-31, 33, 39, 42,
43, 47, 48, 163, 186, 189, 252
morality, 124, 161, 169, 176, 179,
180, 185, 215, 235, 237; instruction, 231; plays, 264

mortality, 31, 63, 106, 169-171, 204,
213
Mortimer, Edmund (1 H IV), 125
Moses, 228; *Revelation of Moses,*
229-231
Moth (LLL), 134
motion, 84, 106; of death, 81; mental, 204; planetary, 24, 73, 204;
power of, 77, 118, 147
"motiveless malignity," 136
Moulton, Richard G., 215
mountains, 26, 50, 55, 56, 91, 205,
207, 234, 235, 257; golden, 91,
195; holy, 230
Mountford, Susan, 222
Mowbray, Thomas (R II), 201, 236
Muir, Kenneth, 12, 250, 265, 271
multitude, the, 96, 109, 181-185 *see*
people, rabble
Munday, Anthony, 255
murder, 46, 53, 124, 154, 179, 184,
221, 222; (fig.), 115; *The Murder
of Gonzago* (Ham), 217
Muriel, 65
Muses, the Nine, 62, 271
music, song, 62, 128, 147, 171, 172,
176, 179, 201-209, 271
mutability, change, 163, 165, 169,
232
Mutius (TA), 125
myth, 50, 166-168, 186, 187, 203,
227

names, 116, 172, 210, 220-222
Nathan, Norman, 261
Nathaniel (LLL), 74
nature, cosmic, 34, 37, 38, 44, 73,
110, 164, 171, 192-200, 223, 225,
229, 230, 233-235, 270, 271;
human, 63, 96, 97, 124, 131,
153-155, 172, 180, 204, 219, 266;
natura creatrix, 197, 200
Navarre, 210
necromancy, 45 *see* witchcraft
Neilson, W. A., 250
Neptune, 211, 212
Nestor (TC), 20; (MV), 132

287

INDEX

Ptolemaic astronomy, 17
puberty, 65, 167
Puck, Robin Goodfellow (MND), 27, 47, 83, 255
pulse, the, 208, 209
puns, 69, 156, 158, 161, 266
Purchas, Samuel, 174, 175, 268
purgation, purgatory, 32, 49-59, 231, 256, 257 see Dante
putrefaction, 28-30, 163-165, 169-171, 266
Puttenham, George, 198, 199, 207, 270, 271
Pygmalion, 197
pyramid (geom.), 68, 71, 72
Pyrrha, 225
Pythagoras, 67, 205

queen, the (Cym), 85; (R II), 124, 134
Quickly, Mrs. (H V), 86; (MWW), 121, 125
Quintilian, 271

rabble, the, 184
Ragnarok, 186
ratiocination, 169
reason, 73, 74, 77, 81, 82, 87, 90, 91, 93-98, 100-104, 106, 107-110, 120, 125, 127, 139, 147, 148, 150, 151, 177, 179, 185-188, 190-193, 202, 204, 214, 232, 262
rebellion, 230
recorder, the (music), 201
Reed, Robert H., 255
Regan (KL), 63, 70, 71, 75, 236
Religion and Ethics, Encyclopedia of, 256
Renaissance, the, 76, 181, 185
repentance, 104, 124
resurrection, 231
revenge, vengeance, 106, 107, 125, 134, 187, 215, 219; "humours of revenge," 125; "winged vengeance," 235
Reynaldo (Ham), 218
Reynolds, Lou A., 252

Rhadamanthus, 50
Rich, Barnaby, 182
Richard I, king (KJ), 123; Richard II (R II), 69, 124, 134, 156, 201, 202; Richard III (3 H VI), 129, (R III), 64, 101, 137, 185
riddles, 159, 201
Rio de Janeiro, 268
Robertson, J. M., 16, 251
Roderigo (Oth), 136
Roman de la Rose, Le, 67
Rome, Romans, 96, 136, 148, 151, 155, 180-185, 226, 272
Romeo (RJ), 38, 48, 51, 83, 85, 89, 92, 101, 116, 126, 133, 134
Rosalind (AYLI), 83, 114; Rosaline (LLL), 123, (RJ), 85, 101, 133
Rosencrantz (Ham), 109, 110, 158, 160, 190
Ross (Mac), 152
rotundity, roundness, 19, 32, 33, 234
Rouse, W. H. D., 273
Ruegg, August, 255-257, 268
Rumour, 21, 23; (2 H IV), 182

sadness, 120, 130-135, 138, 141, 142, 160, 190 see grief
Salanio (MV), 131
Salarino (MV), 131, 132, 135, 215
Salisbury, earl of (KJ), 86
Samuel, spirit of, 46
sanctimony, 70, 112, 113
Sanders, Norman, 10, 273
Sandys, Sir William (H VIII), 201
sanguine temperament, 81, 120-124, 126-128, 131-134, 136-139, 141, 143, 144, 265
sanity, 104
sardonic, Sardonian, 130, 134, 135, 137, 138
Satan, Lucifer, 18, 50, 187
Saturn, Saturnian, 136, 212, 228, 272
satyrs, 91, 99
Saul, 137

290

Silvia (TGV), 116, 223
sin(s), 50-52, 56, 96, 107, 161, 169, 170, 215, 227, 229-231; deadly, 185; original, 161, 169, 170
sirens, 203, 204
Sisson, C. J., 255
Sitter, W. de, 253
Skeat, W. W., 58, 258
Skulsky, Harold, 254
slander, 20, 22, 23, 186, 221, 252
slaves, 138, 139, 151, 172-174, 176, 180
sleep, slumber, 32, 79, 82, 90, 127, 167, 179, 188, 208, 231; sleep-walking, 137
Smith, Charles G., 272, 273; G. Gregory, 250, 270, 271; Hallet, 98, 261; Jonathan, 261
snow, 49, 50, 257; (fig.), 149
Socrates, 223-225
soil tillage, 228-230
solid, a (geom.), 68, 71, 72; solidity, 102, 259; of earth, 33; of flesh, 29; of the spheres, 32, 33 see density, globosity
Solomon, 188, 216
Somers, Sir George, 175
soothsayer, a (AC), 200; (Cym), 209
Sophocles, 225
sorrow, 83, 84, 137, 141, 227, 229 see grief, sadness
souls, human, 11, 27, 32, 36, 38, 41-44, 46, 47, 50, 53-57, 68, 70, 75, 80, 82, 83, 86, 87, 98-118, 138, 146-150, 159-163, 178, 181, 189, 195, 204, 205, 208, 209, 211, 217, 220, 231, 262; exchange of (fig.), 113-118; faculties of the, 76, 105, 122, 146-150, 190, 274, con-cupiscible, 43, 90, 107, 148, 149, 185, 186, irascible, 97, 106, 107, 148, 149, 185, rational, 97, 106, 107, 147, 148, 185, 188, 214; the three-fold soul, 179, rational, 43, 71, 72, 101, 103, 106, 147, 149, 159, 160, 191, 259, sensible, 43,

71, 72, 77, 147, 191, 259, vegetal or vegetable, 71, 72, 147, 191, 259; the world-soul, 31, 68, 73, 101, 110, 204, 205, 253
sources, source hunting, 9, 12, 45, 49, 59, 69, 107, 108, 117, 131, 182, 183, 187, 199, 203, 207, 218, 220, 226, 227, 239
Southampton, earl of, 183
Spanish, the, 173, 218
speculation, in mirror, 85, 86; mental, 23, 104, 105, 168, 172
speech, power of, 74, 95, 173, 174, 224 see language
Spencer, Theodore, 12
Spenser, Edmund, 45, 162, 167, 168, 170, 255, 261, 268
spheres, the (astron.), 18, 19, 21, 22, 31-34, 39, 48, 72, 203-208, 231, 270; a ball, 233 see music
spider's web, a, 102
spirits, bodily, 42, 78, 82, 83, 85-87, 106, 108-110, 122, 123, 128, 132-134, 147, 198, 203, 204, 209; souls, fairies, 42-48, 83, 106, 175, 176, 188, 204 see daemons
Spivack, Bernard, 264
spleen, splenitive, 129, 138, 139, 141
squares, 61, 62, 68, 70-73, 75
stars, 25, 27, 31-34, 45, 58, 60, 189, 203, 204, 206-208 see planets
state, the, 108-110, 155, 181, 182, 191, 202, 209, 220, 232; (fig.), 106, 262
Stephano (Tem), 45, 176, 179
sterility, 190, 191
Sternfeld, F. W., 271
Stirling, Brents, 269
stoicism, 263
stones, 24; (fig.), 204, 205, 207, 224-226, 232, 233
storms, tempests, 33, 34, 44, 46, 47, 49, 56, 80, 88, 95, 101, 111, 234, 254, 268
Stow, John, 178
Strabo, 162
study, 83, 130, 210-212, 223, 233